Contents

Macmillan Education
4 Crinan Street
London N1 9XW
A division of Macmillan Education Limited

Companies and representatives throughout the world

Ferris Wheel Level 1 Teacher's Book 978-1-380-02661-3
Ferris Wheel Level 1 Teacher's Book with Navio App 978-1-380-02659-0

First published 2019

Teacher's Book credits:
Designed by emc design ltd
Character artwork and main illustrations by Animation Group Sp. z o.o. and Jose Ignacio Gómez (Nacho Gómez)
Cover design by emc design ltd
Cover illustration by Animation Group Sp. z o.o
Picture research by Lorraine Beck

Author's acknowledgements
I would like to thank everyone at Macmillan Education in the UK, Spain and Mexico who has contributed to the development and production of these materials. I would also like to thank all the teachers who have taken time to read and pilot the materials, and given invaluable feedback at every stage of writing the course. Special thanks as ever go to my husband, Alan, for his encouragement and support, and to our son and daughter, Jamie and Hannah, from whose early childhood days I learnt so much.

Student's Book credits:

Original design by Clare Webber
Page make-up by emc design ltd.
Illustrated by Animation Group Sp. z.o.o. based on original character designs by Jose Ignacio Gómez (Nacho Gómez)
Cover design by emc design ltd
Cover illustration by Animation Group Sp. z.o.o. based on original character designs by Jose Ignacio Gómez (Nacho Gómez)
Picture research by Lorraine Beck

The publishers would like to thank Alex Tamulis, São Paulo, Brazil; Ayşegül Sezer, İNO Schools, Turkey; Daniela Araujo Pielli, Alt Idiomas, São Bernardo Do Campo, Brazil; Daniela Pugliese, Milton's College, Buenos Aires, Argentina; Esra Ezici, Turkey; Fernanda Domeniconi Nery Amorim, São Paulo, Brazil; Gabriela Iocolari, English Schoolhouse, Buenos Aires, Argentina; Gulbin Cin, Bahcesehir College, Turkey; Mariana Pastorino, Em Pi Instituto de Inglés, Santa Fe, Argentina; Mariné Ortiz, Warrington, Buenos Aires, Argentina; Paola Daniela Tuninetti, Academia Argüello, Córdoba, Argentina; Silvana Paola Accardo, Escuela Cooperativa Mundo Nuevo Instituto Casa de Jesús, Buenos Aires, Argentina.

Printed and bound in Brazil

2025
30

The authors and publishers would like to thank the following for permission to reproduce their photographs:

Alamy Stock Photo/Michael Burrell pp15(eraser), 76(bucket), Alamy Stock Photo/Robert Hicks p15(pencil), Alamy Stock Photo/Martin Lee pp55, 59, 61(sandwich), Alamy Stock Photo/MBI p9(sister), Alamy Stock Photo/Pick and Mix Images p76(spade), Alamy Stock Photo/StockPhotosArt - Sweets pp55, 61(cookie), Alamy Stock Photo/Steve Taylor ARPS p81(crab), Alamy Stock Photo/Andrew Twort p35(hat), Alamy Stock Photo/SABAR UDIN pp75, 76(sea), Alamy Stock Photo/Wavebreak Media ltd pp5, 6(c, grandmother,grandfather), Alamy Stock Photo/Björn Wylezich p15(book); **Getty Images**/AlexStar pp24, 64(modelling clay), Getty Images/aopsan p34(paper plate), Getty Images/artisteer p65(mouse), Getty Images/aurigadesign p71(bl), Getty Images/bazilfoto pp65(bird), 69(r), Getty Images/Corvalol pp55, 61(apple), Getty Images/cynoclub p69(mr), Getty Images/Davies and Starr pp75, 76(crab), Getty Images/Dorling Kindersley p35(tshirt), Getty Images/Eliza317 pp59, 61(water), Getty Images/EyeEm/Cristina Catlin p25(eye), Getty Images/EyeEm/Massimiliano Clari p66(cat), Getty Images/EyeEm/Frank Mcclintock p71(tl), Getty Images/EyeEm/Iain Mcconnell p81(cat), Getty Images/Aaron Foster p81(sea), Getty Images/GlobalP p65(rabbit), Getty Images/Alexandra Grablewski p9(brother), Getty Images/harmpeti pp55, 59, 61(banana), Getty Images/heinteh p35(shorts), Getty Images/Image Source p51(br), Getty Images/iStockphoto p25(mouth), Getty Images/Ivan-balvan p35(shoes), Getty Images/jskiba pp75, 76(shell), Getty Images/kbwills pp59, 61(juice), Getty Images/kickers p25(nose), Getty Images/Dave King p65(fish), Getty Images/lucielang p15(crayon), Getty Images/A. Martin UW Photography p81(fish), Getty Images/Microzoa p81(sea), Getty Images/parinyabinsuk p14(pegs), Getty Images/Jose Luis Pelaez Inc p9(grandmother,grandfather), Getty Images/photovideostock pp75, 76(sand), Getty Images/Ridofranz p9(father), Getty Images/Kinzie Riehm p51(tr), Getty Images/Serg_Velusceac pp14, 24, 34, 44, 54, 64, 74, 84(paints), Getty Images/Techin24 p25(ear); **iStockphoto**/alex_kz pp14, 34, 44, 54, 74, 84(glue); **PHOTODISC** p66(dog); **Shutterstock**/Artazump81(garden), Shutterstock/Johannes Kornelius p69(fish); **Spectrecom** pp9(tr, mother), 12(tr), 19, 22(tr), 29(c,tr), 32(tr), 39, 42(tr), 49(t), 52(tr), 59(tr), 62(tr), 69, 72(tr), 79, 82(tr); **www.imagesource.com** pp14, 54(string).

Commissioned photography by Helen Marsden pp6(tr), 7(tl), 11, 14(tissue paper,wool,1,2,3), 16, 17(tl), 21, 22(tl), 24(1,2,3), 26, 27(tl), 31(ear, eye, boy, girl), 32(Sophie,Tom), 34(wool,1,2,3), 36, 37(tl), 41, 42(bl,bm,br), 44(tissue paper, 1,2,3), 45, 46, 47(tl), 49(scooter,teddy), 51(tl, bl), 54(tissue paper,coathanger,1,2,3), 56, 57(tl), 59(Sophie,Tom), 61(tr), 64(1,2,3), 66(c), 67(tl), 71(tr), 74(tissue paper,1,2,3), 76(c), 77(tl), 81(tr), 84(tissue paper,1,2,3).

A letter from the author

Dear Teacher,

I'm delighted to welcome you to *Ferris Wheel*. Get ready to hop on with your children for what I hope will be a truly enjoyable and successful learning journey!

Before we start, I'd like to introduce you to the imaginary world of the meerkats. The delightful Mimi and her family accompany us through the course and provide a rich source of engaging, and often humorous, stories that young children will want to hear again and again.

Mimi is curious about the world, full of fun, at times mischievous, but also sensible, helpful, loving and kind.

Mimi's younger brother, Dylan, is funny, adorable and sometimes a little silly. Together they make an appealing and loveable pair.

Mimi and Dylan's mommy and daddy work at the Ferris Wheel next to the meerkats' house. Mommy and Daddy share roles such as shopping and cooking, and love sports and dancing, too.

In contrast to the fantasy world of the meerkats, *Ferris Wheel 1* also features two real-life children, Tom and Sophie, whose favorite animated stories are about the meerkat family. Together with Auntie Jenny, Tom and Sophie extend the natural contexts in which children are exposed to English. We meet them in lively videos where they interact in everyday situations, or act out traditional rhymes and songs. These provide a realistic and motivating model that supports children as they learn to communicate in English.

The Ferris Wheel, with its brightly colored pods, represents the course's innovative Hop on & Hop off approach to learning. Instead of working through the units in a linear way, you can teach them in the order that best suits your educational context and the children's curriculum, interests and needs. This gives you flexibility and allows your English program to be in sync with children's learning in other areas of the curriculum.

Before writing *Ferris Wheel*, I carried out extensive research to find out what teachers really need and want from a pre-school English language course. My findings led me to adopt a methodological approach for *Ferris Wheel* that takes into account the priorities and everyday concerns of classroom practitioners, as well as applying what we know from academic research about young children's overall development and language learning. It also incorporates many practical techniques from my own experience of teaching young children.

This is reflected in the methodology of *Ferris Wheel* in the following ways:

- Units with a clear, logical structure that build children's linguistic competence and self-confidence.
- Lesson procedures and activities that are easy to implement and manage, even with large classes.
- A wealth of content to foster children's motivation and develop language skills, including stories, songs, culture, values, real-world content and projects.
- A focus on the development of the whole child, including metacognitive, cognitive, psychological and physical development, social and emotional learning (SEL), life skills and values education.
- A balance between fantasy, which builds on children's natural capacity for creativity and play, and reality, which develops children's curiosity in learning about the real world.
- A wide range of resources to ensure lessons are engaging and dynamic, including the Mimi puppet, the *Ferris Wheel* mat, animated stories, videos, songs, Teacher's and Student's Apps, flashcards, story cards and posters.

Ferris Wheel is dedicated to every pre-school teacher who shares a passion for early language learning and believes in the unique learning potential of every child. I hope you and your children enjoy using *Ferris Wheel* as much as I enjoyed writing it!

All the best,
Carol

Ferris Wheel 1 Syllabus

Unit	Main vocabulary	Key language	Values	Content-based learning	Culture	Project
Hello 	Mimi, Dylan, Mommy, Daddy, boy, girl; red; Ferris Wheel	Hello, I'm (Mimi).				
Family 	mommy, daddy, grandma, grandpa, brother, sister; blue, green, orange, pink, red, yellow	Where's your (grandma)? Here. This is my (mommy). Here we go. Round and round. I love my (mommy). Wheels go round and round.	**I love my family**	**Wheels go round and round:** round, wheel	***The wheels on the bus:*** bus, wheels	A family display
Classroom 	book, chair, crayon, eraser, pencil, table	Sit down. Stand up. Look! It's a (chair). I don't know. I'm (happy). What color is your (book)? It's (red). I care. I'm your friend. I put the (crayon) (in) the (tray). This is the way I say (hello).	**I'm your friend:** care, friend; happy, sad	**Putting classroom objects where they belong:** shelf, tray	***This is the way I say hello:*** bye bye, hello; friends, school	A tray and crayons made from modeling clay
My face 	ear, eye, hair, mouth, nose, teeth	I have (a nose). I have (two) (eyes). It's (a boy) in the water. My (eyes) are special. I (see) with my (eyes). Here is my (nose). Here are my (eyes).	**I'm happy I'm me:** special	**What we do with our ears and eyes:** hear, see	***Here are my ears:*** hands, toes	A faces display
Clothes 	boots, coat, hat, shoes, shorts, T-shirt	Put on your (hat). Take off your (shoes). Where are your (boots)? Here. I'm neat. I put my (coat) away. It's (rainy). I put on my (coat).	**I'm neat:** neat	**Clothes for sunny and rainy weather:** rainy, sunny	***Itsy, bitsy spider:*** spider; rain, sun	A weather display

Unit	Main vocabulary	Key language	Values	Content-based learning	Culture	Project
Toys	ball, car, doll, scooter, teddy, train	What's this? It's a (train). Let's play with the (ball). What's your favorite toy? It's my (teddy). Let's (play) together. I (play) in the (playground).	**We play together:** play, work	**Where we play and where we work:** classroom, playground; play, work	***Bouncy ball:*** big; bouncy, round; numbers 1–3	A toy mobile
Food	apple, banana, cookie, juice, sandwich, water	I like (bananas). I'm hungry. Can I have (a sandwich), please? Here's (a sandwich) for you. / Here you go. Thank you. Are you hungry? I eat (apples). I drink (water).	**I say 'please' and 'thank you':** please, thank you	**Things we drink and things we eat:** drink, eat	***Ten little apples:*** orange; little; tree; numbers 1–10	A picnic blanket and food made from modeling clay
Pets	bird, cat, dog, fish, mouse, rabbit	I have a (mouse). Is this your (mommy)? Yes, it is. / No, it isn't. My (fish) is (orange). I'm kind to you. I help you. Birds fly. Fish swim. Little Peter Rabbit has a fly on his nose.	**I'm kind to you**	**Animals that fly and animals that swim:** fly, swim	***Little Peter Rabbit:*** fly, rabbit	Our favorite pets poster
Beach	bucket, crab, ocean, sand, shell, shovel	I can see (a crab). Me too. How many (little crabs)? (Five). What color are the (shells)? They're (pink). I love the (blue) (ocean). (Fish) live in (water). (Cats) live on (land).	**I love our world:** trees	**Where animals live:** land, water	***One, two, three, four, five:*** crab, fish, shell; numbers 1–10	A beach display

Unit	Main vocabulary
Endmatter	blue, brown, green, orange, pink, purple, red, yellow numbers 1–10 circle, rectangle, square, triangle happy, sad, big, small, up, down
Festivals	Carnival, mask, parade; dance, sing happy, family; mommy, daddy, grandma, grandpa, brother, sister eyes, feet, fur; teddy bear

Ferris Wheel 2 Syllabus

Unit	Main vocabulary	Key language	Content-based learning
Hello	Mommy, Daddy, Mimi, Dylan, Ferris Wheel blue, green, orange, pink, red, yellow numbers 1–6 ball, car, doll, teddy, train, scooter	Hello, I'm (Mimi). Where's the (ball)? Here's the (ball)! It's (blue).	
Classroom	backpack, crayons, glue, paints, paper, pencil, pencil case, scissors	Do you have your/a (pencil)? Yes, I do. / No, I don't. I have (red) (paint). I don't have (scissors).	**Places at school and what we do there:** cafeteria, classroom, library, playground
My body	arms, feet, fingers, hands, head, legs, toes, tummy	I can/can't move my (head). Can you? Can you move your (head)? Yes, I can. / No, I can't. What can you do? I can/can't (dance). Move your (head).	**Things we can do with our bodies:** climb, hop, jump, run
Clothes	coat, dress, pants, shirt, shoes, skirt, socks, sweater	This is my (skirt). These are my (shoes). What are you wearing? I'm wearing (a white) (hat).	**Clothes for hot and cold weather:** gloves, sandals, scarf; cold, hot
Home	bathroom, bedroom, dining room, garage, house, kitchen, living room, yard	Is (Sam) in the (garden)? Yes, he/she is. / No, he/she isn't. Where's (Dylan)? In the (dining room). He's/She's in the (house). He/She isn't in the (garage).	**Putting things away where they belong:** box, closet, recycling bin, shelf
Food	apples, bananas, bread, carrots, cereal, eggs, ice cream, milk	I like (carrots). I don't like (cereal). How about you? Do you like (bananas)? Yes, I do. / No, I don't. Put the (eggs) in the cart.	**Food that grows in the garden:** pears, peas, potatoes, tomatoes
Farm animals	cow, dog, duck, goat, hen, horse, rooster, sheep	There's a (horse). There are (cows). How many (hens)? (Four). The (sheep) goes (baa).	**Animals and their babies:** calf, foal, lamb, puppy
Transportation	bike, boat, bus, car, motorcycle, plane, train, truck	Let's go by (bus)! Yes. / No. I want to go by (car). Do you want to go by (bus)? Yes, I do. / No, I don't.	**Different means of transport and where they go:** air, road, track, water
Space	astronaut, Earth, moon, planet, rocket, sky, star, sun	What's this? It's (the sun). Can you see (the moon)? Yes, I can. / No, I can't. What can you see? How many (stars) can you see?	**What we can see in the sky at night and in the day:** day, night; clouds, rainbow
Endmatter	black, blue, brown, green, orange, pink, purple, red, white, yellow; numbers 1–20; circle, diamond, oval, rectangle, square, star, triangle; hot, cold, noisy, quiet, clean, messy		
Festivals	animals, bird, children, fly, happy, peace, world Carnival, clown, crown, king, pirate, queen; happy children; hug, play, run, talk	I'm a (pirate). I love to (play).	

Ferris Wheel 3 Syllabus

Unit	Main vocabulary	Key language	Content-based learning
Hello	Mommy, Daddy, Mimi, Dylan; Ferris Wheel; blue, green, orange, pink, red, yellow; numbers 1–6	Hello. How are you? I'm fine, thank you. Where's number (one)? It's on (red). I'm (sleepy). Hurry up. Here's your (hat). Goodbye.	
School	color, count, dance, draw, jump, paint, play, run, sing, think	What do you do at school? I (draw) at school. Do you want to (color)? Yes, I do. / No, I don't. I want to (jump). I don't want to (draw).	**Doing exercise:** play soccer, ride my bike, swim, walk (to school)
The park	bench, flowers, grass, merry-go-round, path, pond, seesaw, slide, swing, trees	There's (a path). There are (trees). It's (windy). Is there (a slide)? Are there (swings)? Where's (Mommy)? Under the (tree). On the (bench).	**The life cycle of a plant:** leaves, plant, roots, seed, sun, water
Wild animals	crocodile, elephant, giraffe, hippo, lion, monkey, parrot, snake, tiger, zebra	What's that? It's a (snake). What are those? They're (monkeys). It's (black and white). It has (big teeth). I'm a (crocodile).	**Animal body parts:** claws, fur, tail, whiskers
Daily routines	brush my hair/teeth, get dressed, get up, have breakfast/lunch/dinner, take a shower, wash my face/hands	What do you do every day? I (get up). Do you (wash your hands) (at school)? Yes, I do. / No, I don't. It's time to (get dressed). What do you do at (home)? I (have breakfast) at (home). I don't (have dinner) at (school).	**How and when to wash your hands:** faucet, soap, towel, water; clean
Meals	chicken, fish, pancake, pizza, rice, salad, soup, spaghetti, toast, yogurt	What do you have for (dinner)? I have (soup). Do you want (pancakes)? Yes, please. / No, thank you. I want/don't want (toast).	**Healthy and unhealthy food:** fruit, vegetables; candy, carrots, chips, cupcakes, ice cream, oranges, peas, plums, tomatoes
Town	bookstore, mall, movie theater, museum, park, restaurant, supermarket, swimming pool, toy store, zoo	Do you want to (go to the zoo)? Yes, I do. / No, I don't. Where do you want to go? I want to (go to the museum). Let's (go to the mall).	**Crossing the street safely:** crosswalk, sidewalk, stoplights, street; stop, look, listen
Music	drum, guitar, maracas, piano, recorder, tambourine; clap, dance, listen, sing	What are you doing? I'm (playing the piano). Do you like (playing the maracas)? Yes, I do. / No, I don't. I like (playing the drum).	**Different rhythms:** fast, slow, loud, quiet
Bugs	ant, bee, butterfly, ladybug, snail, worm; legs, spots, stripes, wings	Does (a snail) have (spots)? Yes, it does. / No, it doesn't. Ask the (ladybug), please. It doesn't have (stripes).	**The life cycle of a butterfly:** caterpillar, chrysalis, egg, leaf
Endmatter	black, blue, brown, gray, green, orange, pink, purple, red, white, yellow; numbers 1–100; circle, diamond, oval, rectangle, square, star, triangle; hungry, thirsty, clean, dirty, old, young	It's (red). It's a (star). I can see (three) (diamonds). I'm (hungry). He's/She's/It's (old).	
Festivals	animals, people, pictures, stories, words, world; elephant, gorilla, panda, polar bear, rhino, tiger; beach, countryside, forest, mountains	I like books about (people). I like books with (pictures). Save the (panda). I go to the (countryside). Let's protect the (beach).	

What's in *Ferris Wheel*?

Student's Book

The *Ferris Wheel* Student's Book has a flexible, Hop on & Hop off approach that allows you to adapt to the unique needs and requirements of your class, and align children's English learning with the content and sequence of the wider curriculum. Hop on and off the Ferris Wheel wherever you wish or follow the unit sequence given in the book – it's up to you! Each unit has ten lessons that follow a logical structure in order to develop children's language skills and understanding of the chosen topic.

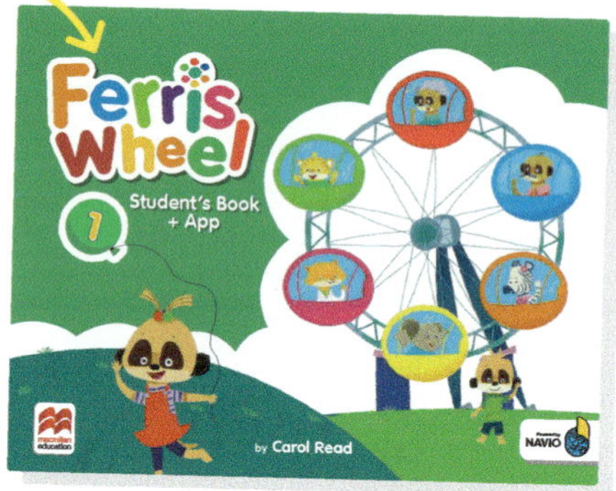

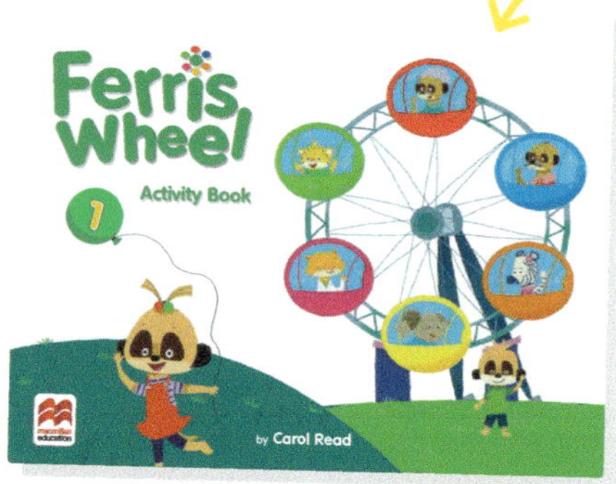

Activity Book

The full-color Activity Book mirrors the Student's Book structure and provides additional practice of key language and content. Activities such as visual discrimination, matching, pre-literacy and numeracy support and develop children's cognitive and fine motor skills.

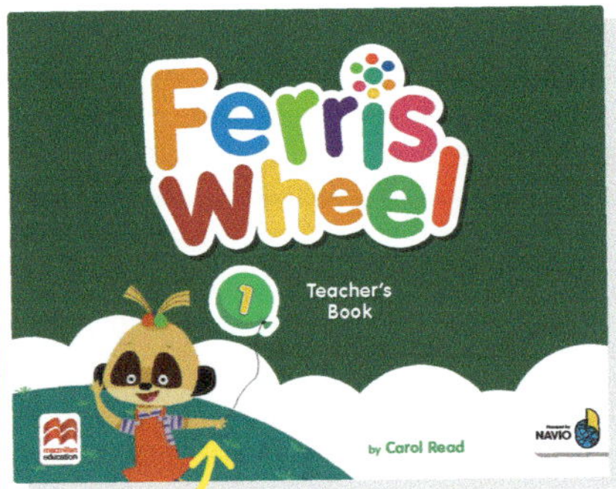

Teacher's Book

Detailed lesson plans, interleaved with the Student's Book pages, allow you to navigate the course with ease. Learning objectives, materials, teacher's tips and audioscripts are all at your fingertips.

***Ferris Wheel* mat**

The *Ferris Wheel* mat is a flexible teaching resource. Place it on the floor during Circle time, or hang it on the wall or board, and put flashcards or real objects in the pockets to play motivating language games. Practical ideas for using the mat can be found on p20.

Mimi puppet

Mimi the meerkat is an engaging puppet who will bring your classes to life. The use of a puppet has a positive impact on children's motivation and participation. Practical ideas for using the puppet can be found on p21.

Teacher's App on Navio

The Teacher's App on Navio offers one-stop access to the digital resources, including Tap & Teach Lessons with integrated audio and video, the Rewards tool to award points for good behavior or success, and a Progress Tracker. You'll also find additional resources in the Resource Bank, including posters, story cards, word cards, worksheets, evaluation materials, extra flashcards, alternative festivals, and letters to parents.

Class CDs

All the audio material, including stories, songs, rhymes, chants, games and dialogues, can be found on the Class CDs.

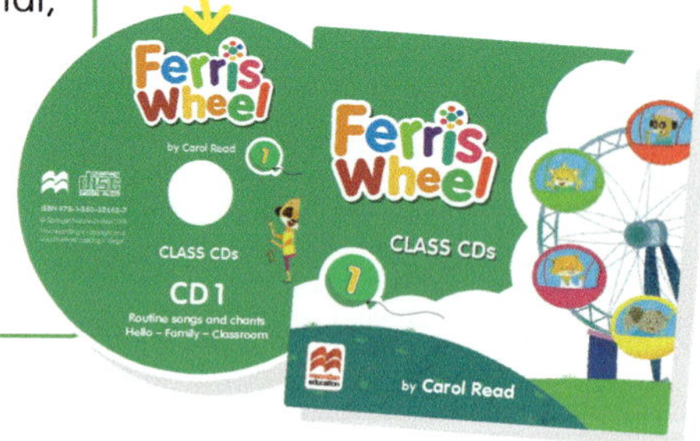

Student's App on Navio

The Student's App allows students to explore Navio's immersive worlds. They complete game-based activities designed to practice and review language and content. The App also includes all the songs, videos and animated stories from the course. The access code can be found on the inside front cover of the Student's Book.

Flashcards

Photographic flashcards are provided for every key vocabulary item. See page 19 for ideas for using the flashcards.

Ferris Wheel's Hop on & Hop off approach

Ferris Wheel's **unique and innovative Hop on & Hop off approach** offers teachers the flexibility to teach the eight core units in any order. Topics can be aligned with the wider curriculum, or sequenced according to your and your class's preferences.

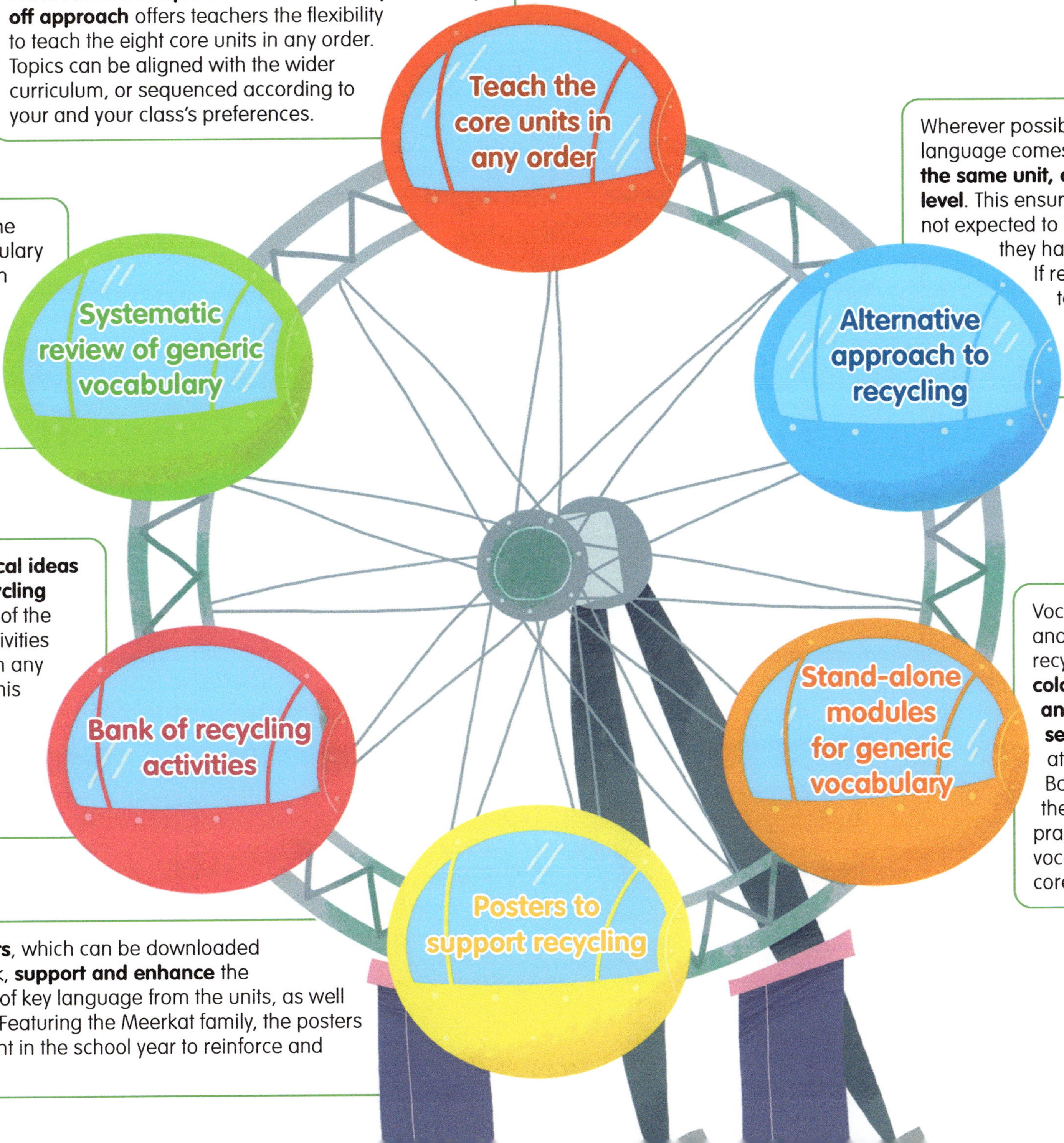

Wherever possible, recycled language comes either from **within the same unit, or from the previous level**. This ensures that children are not expected to use language that they haven't yet covered. If recycled language is taken from other units in the same level, it is for receptive understanding only.

Vocabulary that is generic and can be applied and recycled in any unit, such as **colors**, **numbers**, **shapes and concepts**, appear in **separate short modules** at the back of the Student's Book. This gives teachers the flexibility to present, practice and review this vocabulary outside of the core units.

The *Ferris Wheel* **posters**, which can be downloaded from the Resource Bank, **support and enhance** the teaching and recycling of key language from the units, as well as generic vocabulary. Featuring the Meerkat family, the posters can be used at any point in the school year to reinforce and recycle key language.

There is a **bank of practical ideas and suggestions for recycling known language** on p19 of the Teacher's Book. These activities are designed to work with any vocabulary set or topic. This means you can use them to recycle vocabulary and language from any unit that you have previously covered.

This overall approach to the teaching of generic vocabulary and the recycling of known language allows for **regular and systematic review**, while removing the need to work through the units in chronological order.

About the Student's Book and Activity Book

The *Ferris Wheel* Student's Book and Activity Book have eight core units, plus a *Hello* unit. The course's Hop on & Hop off approach allows you to teach the core units in the order you prefer. Each unit features ten varied lessons to consistently develop a range of skills, as well as motivating children and promoting the use of English in their daily classroom interactions.

Student's Book

Lesson 1, Vocabulary

Children are introduced to **four new topic-based vocabulary items** by Mimi and Dylan. They then practice saying the new words, play a memory game, and stick the vocabulary stickers on the Ferris Wheel.

Lesson 2, Language

The **target language structure and two additional vocabulary items** are introduced through an appealing and memorable song. Children then complete an activity to **demonstrate comprehension and develop skills** such as visual discrimination and matching.

Lesson 3, Story

Children listen to the story using the printable story cards, or watch a **delightful animated version.** They then do a comprehension activity and stick the story sticker.

Lesson 4, Story Song

Children listen to, sing and act out the story song using the audio or an animated version. This **reinforces and reviews the concepts and key language in the story**. They then do a comprehension activity related to the song.

Lesson 5, Speaking

Children watch a **video** showing Tom, Sophie and Auntie Jenny using the **unit language in a realistic context.** Children are then encouraged to use some of the key language in a speaking activity that also practices **life skills.**

Lesson 6, Values

Children sing a song that develops their awareness of a specific value related to the story. They also practice **social and emotional (SEL) skills**.

Lesson 7, Content

Children are introduced to new vocabulary items and learn about **content from the wider world** related to the unit topic.

Lesson 8, Culture

Children are introduced to culture from the English-speaking world through listening to or watching the video of Tom and Sophie singing and acting out a **traditional song**.

Review

With the help of Mimi and Dylan, children **review their learning**. They then complete a **self-evaluation** activity and stick the star sticker.

Project

The unit culminates in a creative and **cooperative project** related to the topic, providing a natural context in which to practice and review known language.

Endmatter

Colors, numbers, shapes and **key concepts** are covered in short modules at the back of the Student's Book. This allows frequently-used vocabulary to be introduced, practiced and reviewed at any stage of the course. This supports *Ferris Wheel*'s Hop on & Hop off approach and facilitates regular recycling. There are also three **Festivals** pages and pull-out **Stickers** pages.

Activity Book

Lessons 1–8, Review and Project

The Activity Book **mirrors the Student's Book unit structure** exactly. The activities are designed to **consolidate children's understanding** of the new language and content presented in the Student's Book, whilst **simultaneously developing skills** such as visual discrimination, pre-literacy, matching, coloring, sequencing, and numeracy.

Endmatter

The Activity Book endmatter provides **further practice of the frequently-used vocabulary** presented in short modules at the back of the Student's Book: **colors, numbers, shapes** and **key concepts**. There are also three Festivals pages with activities to extend and develop this content.

Teacher's and Student's Apps on Navio

The Navio app that accompanies this course offers one-stop access to the wide range of resources that come with *Ferris Wheel*. Tap & Teach Lessons enable you to move seamlessly between the book and digital components. You can track your students' progress using the Progress Tracker and find additional resources in the Resource Bank.

Accessing the app

To access Navio, go to www.macmillaneducationeverywhere.com to create a Macmillan Education account, or log in with your existing account. Then you can enter your access code and download the app for your device (see system requirements at www.macmillaneducationeverywhere.com/system-requirements).

Setting up a class

You can use Navio's Learning Management System to set up a class and register your students with their names and the email address of their parents or guardians. You can then provide login details to parents so that they can log in to the Student's App and enter the code from the inside front cover of the Student's Book to access the 3D worlds and practice activities. Alternatively, parents can register their children directly at www.macmillaneducationeverywhere.com and students can then join your class using a class code.

Managing your downloads

Navio makes it easy to manage the storage space on your device, as you can control how much material you download at one time. Navio makes it clear how much storage space your chosen content will need. You can download the complete Teacher's and Student's Apps at once or, if your device has limited storage capacity, you can choose to download only one or two units. When you complete a unit, you can safely delete the content from your device. You won't lose your students' data, as this information is stored online.

Using the Progress Tracker

All the work your students complete in the app is recorded in the Progress Tracker. You can monitor the progress of a whole class or any individual student. Every activity in the app is mapped against the course learning objectives and skills, so you can easily identify where your students need extra support.

Teaching a lesson

Navio makes it easy to plan and teach your lessons with fully interactive **Tap & Teach Lessons**. Find the lesson you want to teach and click to open it. A thumbnail view of all activities in the lesson is available via the toolbar at the bottom of the page. The toolbar also contains the Tap & Teach tools you need to teach heads-up, whole-class activities, including a timer, pen tool, and mask tool. Lessons include all the audio and video you need for the lesson, as well as some extra tools such as digital flashcards.

Using the Rewards tool

Navio's Rewards tool is a great way to keep your students engaged in class. Much more than just a record of attendance, you can also use it to award points for good behavior or success in activities. You can even organize your class into teams, and you can award points to individuals, groups or the whole class at any time. When students earn points, they appear in the Student's App the next time they log in, so parents can see their performance.

Student's App

As a teacher you can also access a version of the Student's App from the main menu of the Teacher's App. This has all the same content that your students can access at home, but your version is set in teacher mode. This means that all the activities and worlds are already unlocked, and the app does not record any scores to the Progress Tracker. We recommend using teacher mode when students share devices to avoid mixing up students' grades and progress. However, if students have individual devices or are using the app at home, they should always log in with their own username and password. In this way they can earn points and badges, set up and customize their avatar and build a record of their progress in the Progress Tracker.

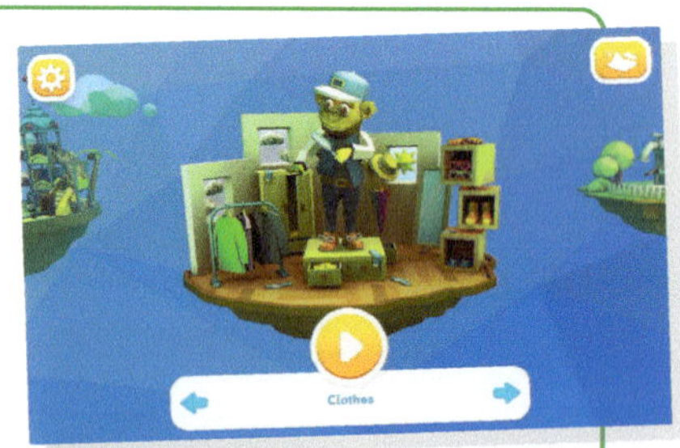

Features of the Teacher's Book

The *Ferris Wheel* Teacher's Book lesson plans are interleaved with the Student's Book pages. Each lesson plan follows the same structure: **Circle time**, **Table time** and **Closing time**.

Each unit begins with an overview of the **vocabulary, language** and **objectives** for the unit.

The audioscripts for the **unit story** and **songs** are also provided at the start of the unit for easy reference.

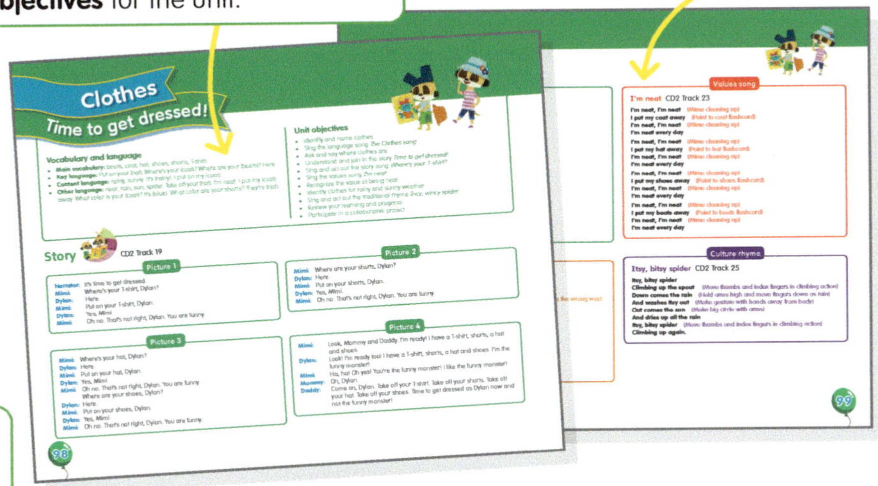

The detailed lesson plans are **interleaved** with full-size reproductions of the Student's Book pages.

Each lesson plan has an overview of the lesson's **learning objectives** and **language aims**, along with the **materials** you need.

A **facsimile and instructions for the Activity Book** are also provided.

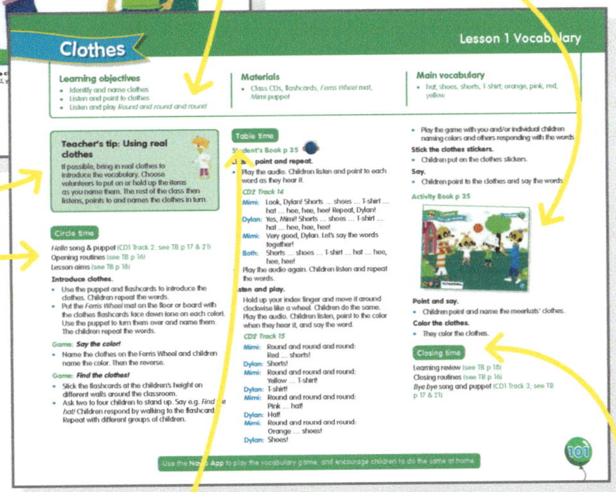

Teacher's tips provide helpful advice and suggestions to enrich the teaching experience.

Each lesson begins with **Circle time**. Children come together for the opening learning routines (see p16). They are also introduced to the lesson aims and then engage in a variety of games and activities using the Mimi puppet and the *Ferris Wheel* mat. Circle time focuses children's attention and is an opportunity for key input and new learning.

During **Table time**, children do a range of language and skills activities in the Student's Book. Step-by-step instructions, as well as audioscripts for the listening activities and chants, allow you to guide children through these activities smoothly and effectively.

Closing time ends the lesson with a learning review (see p18) and closing routines (see p16). Children then sing the *Bye bye song* as they wave goodbye to the Mimi puppet.

Additional resources

Activities Banks with ideas on how to use the Mimi puppet and *Ferris Wheel* mat in class, as well as recycling activities, and ways to specifically promote social and emotional learning, life skills and learning enrichment, can be found on pp19–25. There are also guidelines for how to incorporate **learning reviews** and **learning routines** into your lessons, along with audioscripts for the *Ferris Wheel* routine songs, on pp16–18.

Photocopiable templates specifically designed for the **Project** lessons can be found at the back of the Teacher's Book.

Whole child development

What is whole child development?

Many educators believe that children's learning success, both now and in the future, depends as much on their overall development as on their academic achievements. Developing the whole child means that we not only rely on traditional classroom-based learning, but give children the space and the opportunity to develop their creativity, physical, social and emotional expression, empathy, and understanding of the world around them.

A child's emotional, social, physical, creative and cognitive capacities are all intertwined and of equal importance. As language teachers, we also need to give all aspects of a child's development equal attention in order to achieve well-being, and create the optimal conditions for learning and growth. The development of a child's sense of self-worth and self-determination during the pre-school years is likely to be much more influential on positive long-term outcomes than a focus on standard academic achievements alone.

Ferris Wheel and whole child development

Ferris Wheel aims to integrate whole child development in a holistic way, including natural exposure to meaningful language, with the systematic development of age-appropriate language, thinking and social skills. This ensures that children are given the opportunities they need to develop all aspects of themselves, while simultaneously working towards the language and academic objectives in each unit.

Each level of *Ferris Wheel* was written to reflect the ages and stages of social, emotional, psychological, physical and cognitive development of pre-schoolers. Key child development goals, such as the development of creative thinking, personal autonomy, social and emotional learning, life skills, values, cognitive and metacognitive skills, and deliberate memory, are integrated and addressed throughout the course. On-the-page activities include ordering, matching, sequencing, tracing and visual discrimination to encourage effort, persistence, concentration and the development of early cognitive skills. Many of the songs in *Ferris Wheel* have accompanying actions to develop gross motor skills and coordination. There is a focus on creativity and personal expression, e.g. in the Story and in the Project lessons, and on emotional intelligence, self-esteem and autonomy, e.g. in the Values lessons. Metacognitive skills are developed through regular learning reviews, reflection and self-assessment.

Life skills

Life skills are the strategies needed to deal effectively with the challenges of everyday life. Life skills enable children to effectively problem-solve, adapt, take responsibility for their actions, cooperate and collaborate with others, make decisions, and interact with their peers.

Life skills are integrated across all levels of *Ferris Wheel*. In the Speaking lessons, children watch videos demonstrating how the real-life characters respond and behave in a variety of typical, everyday scenarios that are relevant to young children. On page 23 of the Teacher's Book, you will also find a bank of practical activities to help children develop and practice age-appropriate life skills.

Social and emotional learning (SEL)

Social and emotional learning (SEL) is essential for success at school and in life. Children who develop social and emotional awareness and skills find it easier to manage themselves, relate to others and resolve conflict. This creates positive self-esteem and provides a healthy foundation for children's learning and well-being.

Pre-schoolers are naturally egocentric and are still in the process of learning how to understand and interpret other people's emotions and intentions. This ability to "de-center" or move away from their own limited viewpoint to integrate other people's perspective is a skill that requires practice. SEL is an integrated part of the methodology of *Ferris Wheel* and is also reflected in the learning routines (see p16), unit stories and Values lessons, in which children rehearse strategies for handling their emotions, having empathy for others and making good choices about behavior. On p22, you can also find a bank of activity ideas for the development of social and emotional skills, including self-awareness, self-management, social awareness, relationship skills, responsible decision-making and autonomy.

Values education

The Values education lessons in every unit of *Ferris Wheel* encourage children to think about a range of age-appropriate values in relation to themselves, other people and their immediate environment. The Values lessons link back to a theme or issue that arose in the unit story. Children sing and act out a values-related song and are given options and choices that encourage them to reflect on specific values and apply them to their own lives.

About the projects

Each unit of *Ferris Wheel* culminates with an enjoyable and motivating project, which acts as a final outcome to children's learning in the unit. The projects are simple and achievable, and require only basic materials. The *Ferris Wheel 1* projects include making a toy mobile, creating a display of clothes for sunny and rainy weather, modeling food from clay, and creating a poster of children's favorite pets. Photocopiable templates for the projects can be found in the back of the Teacher's Book.

Cooperative learning, or working together to accomplish **shared goals**, can be beneficial for both the group and the individual. By encouraging children to work with others, we nurture their ability to be **considerate, patient, kind and collaborative**. By following the simple steps in each Project lesson, children work individually, and then in small groups or with the class, to contribute towards a shared outcome. This brings **a sense of satisfaction and boosts self-esteem**.

Three numbered photographs clearly demonstrate **the steps children must follow** to achieve the final outcome, developing **logic and sequencing skills**, and giving them the confidence to attempt the project with **minimal teacher intervention**.

Activities such as painting, gluing and decorating promote the development of **fine motor skills**.

By showing **images of the materials**, rather than a written list, children are empowered to identify and collect the materials they need independently. This promotes **organizational skills and autonomy**.

In the Activity Book, children complete a motivating **art and craft activity** that practices **the key language** from the unit.

There are **photocopiable templates** provided at the back of the Teacher's Book so only **minimal forward planning** is needed.

The project creates a natural context for **production of the unit language**, and any other known language. This opportunity is fully exploited through a group discussion in which children express their personal opinions and give each other positive feedback.

The Teacher's Book provides **step-by-step guidance** on how to prepare children before they embark on their project, as well as **classroom management techniques** to ensure your project lessons run smoothly.

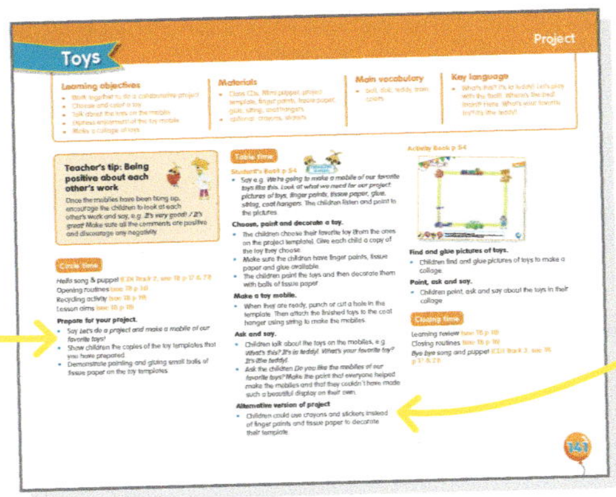

Simpler alternatives are suggested for most projects.

Learning routines

Learning routines are established procedures and patterns of behavior that you teach children and then use to signal and punctuate everyday classroom activities. Learning routines impact positively on children's behavior, participation, and social and emotional well-being, as well as on your ability to manage your classes and hold children's attention. Audioscripts for *Ferris Wheel*'s learning routine songs and chants can be found on p17.

Some typical learning routines include:

- **Opening routines** at the start of lessons, such as greeting the puppet, singing the *Hello song* (see p17), taking the register, identifying the day of the week, or talking about the weather.
- **Activity routines** to create the appropriate atmosphere for specific activities, such as Circle time and Story time.
- **Transition routines** to help children make the transition from one stage of the lesson to another in an orderly way.
- **Classroom routines** for specific tasks, such as giving out and collecting materials.
- **Energy-building routines** to use when children are losing concentration and need a short, physical break.
- **Settling routines** to use when children need to calm down and refocus their attention, e.g. after doing a lively, physical activity.
- **Thinking and feeling routines** to foster certain skills and attitudes, such as explicit thinking, cooperation, mindfulness, and social and emotional learning (SEL).
- **Closing routines** at the end of lessons, such as learning reviews (see p18), cleaning up and singing the *Bye bye song* (see p17).

For **children**, learning routines:

- give security and confidence about what they are expected to do;
- help them manage and regulate their behavior;
- provide frequent, repeated exposure to the same language in a meaningful context;
- provide opportunities for guided interaction and turn-taking in a familiar context;
- develop a sense of responsibility and autonomy in carrying out everyday classroom tasks;
- foster active participation in a safe environment;
- create a sense of community and positively develop social and emotional skills.

For **the teacher**, learning routines:

- allow you to create a safe and caring learning environment;
- allow you to manage your class positively and effectively;
- enable you to carry out essential routine classroom tasks more quickly and efficiently;
- provide for smoother transitions between activities;
- provide opportunities for you to communicate naturally with children;
- cut down on lesson preparation time;
- help you create a positive socio-affective atmosphere in your lessons and develop relationships with all children based on care, respect and trust.

The following guidelines will help you make the most of learning routines in your lessons:

- Decide on the learning routines that you are going to introduce in your lessons and the exact procedure and language you will use to carry out each one. For example, as part of your opening routines, you could:
  i) Hold up a feely bag with the puppet inside. Ask children *Who's here?*
  ii) Encourage children to answer *Mimi* and call to the puppet to come out of the bag.
  iii) Use the puppet to say *Hello, children!* and get children to respond *Hello, Mimi!*
  iv) Get the puppet to greet individual children, e.g. *Hello, Lucía. How are you today?*, and encourage children to respond *Hello, Mimi. I'm fine.*
- Repeat the learning routines in every lesson. To begin with, use exactly the same procedure and language pattern each time. Explicitly model language and be ready to support children in either non-verbal or verbal responses until they become familiar with the routine.
- Once children are responding confidently to a learning routine, you can start to gradually adjust the procedure and extend the language.
- Use opening and closing routines to provide a clear framework and structure to lessons. However, be careful not to spend too long on these stages of the lesson.
- Be aware that although learning routines may feel repetitive for you, children will love to do them over and over again!
- If you have an English Language Area (ELA) (see p25) in your classroom, it is a good idea to resource it with materials you use for learning routines, such as the *Ferris Wheel* mat, flashcards and Mimi puppet, so children can use the learning routines as a starting point for improvisation and free play.

Ferris Wheel 1 learning routine audioscripts

Hello song CD1 Track 2

Ferris Wheel, Ferris Wheel, (Draw a circle in the air with finger)
Hello, hello, hello. (Wave to the Mimi puppet)
Ferris Wheel, Ferris Wheel, (Draw a circle in the air with finger)
Hop on! Hop on! Let's go! (Beckon with hand)
[Repeat]

Bye bye song CD1 Track 3

Ferris Wheel, Ferris Wheel, (Draw a circle in the air with finger)
Bye bye, bye bye, bye bye. (Wave to the Mimi puppet)
Ferris Wheel, Ferris Wheel, (Draw a circle in the air with finger)
Hop off! Hop off! Bye bye! (Wave to the Mimi puppet)
[Repeat]

Story rhyme CD1 Track 4

It's time for a story. (Open palms of hands as if opening a book)
One, two, three. (Hold up three fingers one by one)
Are you ready? (Hold out hand to the class)
Listen to me! (Hold hand to your ear)

Circle time chant CD1 Track 5

Sit down,
Cross your legs,
Hands together,
Just like me!
Ready to learn,
Ready to play,
Let's start our lesson,
One, two, three!
[Repeat]

Table time train chant CD1 Track 6

It's table time, it's table time! (Form a train and lead children to their tables)
Ch-ch-ch-ch, ch-ch-ch-ch
Off we go, off we go!
Ch-ch-ch-ch, ch-ch-ch-ch
[Repeat]

Mimi's action rhyme CD1 Track 7

Follow, follow, follow me. (Signal for children to copy you)
Walk, walk, walk. (Walk purposefully around the classroom)
One, two, three!
Follow, follow, follow me. (Signal for children to copy you)
Run, run, run. (Run slowly around the classroom)
One, two, three!
Follow, follow, follow me. (Signal for children to copy you)
Jump, jump, jump. (Jump around the classroom)
One, two, three!
Follow, follow, follow me. (Signal for children to copy you)
Sit down, shhh … (Sit down and put your finger to your mouth)
One, two, three!

Weather chant CD1 Track 8

Sunny? Cloudy? Rainy? Windy? (Point to pictures of the weather)
What's the weather like today? (Point to the window)
Sunny? Cloudy? Rainy? Windy? (Point to pictures of the weather)
What's the weather? Can you say?

Clean up song CD1 Track 9

Let's clean up, clean up,
And put our things away.
Let's clean up, clean up,
It's time to stop today!
[Repeat]

Mimi's recycling chant CD1 Track 10

Remember, remember,
One, two, three.
Look and say
The words with me! (Hold up six flashcards in turn for children to say the words.)
Very good! Very good!
Great! Hurray!
For all the words
That we can say!

Mimi's clapping chant CD1 Track 11

Clap – like this!
Clap, clap – like this!
Clap, clap, clap, clap – like this!
Clap, clap, clap, clap, clap, clap – like this!
Clap, clap, clap, clap, clap – like this!
[Repeat]

Settle down rhyme CD1 Track 12

I'm quiet as a mouse.
As still as can be.
No noise at all.
Look at me!
[Repeat]

Learning reviews

Much of children's learning during the pre-school years takes place in an implicit, natural way when children are engaged in meaningful and enjoyable activities. However, as teachers, we also need to encourage children to reflect on their learning in child-friendly ways. This helps develop metacognitive skills – children's ability to think about, plan, monitor, reflect on and evaluate their learning. It also allows you to introduce a range of learning strategies that, over time, will inform and support children's learning. As well as providing immediate benefits, such as giving children agency and choice in their learning, this also lays the foundations for becoming responsible and motivated learners in the future.

The learning reviews in *Ferris Wheel* offer children an opportunity to think about both what they are learning (the product) and how they are learning (the process). It is recommended that a short learning review is carried out as a regular part of the Closing time routines at the end of every lesson. At the end of each unit, the Review lesson also offers an opportunity for children to evaluate their learning during the whole unit.

Learning reviews are most effective when they form part of a three-stage learning cycle:

- **Before:** understand the aim and purpose of the lesson;
- **During:** participate in the lesson;
- **After:** think about the outcomes of the lesson and how they were achieved.

Establishing lesson aims

At the start of lessons, briefly explain the lesson aims in simple, child-friendly language. You may like to use the Mimi puppet to do this. Examples of generic lesson aims are as follows:

- **Lesson 1 (Vocabulary):** *Today we're going to learn words for … . We're also going to do some activities to help us learn to say and remember the words.*
- **Lesson 3 (Story):** *Today we're going to listen to, and watch, a story about Mimi and Dylan. We're also going to do activities to check that we understand the story.*

Conducting a learning review

At the end of the lesson, conduct a learning review either in English or in the children's shared language, or using a mixture of the two. Initially, you may wish to use English to name activities and the learning content, and the children's shared language to express ideas about the learning process. You can either do all or select only some of the steps described below:

i) Refer back to the lesson aims communicated to children at the start of the lesson.
ii) Ask children *What did we do first/next/then?* Elicit their ideas. Be ready to use prompts and reminders as necessary.
iii) Ask further questions about each activity, e.g. *What did you learn when we played the* Ferris Wheel *mat game?* Encourage personal responses and make sure it's clear that there are no correct answers.
iv) Extend children's thinking by asking further questions about each activity, e.g. *How did the* Ferris Wheel *mat game help you learn?* Be prepared for children to find questions about the learning process challenging, especially at first. Model possible responses to clarify what you mean, e.g. *The* Ferris Wheel *mat game helped me see pictures of the words in my head.*
v) Ask children for their personal views of the activities they have done, e.g. *Did you like the* Ferris Wheel *mat game? Why? / Why not?* Again make it clear that there are no correct answers.
vi) Refer back to the lesson aims and ask, e.g. *How well did you learn to say and remember the words?* Encourage children to evaluate their work in the lesson positively with a focus on what they have achieved.
vii) Ask children to talk about their progress in the lesson when they go home. Brief parents and carers to show interest, ask further questions and respond positively. When children do the Review lesson, add your own comment, stamp and/or signature to endorse the children's self-evaluation, and make sure that this is shared with parents.

Activities Bank: Recycling

1. Slow reveal
Hide some flashcards from previous units behind a book. Slowly reveal a flashcard so it is just visible over the top of the book. Children say the word as soon as they recognize it.

2. Quick flash
Hold flashcards from previous units facing you. Quickly, show children the top flashcard, then turn it back to you again. Children name the item they saw. If they can't name it, quickly show the same flashcard a second time.

3. Odd one out
Choose three flashcards from two different units, e.g. *hat, T-shirt, ball.* Display the flashcards and encourage children to point and say the odd one out.

4. Point to the …
Display some flashcards from previous units around the classroom. Choose one of the words at random and say *Point to the (chair).* Children point to the correct flashcard.

5. What's in the bag?
Use the flashcards to review vocabulary from a previous unit. Then choose four of the flashcards (or real objects) and place them in a bag without the children seeing. Children talk to a partner and guess which four items are in the bag. Ask different pairs to share their guesses. When children guess correctly, remove the flashcard or object from the bag and show it to the class.

6. Can you remember?
Display six flashcards from different units and allow children to observe them for about 30 seconds. Remove the flashcards and place them face down. Ask children to name the items they remember. Each time a child remembers a word, show the corresponding flashcard to the class.

7. Secret word
Use the flashcards to review vocabulary from a previous unit. Put the flashcards away. If you have space, sit all the children in a circle. If not, have children play this game at their desks in small teams. Choose one of the words you reviewed and whisper it to the child on your left or to one child in each team. That child then whispers the same word to the child on their left. Continue around the circle or team until the word reaches the final child. Ask him/her to say the word aloud. If it is the correct word, show the corresponding flashcard. If not, ask the other children to say the word. (You could also try the game with full sentences, e.g. *I have a hat.*)

8. Order the flashcards
Choose flashcards from previous units and place them on the floor or board. Slowly say three of the words at random. Ask a volunteer to pick up the three corresponding flashcards and put them in the correct order.

9. Stand up!
Give all or some of the children a flashcard from any previous unit and tell them to sit down. Name one of the flashcards. The child holding that flashcard stands up and says the word. If necessary, the rest of the class can help by saying *Stand up, (Jack)!* Ask the class to repeat the word.

10. Which side?
Use the flashcards to review the words from two previous units. Place one flashcard from each set on opposite sides of the room and ask children to stand in the middle of the room. Shuffle the remaining flashcards and place them face down. Take a flashcard from the pile and show it to the class. Children run, jump or walk to the side of the room that has a flashcard from the same unit.

11. I spy
Choose flashcards from previous units that show different-colored objects. Display them around the classroom. Choose a color and say *I spy something (blue).* Children name the item of that color. Allow a child who answers correctly to take your role and play again.

12. Question chain
Choose flashcards from previous units and sit in a circle with the children if you have space. If not, have children play this game in small teams. Take a flashcard and make a question using that word, e.g. *Is this your (scooter)? Where's your (book)?* Pass the flashcard to the child on your left, or the first child in each team, and encourage them to answer the question. They then turn to the child on their left, ask the same question, and pass the flashcard. Children continue asking and answering questions as they pass the flashcards around the circle or team.

13. 20-second time bomb
Use the flashcards to review the vocabulary from several previous units. Put the flashcards away. Set a timer to 20 seconds and name a unit topic, e.g. *Food/Clothes/Pets.* Children must say as many words as they can from that unit before the timer goes off. As children name the words, show the corresponding flashcards.

14. Which one's missing?
Choose five flashcards from previous units and display them on the board. Ask children to close or cover their eyes. Remove one of the flashcards. Ask children to open their eyes and name the missing flashcard.

15. Relay race
Display flashcards from previous units on the board at the children's height. Divide the class into two teams. Ask a child from each team to stand next to each other a few meters away from the board. Name one of the flashcards. The two children race to touch the correct flashcard. The first child to touch the named flashcard wins a point for their team.

16. What do I have?
Place flashcards from previous units face down on the floor or board. Ask a volunteer to pick one up and show it to the class without you seeing it. Ask questions to help you identify the flashcard, e.g. *Is it big? Is it blue? Is it a toy?* When you are ready to guess, ask *Do you have a (ball)?*

17. Twister
Choose flashcards from previous units and stick them face up on the floor so they are secure. Name a flashcard and ask a volunteer to put one hand or foot on that flashcard. Repeat until both the child's hands and feet are touching flashcards, and he/she is in a position that is difficult to maintain. Count to ten with the class and tell the child to try to stay in the same position until you reach number 10. Repeat with different volunteers.

18. No!
Use the flashcards to review vocabulary from different units. Put the flashcards away. Start to name items from the same topic, e.g. *fish, bird, dog, cat.* Then say an item from a different topic, e.g. *shell.* When you say an item from a different topic, the children shout *No!*

19. Yes or no?
Choose flashcards from previous units. Hold up each flashcard in turn and either say the correct name or an incorrect name. If you say the correct name, the children say *Yes* and wave their arms in the air. If you say the incorrect name, they say *No* and fold their arms.

20. Karaoke
Place one flashcard from each previous unit on the board. Ask a child to touch the flashcard from their favorite unit. Play the songs from that unit. Encourage children to sing along and do the actions.

Activities Bank: The *Ferris Wheel* mat

Note: For larger classes, create a *Ferris Wheel* mat learning station (see p25) and do these activities with small groups. When demonstrating a new mat activity, ensure the other learning stations are familiar activities so the rest of the class can work independently.

1. Where's the ...?

Hide six flashcards or objects in different pockets of the mat. Ask *Where's the (teddy)?* Children take turns guessing, e.g. *It's in the (blue) pocket!* or *Is it in the (green) pocket?* When a child guesses correctly, remove the object and show it to the class. Alternatively, ask children *What's in the (blue) pocket?* and encourage them to guess, e.g. *It's the teddy.*

2. Listen and do!

Display some objects or flashcards. Put children in pairs and give each pair an instruction, e.g. *Put the pencil in the pink pocket!* If they follow the instruction correctly, encourage the class to clap and say *Fantastic!* You can also instruct each pair to remove an object, e.g. *Give me the pencil, please.*

3. Remember, remember!

Put six flashcards or objects in different pockets of the mat. Talk to the children as you do this, e.g. *Let's put the ball in the yellow pocket.* Then ask *Can you remember where the (ball) is?* Ask children to raise their hands if they remember. Choose a child and encourage them to say *It's in the (yellow) pocket.* Ask the child to remove the object and show it to the class.

4. My favorite color

Write each child's name on a small piece of white construction paper. Ask children to color their card using their favorite color from the Ferris Wheel. Children take turns naming the color and putting their card inside the corresponding pocket. At the end, count the cards in each pocket. Ask children which pocket has the most cards and say *(Red) is our favorite color!*

5. Hide and seek

Ask children to turn around as you place the Meerkat family flashcards in different pockets of the mat. Leave a small part of each character's body visible. Have children turn around. Ask *Where's (Dylan)?* Ask a volunteer to point and say *(Dylan) is in the (blue) pocket!*

6. Mimi's magic

Hold up the mat. Ask individual children to check the pockets are empty, e.g. *Please look in the green pocket. Nothing there? Thank you!* Turn the mat around so the pockets are facing you and hide a flashcard or object in one of them. Show the mat to the class and have the Mimi puppet wave a "wand" (a ruler or pencil) as you say *Abracadabra! Listen to me. Look in the (red) pocket. What can you see?* Invite a child to remove and name the object.

7. *Ferris Wheel* ride

You will need small passport-sized photos of the children with reusable sticky tac on the back for this activity. Children choose the pod they want to ride in and stick their photo on it. Encourage them to say *I'm in (red)!* Then ask them to make big circles with their arms as they say the following rhyme: *Round and round and round we go! Oh, Ferris Wheel, we love you so!* Alternatively, ask children to bring in a favorite doll or teddy from home. Invite children to place their toys inside the pockets and say *My (teddy) is in (green)!*

8. Color swat!

You will need two plastic fly swatters for this activity. Hang the mat on the wall. Ask two children to stand either side of the mat and give each child a fly swatter. Name a color. The children should swat the correct color on the mat. Alternatively, place the mat on the floor and ask two or three children to walk around the mat. When you name a color, children must quickly touch the correct color.

9. Action game

Hang the mat on the wall. Over several lessons, teach children an action for each color, e.g. *When I say red, jump!* Introduce no more than two actions per lesson, and review the previous colors and actions each time. Once children are familiar with the colors and associated actions, point to a pocket on the mat and say *(Red)!* Children respond by doing the action and saying the word, e.g. *Jump!*

10. Odd one out

Arrange flashcards in six groups of four – three of the items in each group should be from the same lexical set and one should be from a different set. Put each group of flashcards inside a pocket on the mat. Invite a child to choose a color and remove the flashcards from that pocket. The child names each flashcard and then identifies the odd one out.

11. Sorting shapes

Ahead of time, cut out a selection of shapes from construction paper in the colors from the Ferris Wheel. Put children in small groups and give each group a variety of shapes. Ask them to organize them by color. Have a volunteer from each group place the shapes in the same-colored pocket as they say *A (green) (circle).*

12. Musical mat

Place six flashcards in different pockets and lay the mat on the floor. Ask six children to stand around the mat, one next to each pocket. Play music and ask children to dance around the mat. Pause the music and have children stand still. Say a color and ask the child next to that pocket to take out the flashcard and name the item. Ask the class to shout *Yes* and wave their arms if the child is correct and shout *No* and fold their arms if the child is incorrect.

13. Number game

You will need a big dice for this activity (you can make this out of construction paper). Hide a flashcard in each pocket of the mat. Write the numbers 1–6 on pieces of paper and place these clockwise on the pockets of the mat. Ask children to take turns throwing the dice and counting and saying the number. The child then removes the flashcard from the pocket with that number and names the item.

14. Mood mat

You will need pictures of emojis, e.g. happy, sad, scared, surprised, angry, calm, for this activity. Show each emoji and ask children to act out the emotion using facial expression and body language. Ask a child to choose an emoji and place it in the pocket with the color they associate with that emotion. Encourage them to name the emotion and the color. Make sure children understand that there are no correct answers.

15. *Ferris Wheel* role-play

If you like, prepare simple "tickets" for the role-play. Hang the mat on the wall and ask a small group of children to make a line in front of the mat. Use the Mimi puppet to act out a simple role-play with each child. For example: Mimi: *Hello, (David).* / Child: *Hello, Mimi.* / M: *Welcome to the Ferris Wheel! Choose a color.* / C: *(Orange), please.* [the child touches the correct pocket] / M: *Here's your ticket!* / C: *Thank you.*

Activities Bank: The Mimi puppet

The use of a puppet helps create a positive and warm environment for learning and playing in English. Children will develop a familiarity and fondness for Mimi, making the course materials even more engaging and appealing. Using the Mimi puppet as an integral part of your daily activities and routines brings fantasy, magic and humor into the classroom and creates opportunities for children to use English as part of their real-life interactions. Children will feel more secure and confident speaking English to Mimi and are more likely to actively participate, especially as they know she doesn't understand their first language!

1. Daily routines
Use the puppet to greet and say goodbye to children in every lesson. You can also use her for other classroom routines, such as the weather, the day of the week and taking attendance.

2. Social and emotional learning
Use the puppet to show affection towards the children and encourage the children to show affection back. Establish that the puppet has feelings and moods, e.g. happy, sad, tired. Encourage them to empathize with and respect these feelings, as well as telling Mimi how they feel.

3. Boosting confidence and self-esteem
Use the puppet to encourage and praise children. Ask children to show Mimi their work and get her to show interest and give positive feedback. If the class does a task well, use the puppet to praise and reward them with stickers or similar.

4. Demonstrating and modeling activities
Demonstrate and model activities with the puppet, e.g. act out a conversation or role-play. Do a cooperative activity using the puppet as your partner so children can see what to do. You can also use Mimi to drill vocabulary or short sentences. Children repeat what Mimi said in exactly the same way.

5. Linking fantasy and reality
Use the puppet as a bridge between the imaginative world of the Meerkat family and the real world. For example, use the puppet to show how language introduced in the stories is also applicable and relevant to the context of the classroom.

6. Introducing humor
Use the puppet to introduce an element of humor to lessons, e.g. when you want to surprise children or need to get their attention. For example, the puppet can be naughty, moody, make mistakes, answer questions incorrectly, or refuse to follow your instructions.

7. Learning reviews
Use the Mimi puppet when conducting learning reviews and have her take on the role of teacher. Alternatively, pretend she forgot what the children learned and ask them to remind her, or have Mimi answer your questions incorrectly and encourage children to correct her.

8. Managing your class positively
Use the puppet to help you manage your class, e.g. tell children that Mimi's sleeping or has a headache so they need to be quiet, or have Mimi give them instructions to form a line or a circle, e.g. *Come here, please, (Alex).* Similarly, when conflicts arise, have Mimi ask children to say sorry and be friends again. When selecting children to participate in activities, use Mimi to point to children and say a little rhyme, e.g. *Red, yellow, blue. I love YOU!*

9. Role-play and drama
You can use the puppet to act out simple role-plays or short versions of the unit stories, with the puppet taking on Mimi's role and children acting out the other parts.

10. Games and play
Have Mimi take your role in games to engage children's interest. If you have learning stations or an English Language Area (ELA) in your classroom (see p25), put the puppet there along with other resources, such as flashcards, for use during child-led play.

11. Hello, Mimi!
Ask children to sit in a circle. Play music as children pass the puppet around the circle. Whenever you pause the music, the child who has the puppet holds it up and says *Hello, Mimi!* If you wish, encourage the child to tell the puppet something about themselves, e.g. *I'm Maria. I have a ball.* You could also ask children to bring a stuffed animal from home and have their toys greet Mimi.

12. Do what Mimi says
Use the puppet to give instructions for children to follow, e.g. *Stand up. Sit down. Jump. Run. Stop.* Alternatively, display some flashcards and use the puppet to say, e.g. *Touch the (apple).*

13. Guess what Mimi's thinking
Display 3–6 flashcards on the floor or board. Hold up Mimi and put her in a thinking pose. Encourage children to guess which flashcard Mimi is thinking about. Have Mimi nod or shake her head and say *Yes/No.* When a child guesses correctly, Mimi gives them a high five.

14. Guess what's in Mimi's bag
Put several different objects or flashcards in a non-transparent bag. Make the puppet hold up the bag and ask *What's in my bag?* Children take turns guessing. If a child guesses correctly, Mimi removes the object or flashcard from the bag and shows it to the children.

15. Hide and seek
Choose two children and ask them to cover their eyes. Hide the puppet somewhere in the classroom so it is still partially visible. Ask the two children to open their eyes. Ask *Where's Mimi?* As the two children search, encourage the class to say *no, no, no* softly when they are far from the puppet, and *YES, YES, YES!* loudly when they get close to the puppet.

16. Mimi's song choice
When children learn a new song, draw a picture to illustrate it on a piece of construction paper. Keep the cards in a box. Use the puppet to take a card, show it to the class and say *Please sing this song.* Use Mimi as a conductor while children sing by having her hold a pencil or ruler. Hold her high for children to sing more loudly and low for children to sing quietly.

17. Taking Mimi home
Allow children to take turns taking the puppet home. When children bring the puppet back, encourage them to tell the class about the visit, e.g. where Mimi slept and where she went. If you wish, you could ask parents/carers to take photos of the visit and add them to a shared photo album, *Mimi's Travel Diary.*

Activities Bank: Social and emotional learning (SEL)

By integrating the development of social and emotional learning (SEL) skills into your teaching, you will enable children to deal confidently with the psychological, social and academic demands of pre-school, and lay the foundations for their future educational and life success.

1. Social development
Show that you value the way children relate to each other. Encourage children to think through any social difficulties that arise by asking questions such as *How do you feel when someone ...?* This will help children see situations from other people's point of view.

2. Emotional development
Observe children's body language, eye contact, behavior and participation in class. Acknowledge children's emotions, while also making it clear that certain behavior is not acceptable. Provide a positive role model in the way that you express and manage your own emotions. Make discussing your feelings (happy, sad, angry, calm, sleepy, etc.) part of your daily class routine. Sharing your feelings will facilitate an emotional connection with children and give them the confidence to talk about how they feel.

3. Curiosity and confidence
Create a warm and supportive environment in which children feel secure about taking risks, asking questions, sharing ideas or making mistakes. Ask questions to scaffold children's understanding and promote further learning. Give praise and feedback that honestly acknowledges children's achievements and efforts. Make it clear that making mistakes is an important part of learning. Establish regular routines in class so that children feel secure about what is expected of them.

4. Resilience
Resilience is the ability to bounce back and keep going after a difficult or stressful experience. Two significant ways to help children develop resilience are i) to foster positive self-esteem and ii) to reinforce and promote self-belief. A safe and caring learning environment allows children to try to achieve their goals independently while always feeling that they are supported by the adults around them.

5. Responsible decision-making
Children need to practice making positive choices about both their personal and social behavior, and their academic work. Start with simple choices and decisions that are age-appropriate, e.g. the order in which to do activities or which materials to use. Model thinking through the options, making it clear that there are no correct answers. Avoid making decisions for children as, although this may often be quicker and easier, it denies children the opportunity to consider the different options and select the most appropriate action.

6. Self-management
Giving children strategies to control and manage their behavior will contribute to a positive atmosphere in the classroom. After a lively activity, introduce a calming technique to regain children's attention. Ask the children to sit down very slowly while you count down from six. By the time you reach number one, the children should be seated and calm enough to move on to the next activity. Teach children to use language, e.g. *I don't like it when ...*, rather than physical actions to express displeasure. Provide them with strategies to calm down, such as relaxing and breathing deeply or deliberately moving away from the upsetting situation. If possible, create a "peace corner" where children can go when they feel angry or upset. Provide cushions, books and stuffed animals to help children relax and process their emotions.

7. Cooperation and empathy
Pair and group work gives children the opportunity to interact positively and show empathy towards their peers. It is also helpful in developing cooperation skills. Encourage children to listen to and show an interest in others and see things from their point of view. When a child shares something about themselves, encourage them to ask a classmate to do the same by asking *How about you?* Be inclusive at all times and encourage children to behave respectfully towards their classmates by using language such as *please*, *thank you* and *sorry*.

8. Supportiveness and self-esteem
Encourage children to support and help their classmates. Pairing shy children with a more confident classmate can be beneficial for the self-esteem of both children. Encourage children to help and guide each other throughout the day, not only with academic tasks, but also with daily routines, such as putting on coats and shoes, etc. When playing games or doing other activities, remind children to use positive language. If the answer is incorrect, encourage them to say, e.g. *Try again.* If the answer is correct, encourage them to offer praise, e.g. *Great job! Very good!*

9. Autonomy
Little by little, encourage children to become more independent and responsible for their learning and behavior in class. Provide them with simple age-appropriate strategies for everyday tasks, such as putting on their coats, and allow them to make their own choices wherever possible. As part of developing autonomy and metacognitive skills, encourage children to regularly reflect on their learning (see p18). Use the Review lessons in each unit to foster self-awareness and an ability to self-evaluate.

10. Making an effort
Encourage children to believe in their ability to master different skills through effort and persistence. Praise achievement while, at the same time, focusing on the underlying effort. If children find an activity challenging, encourage them not to give up by singing the Level 2 song: *I can do it if I try* (CD1 Track 41). Monitor children's response to their learning in each unit using the self-evaluation in the Review lesson and emphasize that increased effort will lead to more progress.

11. Free play
Child-led play is one of the key ways in which children naturally develop SEL skills, such as relating to friends, managing emotions, solving problems, resolving conflict, developing autonomy and making decisions. An English Language Area (ELA) (see p25) can be a great way to provide opportunities for free play.

Activities Bank: Life skills

Life skills

Pre-school may be children's first experience of extended separation from their family. By teaching basic life skills, you help children adapt to the new social context of life at school. Teaching life skills also enriches children's exposure to English and allows them to acquire new language in a natural and meaningful way.

1. Put on your coat
Show children how to put on their coats by placing the coat on the floor with the hood or collar at their feet. The child inserts their arms in the armholes, and then lifts the coat up and over their head and into position.

2. Find your coat hook or shelf
In addition to labelling coat hooks or shelves with children's first names, add a picture so children can recognize it easily. Provide a selection of pictures showing English vocabulary children already know or will soon learn. Allow children to choose their picture.

3. Look after your clothes
Teach children to put their jacket, hat and gloves into the pockets of their coat before they put it on their coat hook. This way, they will always know where to find them.

4. Clean up
Allow time for children to clean up materials. Ensure everyone knows where each kind of material belongs and have children work together in teams to get the classroom clean and neat. Use the *Clean up song* (see p17) to signal when it's time to clean up.

5. Little helpers
Nominate helpers to give out or collect classroom materials. Rotate the helpers on a daily or weekly basis so everyone gets a turn. This will make children feel valued and help them see the importance of their contribution.

6. Put it in the trash can
Encourage children to use the trash can when clearing up waste paper and snack wrappers. You could also show them how to sharpen their own pencils over the trash can.

7. Make a line or circle
To make a line, use gesture to show that children should stand one behind the other and place their hands on the shoulders or waist of the child in front of them. To make a circle, stand at the front of the line and ask everyone to hold hands. Lead children around to form a circle.

8. Put belongings in your backpack
Encourage children to take responsibility for their own possessions. Give time for children to take out and put away belongings in their backpacks. Praise children who do this independently.

9. Share materials
Encourage children to take turns and share materials. Show that you value a willingness to share materials and cooperate as much as completing the activity.

10. Say "please" and "thank you"
Teach these words early on. Consistently remind children to say *please* and *thank you* both to you and to each other. Make it clear that children are more likely to get a positive response when they use these words.

11. Motor skills and projects
Project work provides an opportunity for the integrated development of both language and fine motor skills, such as rolling modeling clay, tearing tissue paper and using finger paints. Demonstrate these skills before asking children to use them. Praise and value children's efforts.

12. Wash and dry your hands
Teach the procedure for washing hands (see Level 3 Student's Book, p41). Establish when and why it is important for children to wash their hands, e.g. before and after meals, after going to the playground and bathroom, and encourage them to do this independently.

13. Be active
Teach children the importance of moving their bodies every day. Incorporate physical activity into your classroom routines by using action songs and games. This will help develop coordination and gross motor skills. Show children how to place a hand on their heart after physical activity to show that it's beating faster and explain why this is good for them.

14. Wait your turn
Gently insist that children wait their turn to speak, and listen to others without calling out or interrupting. Explain or elicit why this is important. During Circle time, it may help to have an object, e.g. a soft ball, to show whose turn it is to speak. Similarly, when playing classroom games, explain that everyone has equal right to participate and praise children who wait their turn.

15. Cover a cough or sneeze
Explain basic hygiene about spreading germs from coughs and colds. Train children to hold up their arms to cover their mouths when they cough or sneeze. This is preferable to using hands, which they may then use to touch classmates or shared materials.

16. Care with scissors
If children use scissors, make sure that they are holding the scissors correctly. When they get up to put any scraps of paper in the trash can, make sure they leave the scissors on the table.

17. Safe in the sun
Explain to children why it is important to wear a sunhat and sunscreen to protect them from the sun. Ask children to put on their hats before going outside and not to take them off until they come back inside.

18. Bathroom visits
Build in opportunities for children to go to the bathroom either before or after lessons and at recess. Make it clear, however, that if children need to go to the bathroom at any other time, they are free to do so. If the bathrooms are not in the classroom, children could wear a card around their necks to show that they have been authorized to leave the classroom.

19. Drink water
Explain to children why it is important to keep hydrated and drink water throughout the day. Make sure children know that they can ask for water if they feel thirsty.

20. Pleasure in participating
It is important not to force children to participate unless they are willing to do so. At the same time, it is crucial to create an environment in which children take pleasure in participating and learning with their peers. This will help children to develop other life and SEL skills, such as cooperation, tolerance, empathy and respect.

Activities Bank: Learning enrichment

Ferris Wheel provides everything you need to teach children English in an enjoyable and effective way. However, if you also have the time and opportunity to incorporate additional materials, resources and activities, this will enrich children's learning experience and ensure maximum appeal and motivation.

1. Picturebooks

Picturebooks are a great way to expose children to new language in a natural, motivating context. It is a good idea to focus on picturebooks that relate to the topic of the current unit, e.g. Clothes, Food, Pets, and that contain simple and repetitive language. However, keep in mind that children don't need to understand every word to enjoy the story, and you can make use of the illustrations, intonation, facial expression, questions and repetition to support understanding. Once children become familiar with a picturebook, encourage them to join in with repeated phrases and, if appropriate, to act out the story.

You may also like to encourage children to bring English picturebooks from home to share with the class. Put children in small groups to look at their picturebooks together. Encourage them to talk about what they like and can see on each page.

2. Dressing up

Provide a selection of dress-up clothes. Encourage children to practice fine motor skills by putting on and removing the clothes independently, asking for help from their classmates if needed. Encourage children to give each other instructions as they get dressed, e.g. *Put on your hat.* Allow them to play freely and imaginatively with the clothes, e.g. organizing a costume party or drawing pictures of themselves and each other wearing their costumes.

3. Posters and visual images

As well as using the *Ferris Wheel* posters (see Resource Bank) to decorate the classroom walls and reinforce key language, topics and concepts, collect and display other visuals that relate to the topic of the current unit. Make use of the posters to recycle language and play games, e.g. by asking children to run and touch something on the poster. You may also like to use children's artwork for recycling activities. This gives a specific purpose to the work children produce and raises self-esteem.

4. Toys and realia

Wherever the unit topic allows, try to provide real-life objects or toys that children can touch and interact with. This will help create a direct connection in children's minds between their language learning and the real world. It will also make children's learning feel less abstract and more meaningful. Use the toys and objects in place of, or as well as, flashcards when you present and practice vocabulary. You can also use them as props for role-plays, drama and "feely bag" games.

5. Mime and drama

Mime allows children to produce a non-verbal response to language and helps boost confidence and self-esteem. Children can mime what happens as you tell a familiar story about Mimi and Dylan, for example, or they can mime in response to a set of instructions you give. Drama enables you to create a realistic context for children to practice using English they know. For example: you can create simple role-plays using dress-up clothes and props; get children to act out a simplified version of the Mimi and Dylan stories; pretend to be the Meerkat family or the real children; or allow them to take on the role of teacher, as Mimi does in the Review lessons. Use the Mimi puppet to help you transition from the real world to fantasy, and vice versa.

6. Music, movement and dance

Music, movement and dance develop gross motor skills and rhythm, and provide an engaging context in which to respond to simple instructional language. You may like to use the karaoke version of a favorite song from the course as the basis for teaching children a simple dance. It is also beneficial to teach children simple movement sequences, in which you start with one or two instructions, e.g. *Put your arms in the air. Jump three times.*, and build additional actions cumulatively. You can then use these sequences at moments when you feel children's energy levels are getting low and they need to get up and move around.

7. Movies, TV and video clips

In addition to the *Ferris Wheel* animated stories, songs and real-life videos, you may like to select other short movies and video clips from online sources that relate to the current unit topic. You could also occasionally allow children to watch their favorite TV show in the original English language version. This will expose them to natural English being spoken in a familiar context by well-loved characters. You may also like to suggest that parents or carers show children the English version of their favorite TV shows at home.

8. Children's multilingual identities

The children in your class may have diverse cultural backgrounds and speak another language at home, in addition to the shared language of the classroom and English. It is important to show that you respect and value each child's culture and language. Encouraging children to talk about their culture in class will help reinforce a positive sense of identity and create an atmosphere of tolerance and mutual respect. For example, when learning a new word in English, you could ask children to tell you the word in the language they speak at home. Alternatively, you could ask *How many different words do we know for "cat"?* Show your own enthusiasm for learning words in different languages and ask *Do any of the words sound similar?* Similarly, you can ask questions that get children to compare aspects of their culture with North-American culture, e.g. *Do you have a sandwich for lunch? What do you have?*

9. Home-school link

Working in partnership with parents and carers can be a hugely beneficial way to enrich children's learning. Regular letters to parents (see Resource Bank) with information about your approach, content and expectations, along with specific guidance on how parents and carers can support their children's learning, will facilitate communication. It is also a good idea to hold regular meetings with parents and carers, and to ensure they know you are available whenever they have questions or concerns. Given that parents and carers are likely to have had a different experience of learning a foreign language, it may help them understand your approach if they can informally observe a lesson. Alternatively, you could share video clips of your lessons during an explanatory talk. If parents have a good level of English, invite them to visit the class as a volunteer, either to assist children with individual work, read a story or give a short talk related to the current unit topic.

10. Out and about

Whenever appropriate and possible, it is beneficial to take children on trips outside the classroom in order to make the connection between their learning and the real world. This may involve visiting different places within the school, e.g. the playground or music room. If there is a school garden, children could visit the vegetable patch and identify food that is growing there. If possible, plant some seeds, water them regularly and monitor how they grow. Trips further afield might include a visit to a local park for a picnic, or to a farm, zoo or museum.

11. Learning stations

Learning stations provide meaningful, self-directed language practice and develop skills such as autonomy, responsible decision-making and cooperation.
When organized during lesson time, learning stations also provide you with an opportunity to give extra support to small groups of children. Start off with two or three learning stations, and add new stations gradually through the year. Ensure you use activities that children have already practiced with you before they use the station independently. Organize children in pairs or small groups and have them take turns visiting each station. Some ideas for learning stations include:

- **Feely bag:** Children take turns feeling and guessing the objects in a non-transparent bag.
- ***Ferris Wheel* mat games:** see p20.
- **Drawing station:** Children draw their favorite animal, toy, family member, etc.
- **Matching pairs:** Provide two copies of a selection of five to six flashcards, mix them up and place them face down. Children take turns turning over two cards. If they are a matching pair, they keep the cards. If not, they turn them back over in the same place and continue the game.
- **Watch and learn:** Play videos or animations from the current unit or previous units for children to watch and enjoy. For the songs, encourage them to sing along and join in with the actions.
- **Classification station:** Children work together to classify objects or flashcards using different criteria, e.g. colors, shapes, size, etc.

12. English Language Area (ELA)

In some educational contexts, it is usual practice to divide the pre-school classroom into different learning areas or activity centers. These provide opportunities for children to play and experiment with a range of resources and to interact with their peers in an autonomous, child-led way. Typical learning areas or activity centers include: a reading area (with soft cushions, books, audio devices and headphones); a communication and drama area (with props, e.g. store items or kitchen utensils, and dress-up clothes); a science area (with small slides, weights, balances, sand and water); and a modeling and construction area (with building blocks and modeling materials).
You can also create an English Language Area (ELA) using course materials, such as the *Ferris Wheel* mat, the Mimi puppet, a selection of flashcards and story cards, and a computer or tablet with headphones and access to the digital materials. Ensure that the activities and materials are familiar to the children so they can repeat, imitate, and create activities and games closely based on teacher-led activities using known language. For example, children may pretend to take on the role of teacher and use the *Ferris Wheel* mat and flashcards to play a well-known game, or use the Mimi puppet to test a friend on vocabulary, as Mimi does with Dylan in the Review lessons.
As the idea is for the teacher to monitor and observe, but not directly intervene, it is essential for each learning area to have clear rules, e.g. the reading area is strictly for quiet reading and only English can be spoken in the ELA. Observing children as they play in the ELA will also provide you with invaluable feedback on their learning and progress to date.

Hello Welcome!

Vocabulary and language

- **Main vocabulary:** Mimi, Dylan; boy, girl; Mommy, Daddy; Ferris Wheel, red
- **Key language:** Hello, I'm (Mimi).
- **Other language:** blue

Unit objectives

- Identify and name Mimi and Dylan
- Identify and name two colors
- Identify and name Mommy and Daddy
- Sing *Hello, hello, hello*
- Sing *Welcome to the Ferris Wheel*
- Say *hello* and your name
- Say if you're a boy or girl

Songs

Language song

Hello, hello, hello CD1 Track 13

Hello, hello, hello. (Wave)
I'm Mimi. (Hold up Mimi puppet)
I'm Mimi.
Hello, hello, hello. (Wave)
I'm a girl.
I'm a girl.
Hello, hello, hello. (Wave)

Hello, hello, hello. (Wave)
I'm Dylan. (Hold up Dylan puppet)
I'm Dylan.
Hello, hello, hello. (Wave)
I'm a boy.
I'm a boy.
Hello, hello, hello. (Wave)

Language song

Welcome to the Ferris Wheel! CD1 Track 14

Welcome to the Ferris Wheel! (Make a big circle with your hands)
Mimi and Dylan (Point to Mimi and Dylan flashcards)
Mommy and Daddy too (Point to Mommy and Daddy flashcards)
Welcome to the Ferris Wheel! (Beckon)
We love you! (Hug yourself)

Welcome to the Ferris Wheel! (Make a big circle with your hands)
Mimi and Dylan (Point to Mimi and Dylan flashcards)
Mommy and Daddy too (Point to Mommy and Daddy flashcards)
Welcome to the Ferris Wheel! (Beckon)
We love you! (Hug yourself)

Hello Welcome!

Listen, point and sing ***Hello, hello, hello.*** **Stick the stickers of Mimi and Dylan.**
Language: Mimi, Dylan; boy, girl; Hello, I'm (Mimi).

1:13

3

Learning objectives

- Identify and name Mimi and Dylan
- Identify and name two colors
- Sing *Hello, hello, hello*
- Say *hello* and your name
- Say if you're a boy or girl

Materials

- Class CDs, flashcards, *Ferris Wheel* mat, Mimi puppet

Main vocabulary

- Mimi, Dylan; boy, girl

Key language

- Hello, I'm (Mimi).

Teacher's tip: Circle time and Table time

If there isn't space for children to sit on the floor during Circle time, they can sit at their desks. For the *Circle time chant* (see p 17), when it says "hands together," have them hold hands with the children at their table. Table time is when children work with their books. When it's time to do so, ask them to stand up and form a train with the children at their table. All the trains then link up to make a whole-class train. Say the *Table time train chant* (see p 17) as you move around the room, dropping each team off at their table. When each team sits, they give each other a high five!

Circle time

Hello song & puppet (CD1 Track 2; see TB p 17 & 21)

Opening routines (see TB p 16)

Lesson aims (see TB p 18)

Introduce Mimi and Dylan.

- Use the puppet to introduce Mimi. Say *Hello, I'm Mimi.* Use the puppet to wave to the children. Children wave back and say *Hello, Mimi.*
- Hide the puppet behind your back and make it suddenly appear. Each time children see the puppet, they call out *Hello, Mimi.* Repeat several times.
- Use the flashcard to introduce Dylan in the same way.
- Hide the puppet and flashcard behind your back. Produce them in turn and children call out *Hello, Mimi* or *Hello, Dylan* depending who they see.

Tell Mimi and Dylan your name.

- Use the puppet to say *Hello, I'm Mimi* to you and respond by saying *Hello, I'm …* and say your name.
- Repeat with the flashcard of Dylan.
- Use the puppet / flashcard to say *Hello, I'm Mimi / Dylan* to individual children and encourage them to say *Hello, I'm … .*
- Explain that Mimi and Dylan are going to help the children learn English.

Introduce the Ferris Wheel.

- Put the *Ferris Wheel* mat on the floor or board. Explain that Mimi and Dylan live near the Ferris Wheel.
- Put the Mimi puppet on the red pod of the wheel and name the color. Children repeat.
- Put the flashcard of Dylan on the blue pod of the wheel and name the color. Children repeat.
- Say *Red!* and children say *Mimi!* Say *Blue!* and children say *Dylan!*
- Then say the names and children name the colors.

Sing *Hello, hello, hello.*

CD1 Track 13

- Hold up the puppet. Say *Mimi says: "I'm Mimi. I'm a girl."*
- Repeat with the flashcard of Dylan: *I'm Dylan. I'm a boy.*
- Indicate girls and boys in the circle to clarify meaning.
- Say *Let's sing "Hello, hello, hello."*
- Play the song. Hold up Mimi (puppet) and Dylan (flashcard) for each verse and wave when they say hello. Play the song again. Children sing and act out the song (see actions on TB p 27).

Game: *Girl or boy!*

- Hold up the puppet and ask *Girl or boy?* Children respond *Girl!* Repeat with the flashcard of Dylan.
- Go around the circle and encourage children to say with you *Girl, girl, boy,* etc.
- Say *I'm* (your name). *I'm a (girl).* Use the puppet and the flashcard of Dylan to do the same. Encourage confident children to do the same.

Table time

Student's Book p 3

Listen, point and sing *Hello, hello, hello.*

CD1 Track 13

- Point to Mimi and Dylan as children listen.
- Play the audio again. Children join in pointing to Mimi and Dylan.

Stick the stickers of Mimi and Dylan.

- Children put on the stickers of Mimi and Dylan.
- Explain that children will "meet" the other characters on the Ferris Wheel in stories later in the book.

Activity Book p 3

Point and say the names. Trace to circle Mimi and Dylan.

- Children point and say the names of the characters.
- They trace to circle Mimi and Dylan.

Say.

- Children say *Hello, I'm … .*

Closing time

Learning review (see TB p 18)

Closing routines (see TB p 16)

Bye bye song and puppet (CD1 Track 3; see TB p 17 & 21)

Use the **Navio App** to play the vocabulary game, and encourage children to do the same at home.

Lesson 2 Language

Listen, point and sing *Welcome to the Ferris Wheel!* Color the pod red. Say.
Language: Mommy, Daddy, Mimi, Dylan; Ferris Wheel; red

4

Learning objectives

- Identify and name Mommy and Daddy
- Sing *Welcome to the Ferris Wheel*
- Listen and point to the characters

Materials

- Class CDs, flashcards, *Ferris Wheel* mat, Mimi puppet

Main vocabulary

- Mommy, Daddy; Mimi, Dylan; Ferris Wheel; red

Teacher's tip: Forming a bond with the puppet

Allow children to come close and hold Mimi's hand or stroke her head as they greet her. Initially, some children may feel shy, so allow confident children to come out first. At the end of the lesson, invite them again and you may find more children feel confident enough to touch Mimi and begin to form a bond with her.

Circle time

Hello song & puppet (CD1 Track 2; see TB p 17 & 21)
Opening routines (see TB p 16)
Recycling activity (*red, blue*; *Hello, I'm Mimi/Dylan. I'm a girl/boy.*) (see TB p 19)
Lesson aims (see TB p 18)

Introduce Mommy and Daddy.

- Use the flashcards to introduce Mommy and Daddy. Repeat the procedure for introducing Mimi and Dylan in Lesson 1.

Game: *Guess who!*

- Put the *Ferris Wheel* mat on the floor or board.
- Lay out the flashcards of *Mommy, Daddy, Mimi* and *Dylan*. Children name the characters.
- Turn the flashcards face down and mix them up. Put two flashcards on the red pod of the wheel and two flashcards on the blue pod.
- Point to the flashcards in turn and encourage children to guess who's on red and who's on blue, e.g. *Mommy!* Turn the flashcard over. Say *Hurray!* and children clap if it is Mommy. Say *Oh no! It's … (Mimi). Let's try again!* if it isn't Mommy. Repeat several times.

Sing *Welcome to the Ferris Wheel.*

CD1 Track 14

- Lay out the flashcards in the order of the song.
- Say *Let's sing "Welcome to the Ferris Wheel."*
- Play the song. Make a big circle with your arms for *Ferris Wheel* and wave to the flashcards when they are named in the song.
- Repeat. Children sing and act out the song (see actions on TB p 27).

Table time

Student's Book p 4

- Say *Point to Mommy/Daddy/Mimi/Dylan/the Ferris Wheel.* Children point to the pictures in turn.
- Say *Point to red/blue.* Children point to things in the picture that are red or blue, e.g. Daddy's uniform, Mimi's dress.
- Hold up your book. Use children's shared language to explain that Mommy and Daddy run the Ferris Wheel. Mommy works in the office and Daddy sells tickets to go on the wheel. Mimi and Dylan love going on the wheel. Point to the hedgehog and explain that other animals love going on the wheel too.

Listen, point and sing *Welcome to the Ferris Wheel!*

CD1 Track 14

- Play the audio again. Children listen, point to the Ferris Wheel and characters in their books and sing the song.
- Remember that you can use the karaoke version of the song when the children are confident.

Color the pod red. Say.

- Children color the pod on the Ferris Wheel red and then say the word *red*.

Activity Book p 4

Color the circle for Mimi and Dylan in blue. Color the circle for Mommy and Daddy in red.

- Children color the circle between Mimi and Dylan blue. They color the circle between Mommy and Daddy red.

Say.

- They say the names of the four characters.

Closing time

Learning review (see TB p 18)
Closing routines (see TB p 16)
Bye bye song & puppet (CD 1 Track 3; see TB p 17 & 21)

Use the **Navio App** to listen to the song, and encourage children to do the same at home.

Family
The Ferris Wheel

Vocabulary and language

- **Main vocabulary:** mommy, daddy, grandma, grandpa, brother, sister; blue, green, red, yellow
- **Key language:** Where's your (grandma)? Here. This is my (mommy).
- **Content language:** round, wheel; This is a wheel. Wheels go round and round.
- **Other language:** Ferris Wheel, orange, pink, bus; Here we go. Round and round. I love my (mommy). The wheels on the bus go round and round.

Unit objectives

- Identify and name family members
- Sing the language song *Where's your grandma?*
- Ask and say where family members are
- Understand and join in the story *The Ferris Wheel*
- Sing and act out the story song *The Ferris Wheel song*
- Sing the values song *I love my family*
- Recognize the value of loving your family
- Understand that wheels go round
- Sing and act out the traditional song *The wheels on the bus*
- Review your learning and progress
- Participate in a collaborative project

Story

CD1 Track 21

Picture 1

Narrator: Grandma, Grandpa, Mimi and Dylan go on the Ferris Wheel.
Mimi: Where's Grandma?
Grandma: Here! I'm with your brother. In yellow!
Dylan: Where's Grandpa?
Grandpa: Here! I'm with your sister. In orange!
Dylan: Great!
Mimi: Here we go! Round and round.
Dylan: Oh, this is fun.

Picture 2

Zara: Look, Mommy. It's the Ferris Wheel!
Mommy: Hello, Mrs. Zebra. Hello Zara. Hop on!
Zara: Thank you. Here we go! Round and round. This is fun.

Picture 3

Mimi: Oh, look! It's Eddie and his daddy in blue. Hello, Eddie.
Eddie: Hello, Mimi.
Dylan: Oh, look! It's Leo and his grandma in pink. Hello, Leo.
Leo: Hello, Dylan.
Mimi: And look! It's Zara and her mommy. Hello, Zara.
Zara: Hello, Mimi.
Mommy: Time to hop off now!

Picture 4

Mimi, Dylan, Eddie, Zara, Leo: Hurray! I love the Ferris Wheel!
Mimi: I have an idea! Can we go on the Ferris Wheel again, please?
Eddie, Zara, Leo: Oh yes, please! Can we go on the Ferris Wheel again too?
Parents: Yes, of course. Come on!

Songs

Language song

Where's your grandma? CD1 Track 19

Where's your grandma? (Hold out arms questioningly)
Here! (Point to grandma flashcard)
Where's your grandma? (Hold out arms questioningly)
Here! (Point to flashcard)
Where's your grandma? (Hold out arms questioningly)
Where's your grandma? (Hold out arms questioningly)
Here! Here! Here! (Point three times)

Where's your grandpa? (Hold out arms questioningly)
Here! (Point to grandpa flashcard)
(etc)

Where's your mommy? (Hold out arms questioningly)
Here! (Point to mommy flashcard)
(etc)

Where's your daddy? (Hold out arms questioningly)
Here! (Point to daddy flashcard)
(etc)
Where's your brother? (Hold out arms questioningly)
Here! (Point to brother flashcard)
(etc)

Where's your sister? (Hold out arms questioningly)
Here! (Point to sister flashcard)
(etc)

Story song

The Ferris Wheel song CD1 Track 22

Ferris Wheel, Ferris Wheel (Make shape of wheel with arms)
Hop on! Here we go! (Pretend to jump on wheel)
Round and round, round and round. (Make circular movements with one hand)
Round and round we go.
We love the Ferris Wheel (Make shape of wheel with both arms)
The Ferris Wheel is fun (Wave arms in air)
Fun for you, fun for me (Gesture to friend and to yourself)
Fun for everyone. (Gesture to everyone)
(Repeat)

Values song

I love my family CD1 Track 25

I love my family (Hug yourself)
My family loves me. (Point to self)
I love my family. (Hug yourself)
My family loves me. (Point to self)

I love my mommy. (Point to mommy flashcard)
I love my daddy ooh, ooh, ooh. (Point to daddy flashcard)
I love my brother. (Point to brother flashcard)
I love you. (Point to a child)

(Chorus)

I love my grandma. (Point to grandma flashcard)
I love my grandpa ooh, ooh, ooh. (Point to grandpa flashcard)
I love my sister. (Point to sister flashcard)
I love you. (Point to a child)

(Chorus)

Culture song

The wheels on the bus CD1 Track 27

The wheels on the bus go round and round, (Make circular movements with both hands)
Round and round, round and round.
The wheels on the bus go round and round, all through the town.

Brother and sister on the bus go tee, hee, hee, (Pretend to giggle)
Tee, hee, hee, tee, hee, hee
Brother and sister on the bus go tee, hee, hee, all through the town.

Mommy and Daddy on the bus go ssh, ssh, ssh, (Put finger to mouth to be quiet)
Ssh, ssh, ssh, ssh, ssh, ssh.
Mommy and Daddy on the bus go ssh, ssh, ssh, all through the town.
The wheels on the bus go round and round, (Make circular movements with both hands)
Round and round, round and round.
The wheels on the bus go round and round, all through the town.

Family
The Ferris Wheel

Vocabulary Lesson 1

Listen, point and repeat. Listen and play. Stick the family stickers. Say.
Language: mommy, daddy, brother, sister; blue, green, red, yellow

Family

Lesson 1 Vocabulary

Learning objectives

- Identify and name family members
- Listen and point to family members
- Listen and play *Round and round and round*

Materials

- Class CDs, flashcards, *Ferris Wheel* mat, Mimi puppet

Main vocabulary

- mommy, daddy, brother, sister; blue, green, red, yellow

Teacher's tip: Working with stickers

Small children may find it difficult to work with the stickers at first. Demonstrate how to peel them off using a pincer movement with the tip of the forefinger and thumb. Monitor carefully to make sure that children do this slowly, so that they don't tear the stickers.

Circle time

Hello song & puppet (CD1 Track 2; see TB p 17 & 21)
Opening routines (see TB p 16)
Lesson aims (see TB p 18)

Introduce members of the family.

- Use the puppet and flashcards to introduce each member of the family. Say each word and children repeat.
- Put the *Ferris Wheel* mat on the floor or board with the family flashcards face down (one on red, one on blue, one on green, one on yellow). Use the puppet to turn over and name each flashcard. Children repeat the names of the colors and the family words.

Game: *Find Mommy!*

- Name the family members in turn and ask one or two children to find and touch the correct flashcards as fast as they can.

Game: *Say the color!*

- Name the colors and children say the family words. Then the reverse.

Table time

Student's Book p 5

Listen, point and repeat.

- Play the audio. Children listen and point to each word as they hear it.

CD1 Track 16

Mimi: Look, Dylan! Brother … sister… Daddy … Mommy … hee, hee, hee! Repeat, Dylan!
Dylan: Yes, Mimi! Brother … sister … Daddy … Mommy … hee, hee, hee!
Mimi: Very good, Dylan. Let's say the words together!
Both: Brother… sister … Daddy… Mommy… hee, hee, hee, hee!

- Play the audio again. Children listen and repeat the words.

Listen and play.

- Hold up your index finger and move it around clockwise like a wheel. Children do the same. Play the audio. Children listen, point to the color when they hear it, and say the word.

CD1 Track 17

Mimi: Round and round and round: green … Mommy!
Dylan: Mommy!
Mimi: Round and round and round: yellow … Daddy!
Dylan: Daddy!
Mimi: Round and round and round: blue … sister!
Dylan: Sister!
Mimi: Round and round and round: red … brother!
Dylan: Brother!

- Play the game with you and/or individual children naming colors and others responding with the words.

Stick the family stickers. Say.

- Children put on the family stickers.

Say.

- Children point to the family members and say the words.

Activity Book p 5

Trace to circle Daddy in yellow. Trace to circle Mommy in green. Trace to circle brother in red. Trace to circle sister in blue.

- Children trace to circle each family member using the colors specified.

Point and say.

- They point and name the family members and the colors.

Closing time

Learning review (see TB p 18)
Closing routines (see TB p 16)
Bye bye song and puppet (CD1 Track 3; see TB p 17 & 21)

Use the **Navio App** to play the vocabulary game, and encourage children to do the same at home.

Lesson 2 Language

Family

Listen and find the new family members. Listen, point and sing *Where's your grandma?* Color the circle next to Grandpa red. Color the circle next to Grandma blue. Ask and say.
Language: mommy, daddy, grandma, grandpa, brother, sister; Where's your (grandma)? Here.

6

Learning objectives

- Talk about family members
- Identify and name two new family members
- Sing the language song *Where's your grandma?*
- Ask and say where family members are

Materials

- Class CDs, flashcards, *Ferris Wheel* mat, Mimi puppet

Main vocabulary

- mommy, daddy, grandma, grandpa, brother, sister

Key language

- Where's your (grandma)? Here.

Teacher's tip: Children's readiness to speak

At this early stage, you may find children are quiet or reluctant to speak. This is completely normal. It is important not to force any child to speak if he/she is not ready. Encourage children to listen and point in response until they are ready to join in.

Circle time

Hello song & puppet (CD1 Track 2; see TB p 17 & 21)
Opening routines (see TB p 16)
Recycling activity (four family words from Lesson 1) (see TB p 19)
Lesson aims (see TB p 18)

Introduce the new family words.

- Put all six family flashcards on the floor or board. Children identify the two new members of the family.
- Use the puppet to point to and say the words in turn. Children repeat in chorus.
- Turn the two new flashcards face down. Mix them up. Point to one and ask *Grandma or Grandpa?* Children guess. Repeat several times.

Introduce *Where's your (grandma)? Here.*

- Lay out the flashcards and children say the words.
- Hold up the *brother* or *sister* flashcard and ask, e.g. *Where's your mommy?* Encourage children to point to the *mommy* flashcard and model the response: *Here.*
- Repeat asking about different family members.

Game: *Where's your mommy?*

- Stick the family flashcards in different places around the classroom.
- Get children to ask the brother or sister with you in chorus, e.g. *Where's your mommy?* Ask two children to stand up, go and touch the flashcard and say *Here.*
- Repeat several times with different children and flashcards.

***Where's your grandma?* song**

CD1 Track 19

- Leave the flashcards in different places around the classroom.
- Play the song. Children listen and hold out their arms questioningly and point to the flashcards in each verse.
- Repeat once or twice. Children do the actions and sing the song (see TB p 33).

Table time

Student's Book p 6

- Point to Tom and Sophie with Auntie Jenny at the top of the page and say the names. Explain that Tom and Sophie are friends and, together with Auntie Jenny, will help children learn English (as well as Mimi, Dylan and the Meerkat family).

Listen and find the new family members.

- Play the audio. Children listen and find the two new family words. Repeat and children say the words.

CD1 Track 18

Tom: Find … Grandma! Grandma!
Sophie: Grandma! Here!
Tom: Find … Grandpa! Grandpa!
Sophie: Grandpa! Here!

Listen, point and sing *Where's your grandma?*

CD1 Track 19

- Play the song. Children listen, sing and point to the family members in the photo.
- Remember that you can use the karaoke version of the song when the children are confident.

Color the circle next to Grandpa red. Color the circle next to Grandma blue.

- Hold up your book and demonstrate coloring the circle next to Grandpa.
- Play the audio again. Pause after each verse and children color the circles in the correct color.

Ask and say.

- Ask *Where's your (grandma)?* Children point to the photos and say the words.

Activity Book p 6

Find and color Grandma and Grandpa.

- Children find and color Grandma and Grandpa.

Ask and say.

- They ask and answer about all the family members.

Closing time

Learning review (see TB p 18)
Closing routines (see TB p 16)
Bye bye song and puppet (CD1 Track 3; see TB p 17 & 21)

Use the **Navio App** to listen to the song, and encourage children to do the same at home.

Story

Watch. Listen to the story *The Ferris Wheel*. Color the character on the wheel with Zara Zebra. Stick the story sticker. Ask and say. **Language:** mommy, daddy, grandma, grandpa, brother, sister; Ferris Wheel; blue, orange, pink, yellow; Where's (Grandma)? Here.

7

Learning objectives

- Watch, understand and enjoy the story *The Ferris Wheel*
- Make a prediction about the story
- Look and find family members
- Color the character on the wheel in the story

Materials

- Class CDs, printable story cards, flashcards, *Ferris Wheel* mat, Mimi puppet

Main vocabulary

- mommy, daddy, grandma, grandpa, brother, sister; Ferris Wheel; blue, orange, pink, yellow

Key language

- Where's (Grandma)? Here.

Teacher's tip: Using the story resources

Children may find it easier to follow the story if you use the video first. Reinforce comprehension by telling the story again using the printable story cards. Finally, use the book and ask the comprehension questions.

Circle time

Hello song & puppet (CD1 Track 2; see TB p 17 & 21)
Opening routines (see TB p 16)
Recycling activity (*Where's your …?* and family members) (see TB p 19)
Lesson aims (see TB p 18)

Introduce the story *The Ferris Wheel.*

- Say *It's story time!* Play the *Story rhyme* (CD1 Track 4; see TB p 17).
- Say *Tom and Sophie are listening to a story about Mimi and Dylan and the Ferris Wheel. Who goes on the Ferris Wheel in the story?* Listen to children's answers.

Watch or listen to the story.

CD1 Track 21

- Play the audio, watch the video or read the story using the printable story cards. Pause, repeat words, point to the pictures, ask questions. Then say the characters' names and encourage children to point and repeat, e.g. *Mimi, Leo,* etc.
- Ask *Who goes on the Ferris Wheel in the story? (Mimi, Dylan, Grandma, Grandpa, Zara and her mommy, Leo and his grandma, Eddie and his daddy).*
- Repeat the story. Encourage children to join in with the words and phrases in the story.
- Ask *Do you like the story? Do you want to go on the Ferris Wheel?*

Look and find.

- Say e.g. *Find Grandma!* Children look at the story and point to Grandma as fast as they can.
- Repeat with other family members and colors (red, blue, green and yellow) of the Ferris Wheel

Table time

Student's Book p 7

Watch. Listen to the story *The Ferris Wheel.*

CD1 Track 21

- Play the story again. Children listen and point to the pictures in their books.

Story questions

Picture 1
Where's Grandma? *(In yellow)*
Where's Grandpa? *(In orange)*

Picture 2
Who does Mommy see? *(Mrs. Zebra/Zara)*
Does Zara like the Ferris Wheel? *(Yes)*

Picture 3
Where are Eddie and his daddy? *(In blue)*
Where are Leo and his grandma? *(In pink)*

Picture 4
Do the children like the Ferris Wheel? *(Yes)*
Do they go on the Ferris Wheel again? *(Yes)*

Color the character on the wheel with Zara Zebra.

- Demonstrate coloring the character on the wheel with Zara Zebra (i.e. her mommy).

Stick the story sticker.

- Children stick on the story sticker.

Ask and say.

- Children ask and answer questions.
- Ask e.g. *Do Mimi and Dylan go on the Ferris Wheel again at the end of the story? Who with? Do you want to go on the Ferris Wheel?*

Activity Book p 7

Color the pod with Dylan and Grandma yellow.
Color the pod with Mimi and Grandpa orange.

- Children color the two pods.

Ask and say.

- They ask and answer about all the family members.

Closing time

Learning review (see TB p 18)
Closing routines (see TB p 16)
Bye bye song and puppet (CD1 Track 3; see TB p 17 & 21)

Use the **Navio App** to watch the video, and encourage children to do the same at home.

Lesson 4 Story Song

Family

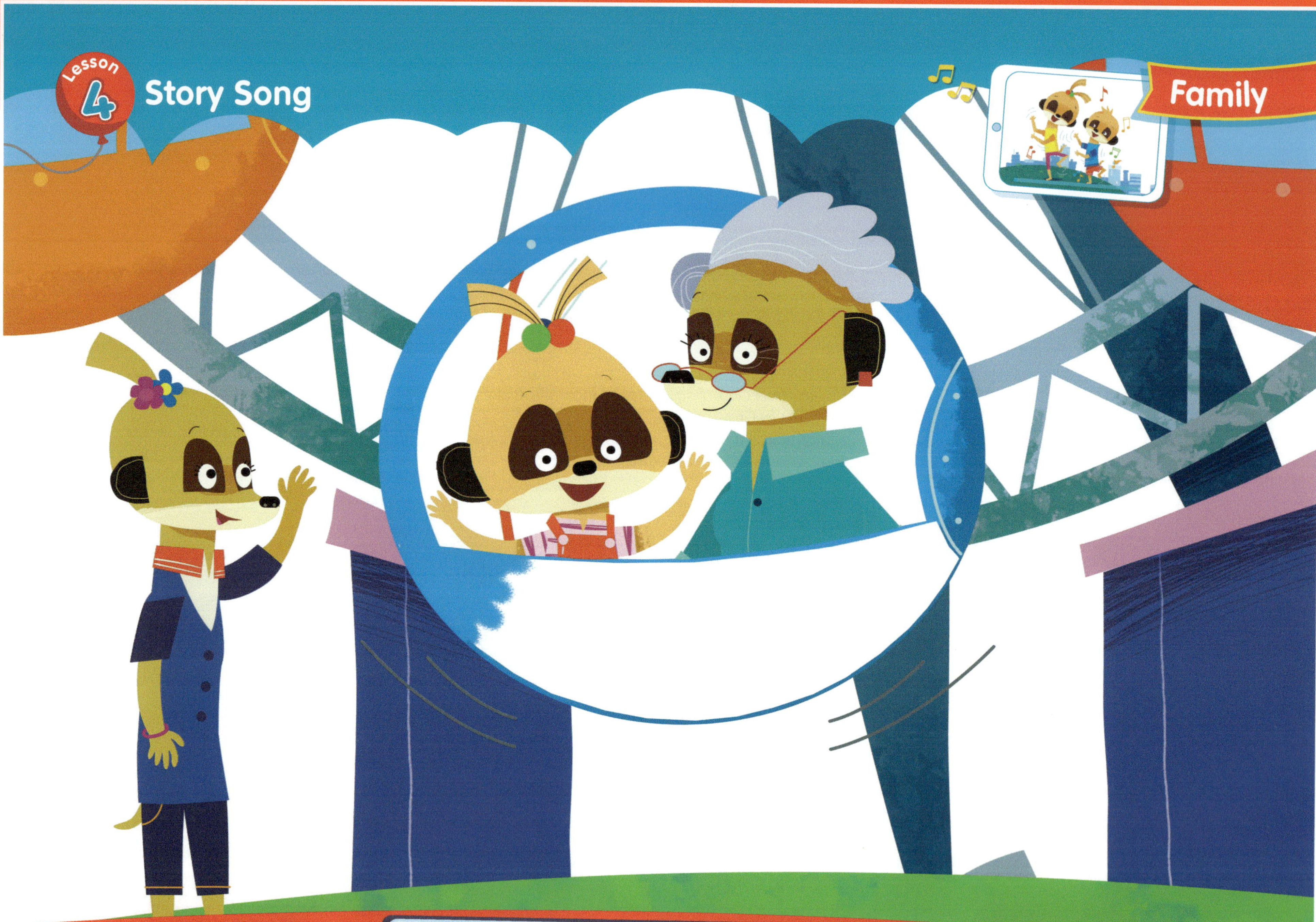

Watch. Listen, point and sing *The Ferris Wheel song*. Color the pod blue. Say.
Language: mommy, grandma, sister; Ferris Wheel; Here we go. Round and round.

8

Learning objectives

- Watch, sing and act out the story song *The Ferris Wheel song*
- Listen to the story again and identify the family members
- Play *Round and round*
- Color Mimi and say where she is
- Trace the movement of the Ferris Wheel

Materials

- Class CDs, printable story cards, flashcards, *Ferris Wheel* mat, Mimi puppet

Main vocabulary

- mommy, grandma, sister; Ferris Wheel

Key language

- Here we go. Round and round.

Teacher's tip: Being positive about each other's work

Demonstrate being positive about children's work by pointing to their completed pictures and saying, e.g. *Very good* or giving a thumbs up. Once the children have finished coloring Mimi, get them to show their pictures to the child next to them and to be positive about each other's work. Make sure you discourage any negativity and encourage them to show they appreciate each other's efforts.

Circle time

Hello song & puppet (CD1 Track 2; see TB p 17 & 21)
Opening routines (see TB p 16)
Recycling activity (family vocabulary) (see TB p 19)
Lesson aims (see TB p 18)

Retell the story *The Ferris Wheel*.

- Play the audio, video or read the story using the printable story cards.
- Demonstrate that children should wave their arms in the air every time they hear a family word in the story.

Game: *Round and round*

- Say *The Ferris Wheel goes round and round.* Move your arm in a circle and children do the same. Say *The Ferris Wheel stops* and freeze in position.
- Repeat several times and children respond.

The Ferris Wheel song

CD1 Track 22

- Play the video or audio of the story song. Children watch/listen and make the shape of a wheel with their arms every time they hear *Ferris Wheel* in the song.
- Play the song again. Children stand in a circle, listen, sing and act out the song (see TB p 33).
- Repeat once or twice.

Table time

Student's Book p 8

Watch. Listen, point and sing *The Ferris Wheel song*.

CD1 Track 22

- Play the audio of the song. Children listen, sing and point to the Ferris Wheel.
- Remember that you can use the karaoke version of the song when the children are confident.

Color Mimi.

- Children color the picture of Mimi on the Ferris Wheel.

Say.

- Children ask and answer questions about their picture, e.g. *Where's Mimi? Here! In blue!*

Activity Book p 8

Trace the Ferris Wheel going round.

- Children trace the line around the Ferris Wheel.

Color the pod you want to go in.

- Children color the pod they want to go in.

Ask and say.

- They point and say *Round and round.* Then they ask and answer about the characters.

Closing time

Learning review (see TB p 18)
Closing routines (see TB p 16)
Bye bye song and puppet (CD1 Track 3; see TB p 17 & 21)

Use the **Navio App** to watch the video, and encourage children to do the same at home.

Lesson 5

Speaking

Life skills

1:24

hello

Watch. Listen and point. Follow and draw a path to connect the pictures in order. Trace around Mommy. Ask and say. **Language:** mommy, daddy, grandma, grandpa, brother, sister; Where's your (sister)? Here. This is my (mommy).

9

Learning objectives

- Ask and answer questions about where family members are
- Watch, understand and enjoy a video
- Identify family members in the video

Materials

- Class CDs, flashcards, *Ferris Wheel* mat, Mimi puppet

Main vocabulary

- mommy, daddy, grandma, grandpa, brother, sister

Key language

- Where's your (sister)? Here. This is my (mommy).

Teacher's tip: Starting to work in pairs

Life skills

Encouraging children to work in pairs right from the start is a great way to set them off on the road to working together cooperatively. Show them how to place one book on top of another so that they can work together while they listen to the audio and point to the pictures.

Circle time

Hello song & puppet (CD1 Track 2; see TB p 17 & 21)
Opening routines (see TB p 16)
Recycling activity (story song) (CD1 Track 22; see TB p 19)
Lesson aims (see TB p 18)

Game: *Where's your (sister)?*

- Give out the family flashcards to individual children.
- Ask e.g. *Where's your sister?* The child with the flashcard stands up and says *Here!*
- Repeat with the other flashcards.

Game: *Guess where!*

- Put the flashcards face down on the floor or board and mix them up.
- Ask e.g. *Where's Grandma?* and invite a child to guess and turn over one of the flashcards. Say *Hurray!* and children clap if it is Grandma. Say *Oh no! It's …* (naming the family member). *Let's try again!* if it isn't Grandma. Repeat several times.

Watch the video.

- Explain that Auntie Jenny comes to Tom and Sophie's house and asks about the family.
- Play the video of Sophie, Auntie Jenny and Tom.
- Ask *Who's in the family? (mommy, daddy, grandma, grandpa, brother, sister).*
- Watch again. Pause and children repeat the questions and what Sophie and Tom say.

Table time

Student's Book p 9 Life skills

Watch. Listen and point.

- Children identify Tom, Sophie and Auntie Jenny in the photo.
- Play the audio or video. Use the pause button. Children point to the family members.

CD1 Track 24

Sophie:	Hi, Auntie Jenny. Hello, Tom. This is my photo album. This is my family.
Auntie Jenny:	Great! Where's your sister?
Sophie:	Here. This is my sister.
Tom:	Where's your daddy?
Sophie:	Here. This is my daddy.
Auntie Jenny:	Where's your grandma?
Sophie:	Here. This is my grandma.
Tom:	Where's your grandpa?
Sophie:	Here. This is my grandpa.
Auntie Jenny:	Where's your brother?
Sophie:	Here. This is my brother.
Auntie Jenny:	Where's your mommy?
Sophie:	Here. This is my mommy.
Sophie:	Here. This is my mommy!
Mommy:	Hello!
All:	Hello!

Follow and draw a path to connect the pictures in order.

- Play the audio again. Children follow the path with their finger and point to the different members of the family as they listen.
- They then draw the path to show the order of the pictures.

Trace around Mommy.

- Children trace around the photo of Mommy.

Ask and say.

- Children ask and say as if talking to Sophie, e.g. *Where's your mommy? Here!*

Activity Book p 9

Draw and color you and your family.

- Children draw and color themselves on the silhouette and any family members they choose in the rest of the frame.

Ask and say.

- Children ask and answer about the family members in their picture.

Closing time

Learning review (see TB p 18)
Closing routines (see TB p 16)
Bye bye song and puppet (CD1 Track 3; see TB p 17 & 21)

Use the **Navio App** to watch the video, and encourage children to do the same at home.

Values I love my family

Listen, point and sing ***I love my family***. Color the frame red. Say.
Language: mommy, daddy, grandma, grandpa, brother, sister; I love my (mommy).

SOCIAL AND EMOTIONAL LEARNING

10

Learning objectives

- Recognize the value of loving your family
- Sing the values song *I love my family*
- Say *I love my (mommy)*

Materials

- Class CDs, flashcards, *Ferris Wheel* mat, Mimi puppet

Main vocabulary

- mommy, daddy, grandma, grandpa, brother, sister

Key language

- I love my (mommy).

Teacher's tip: Creating a caring corner

Before the lesson, ask the children to bring in a photo of themselves with a member of their family. Alternatively, they can draw a picture. Stick all the photos and pictures into a scrapbook. Get children to look at the photos and pictures together and say *I love my (mommy)*. Keep the scrapbook in an accessible place so that any children who start to miss family members during the school day can look at it with a classmate.

Circle time

Hello song & puppet (CD1 Track 2; see TB p 17 & 21)
Opening routines (see TB p 16)
Recycling activity (*Where's your … ? Here!*) (see TB p 19)
Lesson aims (see TB p 18)

Watch *The Ferris Wheel* story video.

- Play the story video.
- Children watch and repeat every time they hear a family word.
- Draw a heart on the board and explain the meaning of *love*. Ask e.g. *Who does Mimi say she loves in the story? (Mommy, Daddy, Grandma, Grandpa). Do you love your family?*

***I love my family* song**

CD1 Track 25

- Stick the family flashcards on the board.
- Use the Mimi puppet to say *Listen and find out. Who do we love in the song?*
- Play the audio. The children point to the flashcards and name the family members in the song *(mommy, daddy, grandma, grandpa, brother, sister)*.
- Play the audio again. The children sing the song and do the actions (see TB p 33).

Table time

Student's Book p 10

Listen, point and sing *I love my family*.

CD1 Track 25

- Play the audio of the song. Children sing and point to the members of the family.

Color the frame red.

- Children color the frame around the photo red.

Say.

- Children talk about their own family members and say, e.g. *I love my daddy*.

Activity Book p 10

Color the circles to show the family members you love.

- Children color the circles next to the family members they love.

Say.

- Children say who they love.

Closing time

Learning review (see TB p 18)
Closing routines (see TB p 16)
Bye bye song and puppet (CD1 Track 3; see TB p 17 & 21)

Use the **Navio App** to listen to the song, and encourage children to do the same at home.

1:26

hello

Listen and point. Color the wheels. Say.
Language: round, wheel; This is (a wheel). Wheels go round and round.

11

Learning objectives

- Understand that wheels go round
- Listen and understand a dialogue about wheels
- Identify and talk about wheels in the classroom
- Count and say how many wheels

Materials

- Class CDs, printable flashcards, *Ferris Wheel* mat, Mimi puppet

Main vocabulary

- round, wheel

Key language

- This is a (wheel). Wheels go round and round.

Teacher's tip: Reinforcing the concept of round and round

Once the children have finished coloring the wheels in their books, encourage them to go around the wheels with a finger, saying *round and round, round and round*. Remind the children that the Ferris Wheel also goes round and round. Have them stand up and join hands to make a large circle. Slowly walk round and round like the Ferris Wheel. Encourage the children to say *Round and round* as they walk.

Circle time

Hello song & puppet (CD1 Track 2; see TB p 17 & 21)
Opening routines (see TB p 16)
Recycling activity (see TB p 19)
Lesson aims (see TB p 18)

Introduce content vocabulary.

- Use the printable flashcards and the puppet to introduce the content words *(wheel, round)*. Children repeat.
- Say *Wheels go round and round.* Demonstrate what you mean and children make a circular movement with their arms.

Game: *Round and round*

- Remind children of the Ferris Wheel in the story and story song.
- Lay out the printable flashcards. Say *This is a wheel and it goes round and round.*
- Repeat the game from Lesson 4. Say *The wheel goes round and round.* Move your arm in a circle and children do the same. Say *The wheel stops* and freeze in position.
- Repeat several times and children respond.

Find wheels in the classroom.

- Make sure that classroom toys with wheels, such as toy cars or trucks, or picture books or posters of things with wheels are visible.
- Invite pairs of children to take turns standing up and finding something with wheels in the classroom. Respond by saying, e.g. *Yes, very good. And the wheels go round and round like this.*

Table time

Student's Book p 11

Listen and point.

- Say *Sophie and Tom are talking to Auntie Jenny about wheels.*
- Play the audio. Children listen and point to the wheels in turn. Use the pause button as necessary.

CD1 Track 26

Sophie: This is a wheel. This is a wheel.
Tom: This is a wheel. This is a wheel.
Auntie Jenny: Yes, very good. Wheels go round and round.
Sophie: Round and round; round and round.
Tom: Yes, wheels go round and round; round and round.

Color the wheels. Say.

- Children color the wheels.
- Play the audio again. Use the pause button. Children repeat the sentences and point to the completed pictures in their books.

Activity Book p 11

Trace the wheels.

- Children trace the wheels.

Count and say.

- Children count the wheels on the scooter and the bike and say how many.

Closing time

Learning review (see TB p 18)
Closing routines (see TB p 16)
Bye bye song and puppet (CD1 Track 3; see TB p 17 & 21)

Use the **Navio App** to play the vocabulary and language games, and encourage children to do the same at home.

Lesson 8 Culture

Watch. Listen, point and sing *The wheels on the bus.* Color the circles under the family members in the song. Say. **Language:** mommy, daddy, brother, sister; bus, wheels; The wheels on the bus go round and round.

12

Learning objectives

- Watch, sing and act out the traditional song *The wheels on the bus*
- Play an action game
- Identify and name the people in the song

Materials

- Class CDs, flashcards, *Ferris Wheel* mat, Mimi puppet

Main vocabulary

- mommy, daddy, brother, sister; bus, wheels

Key language

- The wheels on the bus go round and round.

Teacher's tip: Acting out a simple role play

Seat the children on the floor in pairs as if they are on a bus. Choose one child to sit at the front and be the driver. Allow the children to choose a role: mommy, daddy, brother or sister. Play the audio of the song and the children act out their part. If space is limited, have children take turns coming to the front and acting out the song in groups of five.

Circle time

Hello song & puppet (CD1 Track 2; see TB p 17 & 21)
Opening routines (see TB p 16)
Recycling activity (see TB p 19)
Lesson aims (see TB p 18)

Game: *Mimi says (the wheels go round).*

- Use the puppet to say *Mimi says the wheels go round* and children respond by making circular movements with both their hands.
- Say *Mimi says the wheels stop* and children freeze in position.
- Alternate the instructions and go faster as children get more confident in responding.

***The wheels on the bus* song**

CD1 Track 27

- Show children a picture or toy bus and introduce the word.
- Say *Stand up. Let's learn the song "The wheels on the bus."*
- Play the audio. The children listen and do the actions for the song (see TB p 33).
- Repeat. The children sing and do the actions.

Watch *The wheels on the bus* song video.

- Children watch the video and join in singing the song and doing the actions with Tom and Sophie.

Table time

Student's Book p 12

Watch. Listen, point and sing *The wheels on the bus.*

CD1 Track 27

- Play the audio. Children listen, sing and point to the pictures of the wheels and family members as they hear the words in the song.

Color the circles under the family members in the song. Say.

- Children color the circles under each of the family members in the song (i.e. all of them).
- Children point to and name the family members on the bus, e.g. *brother.*

Activity Book p 12

Draw your family or friends on the bus. Color the wheels.

- Children draw four of their family members or friends on the bus. Then they color the wheels.

Point and say.

- Children point and name the people they drew.

Closing time

Learning review (see TB p 18)
Closing routines (see TB p 16)
Bye bye song and puppet (CD1 Track 3; see TB p 17 & 21)

Use the **Navio App** to watch the video, and encourage children to do the same at home.

Review

Family

Listen, point and say. Color the pods to show the family members you know. Stick the star sticker. Ask and say. Language: mommy, daddy, grandma, grandpa, brother, sister; blue, green, orange, pink, red, yellow; Where's your (sister)? Here. This is my (brother).

13

Learning objectives

- Review your learning and progress
- Ask and say where family members are
- Stick on a star sticker for achievement

Materials

- Class CDs, flashcards, *Ferris Wheel* mat, Mimi puppet

Main vocabulary

- mommy, daddy, grandma, grandpa, brother, sister; blue, green, orange, pink, red, yellow

Key language

- Where's your (sister)? Here. This is my (brother).

Teacher's tip: Introducing the concept of self-evaluation

The concept of self-evaluation is likely to be new to children. Explain and demonstrate that they should only color the pods of the family members they know. Encourage them to say the words as they do this. Give lots of encouragement and praise, pointing out the things they learned and achieved in this unit.

Circle time

Hello song & puppet (CD1 Track 2; see TB p 17 & 21)
Opening routines (see TB p 16)
Recycling activity (see TB p 19)
Lesson aims (see TB p 18)

Family flashcard games

- Choose one or two flashcard games with the *Ferris Wheel* mat and/or the puppet to review key vocabulary (see TB p 20 & 21).

Sing *Where's your grandma?*

CD1 Track 19

- Lay out the flashcards. Children name the family members.
- Play the audio. Children sing and point to the flashcards.
- Children ask and answer questions about all the family members.

Game: *Where's mommy?*

- Stick the flashcards at the children's height on different walls around the classroom. Say *Where's mommy?* Children point to the corresponding flashcard and say *Here!*

Game: *I love my daddy.*

- With the flashcards still in position around the classroom, say, *I love my daddy!* Choose a volunteer to pick up the corresponding flashcard and mime giving "daddy" a hug.

Watch the story video.

- Children watch the story video. Ask *Who's in orange? (Mimi and Grandpa) Who's in yellow? (Dylan and Grandma) Who helps in the story? (Mommy and Daddy).*

Table time

Student's Book p 13

Listen, point and say.

- Say e.g. *Find daddy!* and children point to the correct pod.
- Play the audio. Children listen, point to the pictures and say the words.

CD1 Track 28

Mimi: I'm the teacher! Can you remember our family, Dylan?
Dylan: Yes, I can. Mommy.
Mimi: Mommy.
Dylan: Daddy.
Mimi: Daddy.
Dylan: Brother
Mimi: Brother.
Dylan: Sister.
Mimi: Sister.
Dylan: Grandma.
Mimi: Grandma.
Dylan: Grandpa.
Mimi: Grandpa. Great job, Dylan. Very good!

Color the pods to show the family members you know.

- Children color the pods of the family members they know.

Stick the star sticker.

- Children stick on the star sticker for achievement.
- Monitor and encourage children to think positively about their progress.

Ask and say.

- Children ask and answer questions about the family, e.g. *Where's Grandma? Here!*

Activity Book p 13

Color the faces to show the family members you know. Ask and say.

- Children color the faces next to the family members they know. They imagine they are Mimi or Dylan and ask and answer about the family members.

Think and color the stars to show your progress.

- Children color the number of stars that they feel shows their progress in this unit.

Closing time

Learning review (see TB p 18)
Closing routines (see TB p 16)
Bye bye song and puppet (CD1 Track 3; see TB p 17 & 21)

Use the **Navio App** to review what children have learned in this unit, and encourage children to do the same at home.

Project

COOPERATIVE LEARNING

1

2

3

Choose a member of your family. Paint and decorate your picture. Make a family display. **Ask and say.** Language: mommy, daddy, grandma, grandpa, brother, sister; Where's your (grandpa)? Here. This is my (sister). I love my (daddy).

14

Learning objectives

- Work together to do a collaborative project
- Make a family member for the display
- Talk about the family display
- Express enjoyment of the family display

Materials

- Class CDs, Mimi puppet, project template, finger paints, yarn, tissue paper, glue, clothes line and clothespins for display
- optional: crayons

Main vocabulary

- mommy, daddy, grandma, grandpa, brother, sister

Key language

- Where's your (grandpa)? Here. This is my (sister). I love my (daddy).

Life skills

Teacher's tip: Reinforcing how to hold a crayon

Coloring with crayons encourages the correct hold the children will need to establish for writing. Children of this age group may need to be shown how to hold a crayon correctly. Demonstrate the correct hold and gently adjust the hold of any children using an incorrect grip.

Circle time

Hello song & puppet (CD1 Track 2; see TB p 17 & 21)
Opening routines (see TB p 16)
Recycling activity (see TB p 19)
Lesson aims (see TB p 18)

Prepare for your project.

- Say *Let's do a project and make a family display!*
- Show children the copies of the family templates that you have prepared.
- Demonstrate painting the templates with finger paints or making small balls of tissue paper and gluing them on the template for clothes and gluing pieces of yarn on the template for hair.

Table time

COOPERATIVE LEARNING

Student's Book p 14

- Say e.g. *We're going to make a family display like this. Look at what we need for our project: pictures of the family, finger paints, yarn, tissue paper, glue, string, clothespins.* Children listen and point to the pictures.
- Divide the children into groups or tables.

Choose a member of your family. Paint and decorate your picture.

- Children choose the family template they want to complete or you can assign this.
- Make sure children have finger paints, yarn, tissue paper and glue available.
- Children use finger paints, yarn and tissue paper to paint and decorate their family template.

Make a family display.

- When they are ready, children hang their completed template on the string clothes line you have prepared. Each table or group makes one family.

Ask and say.

- Children identify the different members of each family in their display. Make the point that all families are different but equally special.
- Ask children *Do you like our family display?* Make the point that everyone helped make it and that they couldn't have made such a beautiful display on their own.

Alternative version of project

- Children could color their template with crayons instead of painting and decorating it.

Activity Book p 14

Glue a photo or draw and color a picture of your family.

- Children either glue a photo or draw and color a picture of their family.

Point, ask and say. Talk about your family.

- Children use their picture to ask and talk about their family.

Closing time

Learning review (see TB p 18)
Closing routines (see TB p 16)
Bye bye song and puppet (CD1 Track 3; see TB p 17 & 21)

Classroom

Mimi's first day at school

Unit objectives

- Identify and name classroom objects
- Sing the language song *Stand up! Sit down!*
- Ask and say where things are
- Understand and join in the story *Mimi's first day at school*
- Sing and act out the story song *Where's your book?*
- Sing the values song *I'm your friend*
- Recognize the value of friendship
- Identify and name where things go in the classroom
- Sing and act out the traditional song *This is the way I say hello*
- Review your learning and progress
- Participate in a collaborative project

Vocabulary and language

- **Main vocabulary:** book, chair, crayon, eraser, pencil, table
- **Key language:** Sit down. Stand up. Look! It's (a chair). Where's your (book)? Here.
- **Content language:** shelf, tray; I put the (crayon) (in) the (tray).
- **Other language:** happy, sad, care, friend, school; bye bye, hello; I don't know. I'm (sad). What color is your (book)? It's (blue). I care. I'm your friend. This is the way I say (hello). Where's the (blue) crayon?

Story

CD1 Track 34

Picture 1

Narrator: It's Mimi's first day at school.
Mimi: My book … my pencil … my eraser … my crayon.
Mommy: Time to go, Mimi.
Mimi: Yes, Mommy.
Daddy: Hurry! Come on!
Mimi: Yes, Daddy. I'm happy!

Picture 2

Narrator: Mimi walks to school with Mommy and Daddy. Leo and Zara walk to school too.
Leo: Look! It's a book.
Zara: Look! It's a pencil.
Leo: Look! It's an eraser.
Zara: Look! It's a crayon. Come on. Hurry. We're late.

Picture 3

Narrator: Mrs. Cat is the teacher.
Mrs. Cat: Hello Mimi. Welcome to school. Go to your table. Sit down on your chair. Open your book. Get out a pencil, an eraser and a crayon.
Mimi: Oh no!
Eddie: Where's your book?
Mimi: I don't know.
Eddie: Where's your pencil?
Mimi: I don't know.
Eddie: Where's your eraser?
Mimi: I don't know.
Eddie: Where's your crayon?
Mimi: I don't know. I'm sad. Boo-hoo.
Mrs. Cat: Please don't cry, Mimi.

Picture 4

Narrator: Leo and Zara come into the classroom.
Leo: Hello, Mrs. Cat.
Zara: Sorry, we're late. Look! A book … a pencil … an eraser … a crayon.
Mrs. Cat: Aha, very good. Where's your book, Mimi?
Mimi: Here!
Mrs. Cat: Where's your pencil?
Mimi: Here!
Mrs. Cat: Where's your eraser?
Mimi: Here!
Mrs. Cat: Where's your crayon?
Mimi: Here! Oh, thank you, Leo. Thank you, Zara. Thank you, Mrs. Cat. I'm happy now.
Eddie, Zara, Leo: And we're all friends!

Songs

Language song

Stand up! Sit down! CD1 Track 32

Stand up! Sit down! (Stand up and sit down again)
Look! Look! It's a chair, chair, chair. (Point to chair flashcard)

Stand up! Sit down! (Stand up and sit down again)
Look! Look! It's a table, table, table. (Point to your eye, then to the table flashcard)

Stand up! Sit down! (Stand up and sit down again)
Look! Look! It's a book, book, book. (Point to book flashcard)

Stand up! Sit down! (Stand up and sit down again)
Look! Look! It's a pencil, pencil, pencil. (Point to pencil flashcard)

Stand up! Sit down! (Stand up and sit down again)
Look! Look! It's a crayon, crayon, crayon. (Point to crayon flashcard)

Stand up! Sit down! (Stand up and sit down again)
Look! Look! It's an eraser, eraser, eraser. (Point to eraser flashcard)

Story song

Where's your book? CD1 Track 35

Where's your book? Where's your book? (Hold out arms questioningly)
I don't know. (Make expression to show you don't know)
Where's your pencil? Where's your pencil? (Hold out arms questioningly)
I don't know. (Show surprise that it's lost)
Where's your eraser? Where's your eraser? (Hold out arms questioningly)
I don't know. (Show surprise that it's lost)
Where's your crayon? Where's your crayon? (Hold out arms questioningly)
I don't know. I'm sad. I'm sad. (Show surprise that it's lost)
Where's your book? Where's your book? (Hold out arms questioningly)
Here! Here! (Point to or hold up the object or flashcard)
Where's your pencil? Where's your pencil? (Hold out arms questioningly)
Here! Here! (Wave arms in the air to show you're happy it's found)
Where's your eraser? Where's your eraser? (Hold out arms questioningly)
Here! Here! (Wave your arms in the air to show you're happy it's found)
Where's your crayon? Where's your crayon? (Hold out arms questioningly)
Here! Here! I'm happy. I'm happy. Hurray! (Wave arms in the air happily)

Values song

I'm your friend CD1 Track 38

I'm your friend (Look at a friend and hold their hand)
When you're happy, happy, happy (Make a happy face)
I'm your friend (Look at a friend and hold their hand)
When you're sad, sad, sad (Look at a friend and make sad face)
I'm your friend (Put arm around a friend as if looking after them)
I care, care, care
I'm your friend (Put arm around a friend as if looking after them)
Oh, yeah, yeah, yeah! (Wave other arm in the air)

I'm your friend (Look at a friend and hold their hand)
When you're happy, happy, happy
I'm your friend (Look at a friend and hold their hand)
When you're sad, sad, sad
I'm your friend (Put arm around a friend as if looking after them)
I care, care, care
I'm your friend (Put arm around a friend as if looking after them)
Oh, yeah, yeah, yeah! (Wave other arm in the air)

Culture song

This is the way I say hello CD1 Track 40

This is the way I say hello (Wave and smile)
Say hello, say hello
This is the way I say hello
To my friends at school. (Point to different children)

This is the way I say bye bye (Wave sadly and slightly turn away)
Say bye bye, say bye bye
This is the way I say bye bye
To my friends at school (Point to different children)
(Repeat)

Vocabulary Lesson 1

Classroom

Mimi's first day at school

Listen, point and repeat. Listen and play. Stick the classroom object stickers. Say.
Language: book, crayon, eraser, pencil; blue, orange, pink, yellow

15

Classroom

Lesson 1 Vocabulary

Learning objectives

- Identify and name classroom objects
- Listen and point to classroom objects
- Listen and play *Round and round and round*

Materials

- Class CDs, flashcards, *Ferris Wheel* mat, Mimi puppet

Main vocabulary

- book, crayon, eraser, pencil; blue, orange, pink, yellow

Teacher's tip: Using a "feely bag"

For additional practice, put the real classroom objects you have brought into a "feely bag" (an opaque, soft cloth bag, e.g. for keeping shoes or bread). Gather the children close so that they can see and name the items as you gradually reveal them one by one.

Circle time

Hello song & puppet (CD1 Track 2; see TB p 17 & 21)
Opening routines (see TB p 16)
Lesson aims (see TB p 18)

Introduce classroom objects.

- Have ready a real book, pencil, eraser and crayon, and introduce the words. The children repeat the words.
- Repeat with the classroom object flashcards.
- Ask individual children to put each real object on the corresponding flashcard. The children say *Hurray!* and repeat the words as they do this.
- Put the *Ferris Wheel* mat on the floor or board with the classroom object flashcards face down (one on each color). Use the puppet to turn them over and name them. The children repeat the names of the colors and the classroom objects.

Game: ***Say the color!***

- Name the classroom objects on the Ferris Wheel and children name the color. Then the reverse.

Game: ***Pass the object!***

- Give out the real objects and the flashcards in random order to different children.
- Children take turns holding up their object or flashcard and the rest of the class says the word.
- Children pass their object or flashcard clockwise around the circle or around their table. When you say *Stop!*, children repeat the procedure as above.

Table time

Student's Book p 15

Listen, point and repeat.

- Play the audio. Children listen and point to each object as they hear it.

CD1 Track 29

Mimi: Look, Dylan! Pencil … eraser … book … crayon … hee, hee, hee! Repeat, Dylan!
Dylan: Yes, Mimi! Pencil … eraser … book … crayon … hee, hee, hee!
Mimi: Very good, Dylan! Let's say the words together.
Both: Pencil … eraser … book … crayon … hee, hee, hee!

- Play the audio again. Children listen and repeat the words.

Listen and play.

- Hold up your index finger and move it around clockwise like a wheel. Children do the same. Play the audio. Children listen, point to the color when they hear it, and say the word.

CD1 Track 30

Mimi: Round and round and round: yellow … book!
Dylan: Book!
Mimi: Round and round and round: blue … pencil!
Dylan: Pencil!
Mimi: Round and round and round: pink … crayon
Dylan: Crayon!
Mimi: Round and round and round: orange … eraser!
Dylan: Eraser!

- Play the game with you and/or individual children naming colors and others saying the words.

Stick the classroom object stickers.

- Children put on the classroom object stickers.

Say.

- Children point to the objects and say the words.

Activity Book p 15

Color the classroom objects.

- Children color the classroom objects.

Point and say.

- They point and name the objects.

Closing time

Learning review (see TB p 18)
Closing routines (see TB p 16)
Bye bye song and puppet (CD1 Track 3; see TB p 17 & 21)

Use the **Navio App** to play the vocabulary game, and encourage children to do the same at home.

Lesson 2 Language

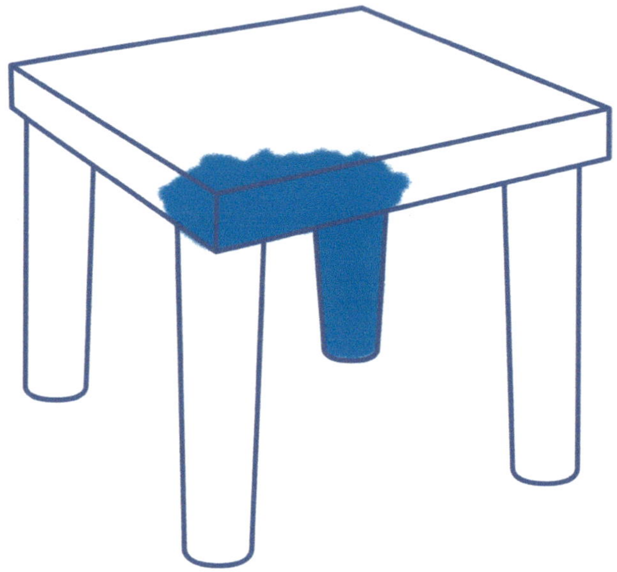

Listen and find the new classroom objects. Listen, point and sing *Stand up! Sit down!* Color the chair red and the table blue. Point and say. Language: book, chair, crayon, eraser, pencil, table; Sit down. Stand up. Look! It's (a chair).

16

Learning objectives

- Talk about classroom objects
- Identify and name two new classroom objects
- Sing the language song *Stand up! Sit down!*
- Give and follow instructions *(Sit down. Stand up)*
- Identify the odd one out

Materials

- Class CDs, flashcards, *Ferris Wheel* mat, Mimi puppet

Main vocabulary

- book, chair, crayon, eraser, pencil, table

Key language

- Sit down. Stand up. Look! It's (a chair).

Teacher's tip: Calming children down

After the lively action song, the children may need some help to calm down and refocus. Put your finger to your lips, keep very still, and say *shh, shh, shh*, rhythmically and repeatedly in a soft voice encouraging them to join in with you until they are calm again.

Circle time

Hello song & puppet (CD1 Track 2; see TB p 17 & 21)
Opening routines (see TB p 16)
Recycling activity (four classroom words from Lesson 1) (see TB p 19)
Lesson aims (see TB p 18)

Introduce the new classroom objects.

- All six classroom object flashcards on the floor or board.
- Children identify the two new classroom objects.
- Use the puppet to point to and say the words in turn. Children repeat in chorus.
- Turn the two new flashcards face down. Mix them up. Point to one and ask *Table or chair?* Children guess. Repeat several times

Game: *Touch the chair!*

- Give pairs of children instructions in turn, e.g. *Touch the table / chair!* Children stand up and respond. Everyone claps, repeats the word and says *Hurray!* if they do this correctly.
- Repeat several times with different pairs.

Introduce *Look! It's (a chair).*

- Hide a flashcard behind a book. Gradually reveal the picture. Say *Look! It's (a crayon)*, once it's possible to identify it.
- Children repeat the sentence.

Game: *Repeat if it's true!*

- Lay out the flashcards face down.
- Invite a child to choose and turn over one of the flashcards. Use the puppet to say e.g. *Look! It's a pencil.* Children repeat the sentence if it's true and cross their arms and stay silent if not.

***Stand up! Sit down!* song**

CD1 Track 32

- Say *Stand up! / Sit down!* several times and children respond.
- Put the classroom object flashcards face up on the floor or board.
- Play the song. Children listen, point to the flashcards as they hear them and do the actions (see TB p 55).

Table time

Student's Book p 16

Listen and find the new classroom objects.

- Hold up your book. Point to the photo of Tom and Sophie and say their names.
- Play the audio. Children listen, find the two new classroom objects and say the words.

CD1 Track 31

Sophie: Find the … table! Table!
Tom: Table! Here!
Sophie: Find the … chair! Chair!
Tom: Chair! Here!

Listen, point and sing *Stand up! Sit down!*

CD1 Track 32

- Play the song. Children listen, sing and point to the classroom objects in the photos.
- Remember that you can use the karaoke version of the song when the children are confident.

Color the chair red and the table blue.

- Children color the chair red and the table blue, the same as in the photo.

Point and say.

- Children point and say the words.

Activity Book p 16

Point and say.

- Children point and name the objects in each row.

Color the classroom object in each row that is different.

- They color the object in each row that is different.

Closing time

Learning review (see TB p 18)
Closing routines (see TB p 16)
Bye bye song and puppet (CD1 Track 3; see TB p 17 & 21)

Use the **Navio App** to listen to the song, and encourage children to do the same at home.

Lesson 3

Story

Watch. Listen to the story *Mimi's first day at school*. Color the characters who find the classroom objects. Stick the story sticker. Ask and say. **Language:** book, crayon, eraser, pencil; happy, sad; Look! It's (a crayon). Where's your (book)? Here. / I don't know. I'm (happy).

17

Learning objectives

- Watch, understand and enjoy the story *Mimi's first day at school*
- Make a prediction about the story
- Look and find classroom objects
- Color the characters who find classroom objects in the story

Materials

- Class CDs, printable story cards, flashcards, *Ferris Wheel* mat, Mimi puppet

Main vocabulary

- book, crayon, eraser, pencil; happy, sad

Key language

- Look! It's (a crayon). Where's your (book)? Here. / I don't know. I'm (happy).

Teacher's tip: Managing feelings

Pre-schoolers are still developing the ability to identify their own feelings. After the story, get children to act out being happy or sad. This can help them identify their own emotions.

Circle time

Hello song & puppet (CD1 Track 2; see TB p 17 & 21)
Opening routines (see TB p 16)
Recycling activity (*Look! It's a/an …* and classroom objects) (see TB p 19)
Lesson aims (see TB p 18)

Introduce the story *Mimi's first day at school.*

- Say *It's story time!* Play the *Story rhyme* (CD1 Track 4; see TB p 17).
- Say *Tom and Sophie are listening to a story about Mimi's first day at school. Is Mimi happy or sad at school?* Demonstrate what you mean and encourage children to guess.

Watch or listen to the story.

CD1 Track 34

- Play the audio, watch the video or read the story using the printable story cards. Pause, repeat words, point to the pictures, ask questions.
- Ask again *Is Mimi happy or sad at school?* Establish that she's sad when she can't find her things and happy at the end of the story.
- Repeat the story. Encourage children to join in with the words and phrases in the story.
- Ask *Do you like the story? Are you happy at school?*

Look and find.

- Say e.g. *Find Mimi's pencil!* Children look at the story, point to Mimi's pencil and repeat the word.
- Repeat with other classroom objects.

Table time

Student's Book p 17

Watch. Listen to the story *Mimi's first day at school.*

CD1 Track 34

- Read or play the story again. Children listen and point to the pictures in their books.

Story questions

Picture 1
Where's Mimi going? *(School)*
Is Mimi happy? *(Yes)*

Picture 2
What does Leo see? *(Book/eraser)*
What does Zara see? *(Pencil/crayon)*

Picture 3
Does Mimi have her (book/pencil/eraser/crayon)? *(No)*
Is Mimi happy? *(No)*

Picture 4
Where's Mimi's (book/pencil/eraser/crayon)? *(Here)*
Is Mimi happy? *(Yes)*

Color the characters who find the classroom objects.

- Demonstrate coloring the characters who find the classroom objects in the story (i.e. Zara and Leo).

Stick the story sticker.

- Children stick on the story sticker.

Ask and say.

- Children ask and answer questions, e.g. *Where's your (book)? Here.*
- Ask e.g. *Is Mimi happy at the end of the story? Who are Mimi's friends?* and children respond.

Activity Book p 17

Color Mimi's book, eraser, pencil and crayon.

- Children color the four classroom objects.

Point, ask and say.

- They then point, ask and answer about the objects.

Closing time

Learning review (see TB p 18)
Closing routines (see TB p 16)
Bye bye song and puppet (CD1 Track 3; see TB p 17 & 21)

Use the **Navio App** to watch the video, and encourage children to do the same at home.

Story Song

Watch. Listen, point and sing *Where's your book?* Follow and draw the path through the maze. Ask and say. **Language:** book, crayon, eraser, pencil; happy, sad; Where's your (book)? Here. / I don't know. I'm (happy).

18

Learning objectives

- Watch, sing and act out the story song *Where's your book?*
- Listen to the story again and identify the classroom objects
- Play *I'm happy! I'm sad!*
- Ask and say where classroom objects are
- Complete a sequence

Materials

- Class CDs, printable story cards, flashcards, *Ferris Wheel* mat, Mimi puppet

Main vocabulary

- book, crayon, eraser, pencil; happy, sad

Key language

- Where's your (book)? Here. / I don't know. I'm (happy).

Teacher's tip: Joining in a song in stages

Children of this age group may need to listen to the story song a number of times before starting to join in. Encourage them to join in first with the actions, then with the key words and chunks of language until they are joining in with the whole song.

Circle time

Hello song & puppet (CD1 Track 2; see TB p 17 & 21)
Opening routines (see TB p 16)
Recycling activity (classroom objects vocabulary) (see TB p 19)
Lesson aims (see TB p 18)

Retell the story *Mimi's first day at school*.

- Play the audio, video or read the story using the printable story cards.
- Demonstrate that children should wave their arms in the air every time they hear the name of a classroom object in the story.

Game: *I'm happy! I'm sad!*

- Use the puppet to say in turn *I'm happy. / I'm sad.* Model expressions to show both feelings and children respond.
- Repeat several times alternating the sentences. As children make happy or sad expressions, get them to say the sentences with you.

***Where's your book?* song**

CD1 Track 35

- Play the video or audio of the story song. Children watch/listen and make happy or sad expressions at the end of each verse as per the song.
- Play the song again. Children sing and act out the song (see TB p 55).
- Ask questions, e.g. *Where's your book?* Children respond by pointing to or holding up classroom objects and saying *Here.*

Game: *Ask Mimi.*

- Lay out the flashcards of the book, pencil, crayon and eraser.
- Hold up the puppet. Ask Mimi questions and encourage children to join in asking with you, e.g. *Where's your book, Mimi? / Here!*
- Us the puppet to ask individual children questions in the same way.

Table time

Student's Book p 18

Watch. Listen, point and sing *Where's your book?*

CD1 Track 35

- Play the audio of the song. Children listen, sing and point to the classroom objects in the maze.
- Remember that you can use the karaoke version of the song when the children are confident.

Follow and draw the path through the maze.

- Demonstrate following the path through the maze with your finger.
- Children draw the path themselves.

Ask and say.

- Children ask and answer questions, e.g. *Where's your (book)? Here.*

Activity Book p 18

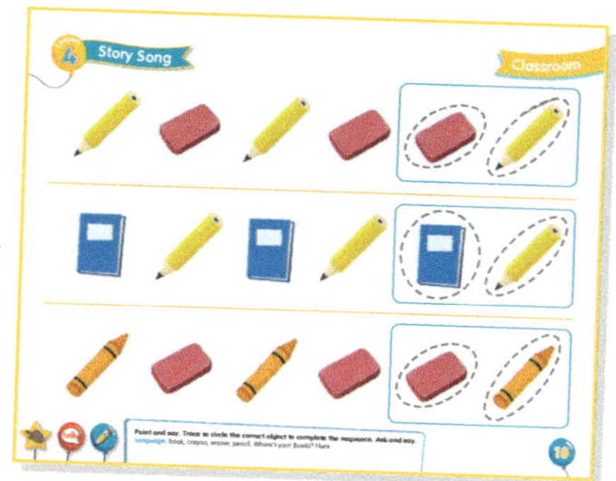

Point and say.

- Children point and name the objects in each sequence.

Trace to circle the correct object to complete the sequence. Ask and say.

- Children trace to circle the correct object to complete each sequence. Then they ask and answer about the objects.

Closing time

Learning review (see TB p 18)
Closing routines (see TB p 16)
Bye bye song and puppet (CD1 Track 3; see TB p 17 & 21)

Use the **Navio App** to watch the video, and encourage children to do the same at home.

Lesson 5 Speaking

Life skills

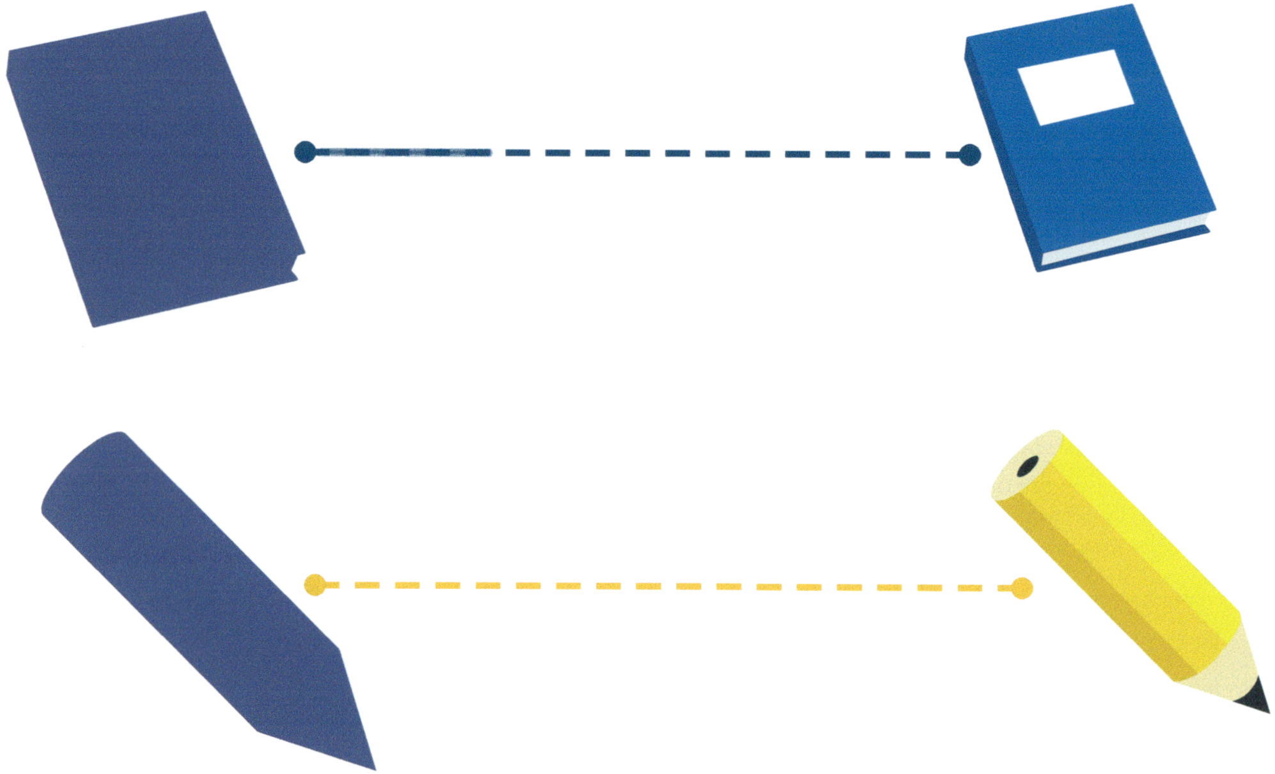

Watch. Listen and point. Trace to match the classroom objects. Ask and say. **Language:** book, pencil; blue, yellow; Where's your (book)? Here. What color is your (book)? It's (blue).

19

Classroom

Learning objectives

- Ask and answer questions about where classroom objects are
- Watch, understand and enjoy a video
- Identify classroom objects in the video

Materials

- Class CDs, flashcards, *Ferris Wheel* mat, Mimi puppet

Main vocabulary

- book, pencil; blue, yellow

Key language

- Where's your (book)? Here. What color is your (book)? It's (blue).

Teacher's tip: Learning to be organized

Life skills

It's important that children can identify their own belongings. If they sit at color coded tables, put a sticker of the corresponding color on the cover of their books to help with the identification process.

Circle time

Hello song & puppet (CD1 Track 2; see TB p 17 & 21)
Opening routines (see TB p 16)
Recycling activity (story song) (CD1 Track 35; see TB p 19)
Lesson aims (see TB p 18)

Game: *Where's your pencil?*

- Give out the classroom object flashcards to individual children.
- Ask e.g. *Where's your pencil?* The child with the flashcard stands up and says *Here*.
- Repeat with the other flashcards.

Game: *Guess where!*

- Put the flashcards face down on the floor or board and mix them up.
- Ask e.g. *Where's the crayon?* and invite a child to guess and turn over one of the flashcards. Say *Hurray!* and children clap if it is the crayon. Say *Oh no! It's the …* (naming the classroom object). *Let's try again!* if it isn't the crayon.
- Repeat several times.

Watch the video.

- Explain that Auntie Jenny is helping Tom and Sophie get ready for school.
- Play the video of Auntie Jenny, Tom and Sophie.
- Ask *What color is Sophie's book? (Blue) What color is Tom's pencil? (Yellow) Are Tom and Sophie ready for school?*
- Watch again. Pause and children repeat the questions and answers with *Where*.

Table time

Student's Book p 19 Life skills

Watch. Listen and point.

- Children identify Tom, Sophie and Auntie Jenny in the photo.
- Point to the classroom objects and children say the words.
- Play the audio or video. Children listen and point to the pictures.

CD1 Track 37

Auntie Jenny: Are you ready for school, Sophie?
Sophie: Yes, I am.
Auntie Jenny: Where's your book?
Sophie: Here.
Auntie Jenny: What color is your book?
Sophie: It's blue.
Auntie Jenny: Are you ready for school, Tom?
Tom: Yes, I am.
Auntie Jenny: Where's your pencil?
Tom: Here.
Auntie Jenny: And what color is your pencil?
Tom: It's yellow.
Auntie Jenny: Great. So you're both ready for school now!
Tom & Sophie: Yes!
Auntie Jenny: Come on! Tom! Your bag!

Trace to match the classroom objects.

- Children trace the lines to match the classroom objects.
- Play the audio again. Use the pause button. Children listen and point to the classroom objects in their books.

Ask and say.

- Pretend to be Auntie Jenny. Ask children questions as if they are Tom and Sophie as in the audio. Use the flashcards as prompts. Children ask and answer questions, e.g. *Where's your (book)? Here.*

Activity Book p 19

Draw and color the objects you take to school inside the backpack.

- Children draw and color the objects they take to school in the backpack.

Point, ask and say.

- They ask and answer about the objects they drew.

Closing time

Learning review (see TB p 18)
Closing routines (see TB p 16)
Bye bye song and puppet (CD1 Track 3; see TB p 17 & 21)

Use the **Navio App** to watch the video, and encourage children to do the same at home.

Lesson 6

Values *I'm your friend*

Listen, point and sing *I'm your friend*. Draw and color a picture of a friend. Say. Language: care, friend, happy, sad; I care. I'm your friend.

SOCIAL AND EMOTIONAL LEARNING

20

Learning objectives

- Recognize the value of friendship
- Sing the values song *I'm your friend*
- Say *I'm your friend*

Materials

- Class CDs, flashcards, *Ferris Wheel* mat, Mimi puppet

Main vocabulary

- care, friend, happy, sad

Key language

- I care. I'm your friend.

Teacher's tip: Learning to make friends

Give opportunities for children to show empathy towards each other and learn to make friends with all their classmates, despite any differences they may have. After singing the song, encourage the children to walk around the classroom and say *I'm your friend* to as many classmates as possible.

Circle time

Hello song & puppet (CD1 Track 2; see TB p 17 & 21)
Opening routines (see TB p 16)
Recycling activity (*Where's your …? Here!*) (see TB p 19)
Lesson aims (see TB p 18)

Watch the *Mimi's first day at school* story video.

- Play the story video.
- Children watch and repeat every time they hear a classroom object.
- Ask e.g. *Who are Mimi's friends in the story? (Eddie, Zara and Leo). Do you have friends?*

***I'm your friend* song**

CD1 Track 38

- Use the Mimi puppet to say *Let's sing the song "I'm your friend."*
- Play the song. Children listen and make happy and sad faces when they hear the words *happy* and *sad* in the song.
- Play the song again. Children sing and act out the song (see TB p 55).

Table time

Student's Book p 20

Listen, point and sing *I'm your friend.*

CD1 Track 38

- Play the song. Children sing and point to the pictures of Mimi and her friends.

Draw and color a picture of a friend.

- Children draw and color a picture of one of their friends.

Say.

- Children say sentences to their friends, e.g. *I'm your friend.*

Activity Book p 20

Color the frame of the happy friends yellow and the sad friend blue.

- Children color the frame around the picture of the happy friends yellow. They color the frame around the picture of the sad friend blue.

Say.

- They find a friend and say *I care. I'm your friend.*

Closing time

Learning review (see TB p 18)
Closing routines (see TB p 16)
Bye bye song and puppet (CD1 Track 3; see TB p 17 & 21)

Use the **Navio App** to listen to the song, and encourage children to do the same at home.

Content

Classroom

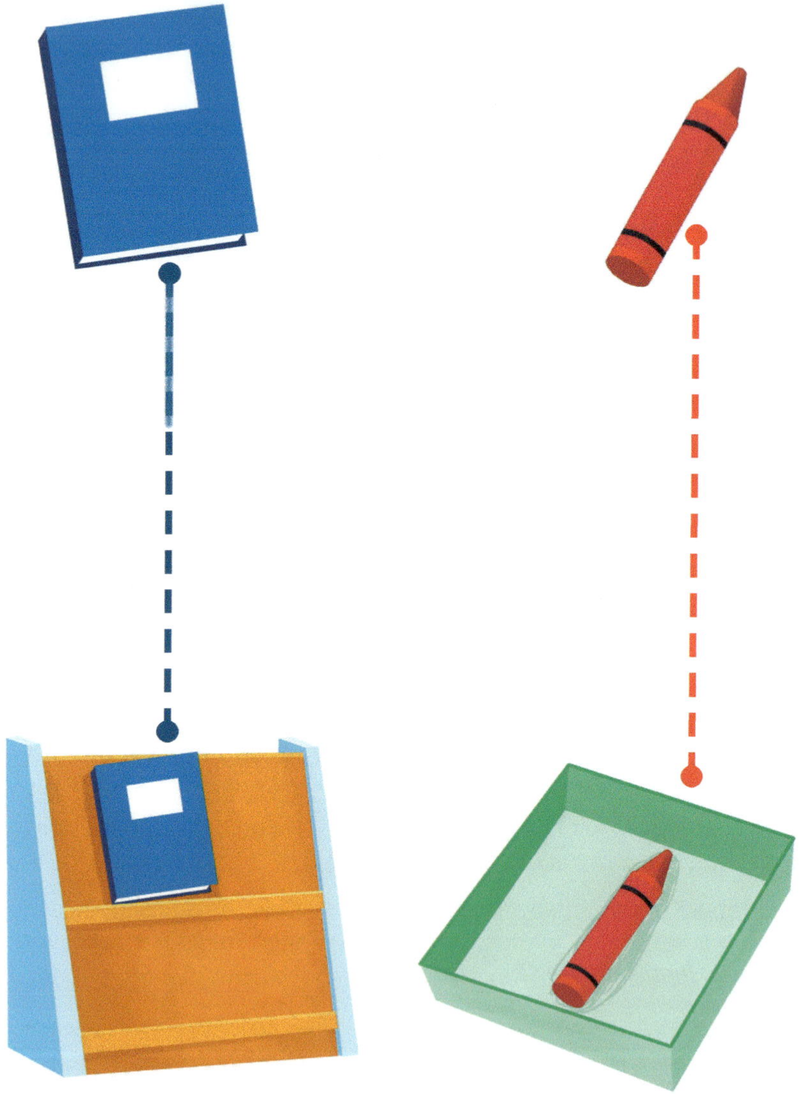

Listen and point. Trace to match the book and crayon to where they belong. Say.
Language: book, crayon; shelf, tray; I put the (crayon) (in) the (tray).

21

Learning objectives

- Identify and name places where things go in the classroom
- Listen and understand a dialogue about putting things away
- Say where you put things in the classroom

Materials

- Class CDs, printable flashcards, *Ferris Wheel* mat, Mimi puppet

Main vocabulary

- book, crayon; shelf, tray

Key language

- I put the (crayon) (in) the (tray).

Teacher's tip: Learning to put things away in the classroom

Life skills

Point out to the children the importance of helping out when it's time to clean up. Introduce more ways they can help out in the classroom by putting crayons in the trays and putting their books on the shelf. Encourage them to look on the floor and clean up any materials that may be lying around.

Circle time

Hello song & puppet (CD1 Track 2; see TB p 17 & 21)
Opening routines (see TB p 16)
Recycling activity (see TB p 19)
Lesson aims (see TB p 18)

Introduce content vocabulary.

- Use the printable flashcards and the puppet to introduce the new words (*shelf, tray*). Children repeat the words.
- Lay out the two new printable flashcards face up.
- Hold up the flashcards of the book and the crayon. Say *I put the book on the shelf. / I put the crayon in the tray* and put each one on the corresponding printable flashcard.
- Repeat and children say the sentences with you.

Game: ***I put the book on the shelf.***

- Lay out the printable flashcards of the shelf and the tray on opposite sides of the circle. Put the classroom object flashcards (except the table and chair) as well as real classroom objects in the centre of the circle.
- Say e.g. *I put the eraser on the shelf. / I put the pencil in the tray.* Children respond by picking up and moving the flashcard or an object you name to the correct side of the circle.
- Repeat several times with different instructions and children respond.

Game: ***Touch the tray!***

- Get children to identify a shelf and a tray in the classroom.
- Give instructions to pairs of children in turn, e.g. *Touch the shelf! Touch the tray!* Children stand up and respond. Everybody claps and says *Hurray!* if they do this correctly.
- Repeat several times giving instructions to different pairs.

Table time

Student's Book p 21

Listen and point.

- Say *Tom and Sophie are putting books on the shelf and crayons in the tray.*
- Play the audio. Children listen and point to the photos as Tom and Sophie respond. Use the pause button after each sentence.

CD1 Track 39

Teacher: Put the book on the shelf, please.
Tom: I put the book on the shelf.
Sophie: I put the book on the shelf.
Teacher: Very good. Thank you.
Teacher: Put the crayon in the tray, please.
Sophie: I put the crayon in the tray.
Tom: I put the crayon in the tray.
Teacher: Very good. Thank you.

Trace to match the book and crayon to where they belong.

- Demonstrate that children should match the book and crayon to where they belong (i.e. the book to the shelf and the crayon to the tray).

Say.

- Play the audio of Tom and Sophie again. Children point to the pictures and repeat the sentences.

Activity Book p 21

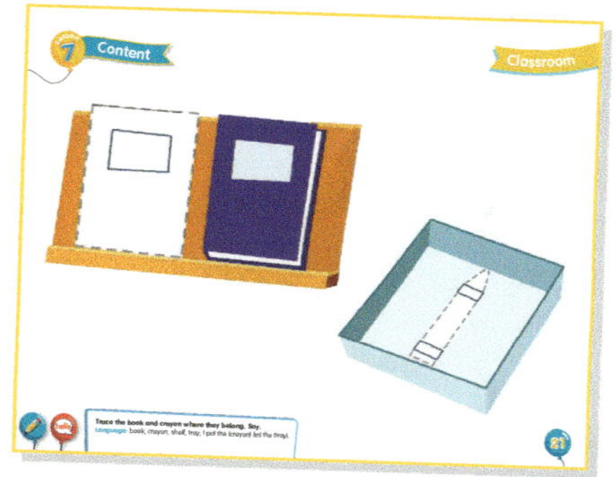

Trace the book and crayon where they belong.

- Children trace the book on the shelf and the crayon in the tray.

Say.

- They point and say *I put the (book) (on) the (shelf).*

Closing time

Learning review (see TB p 18)
Closing routines (see TB p 16)
Bye bye song and puppet (CD1 Track 3; see TB p 17 & 21)

Use the **Navio App** to play the vocabulary and language games, and encourage children to do the same at home.

Lesson 8 Culture

Watch. Listen, point and sing *This is the way I say hello*. Follow and draw the path from Sophie and Tom to the school. Say.
Language: bye bye, hello; friends, school; This is the way I say (hello).

22

Learning objectives

- Watch, sing and act out the traditional song *This is the way I say hello*
- Play an action game
- Act out saying *hello* and *bye bye*

Materials

- Class CDs, flashcards, *Ferris Wheel* mat, Mimi puppet

Main vocabulary

- bye bye, hello; friends, school

Key language

- This is the way I say (hello).

Teacher's tip: Exploiting the Culture song for children's social development

Incorporate the verses from the song into your daily routines. Encourage the children to sing *This is the way I say hello* as they arrive in the morning or at the beginning of the session and *This is the way I say bye bye* at the end of the session.

Circle time

Hello song & puppet (CD1 Track 2; see TB p 17 & 21)
Opening routines (see TB p 16)
Recycling activity (see TB p 19)
Lesson aims (see TB p 18)

Game: *Mimi says hello*

- Use the puppet to say *Mimi says hello* and demonstrate greeting the children.
- Use the puppet to say *Mimi says bye bye* and demonstrate waving bye bye.
- Use the puppet to alternate instructions and children respond. Speed up as children get more confident in responding.

***This is the way I say hello* song**

CD1 Track 40

- Say *Stand up. Let's learn the song "This is the way I say hello."*
- Play the audio. Children listen and mime saying *hello* and *bye bye* with you in each verse.
- Repeat. Children join in singing and acting out the song (see TB p 55).

Watch the *This is the way I say hello* song video.

- Children watch the video and join in singing the song and doing the actions with Tom and Sophie.

Table time

Student's Book p 22

Watch. Listen, point and sing *This is the way I say hello.*

CD1 Track 40

- Play the audio. Children listen, sing and point to Sophie and Tom.

Follow and draw the path from Sophie and Tom to the school.

- Play the audio again. Children listen and follow the path from the photo of Sophie and Tom to school with their finger.
- Children draw a line to follow the path to school.

Say.

- Children act out saying *hello* and *bye bye* to their friends.

Activity Book p 22

Trace to match the children saying 'hello' and 'bye bye'.

- Children trace the blue line to match the children saying *hello*. They trace the red line to match the children saying *bye bye*.

Point and say.

- They point and say *This is the way I say (hello).*

Closing time

Learning review (see TB p 18)
Closing routines (see TB p 16)
Bye bye song and puppet (CD1 Track 3; see TB p 17 & 21)

Use the **Navio App** to watch the video, and encourage children to do the same at home.

Review

Classroom

Listen, point and say. Color the words you know. Stick the star sticker. Ask and say. **Language:** book, chair, crayon, eraser, pencil, table; colors; It's (a crayon). Where's your (book)? Here. What color is your (book)? It's (blue).

Learning objectives

- Review your learning and progress
- Talk about classroom objects
- Ask and say where family members are
- Stick on a star sticker for achievement

Materials

- Class CDs, flashcards, *Ferris Wheel* mat, Mimi puppet

Main vocabulary

- book, chair, crayon, eraser, pencil, table; colors

Key language

- It's (a crayon). Where's your (book)? Here. What color is your (book)? It's (blue).

Teacher's tip: Checking the vocabulary in pairs

As an alternative to working on their own, put the children in pairs and demonstrate that they should take turns pointing to and naming the vocabulary before they begin to color. Remind children that they should only color the items they remember.

Circle time

Hello song & puppet (CD1 Track 2; see TB p 17 & 21)
Opening routines (see TB p 16)
Recycling activity (see TB p 19)
Lesson aims (see TB p 18)

Classroom object flashcard games

- Choose one or two flashcard games with the *Ferris Wheel* mat and/or the puppet (see TB p 20 & 21).

Sing *Stand up! Sit down!*

CD1 Track 32

- Lay out the classroom object flashcards.
- Play the audio. Children sing, do the actions and point to the flashcards.

Game: ***Look! It's (a pencil).***

- Choose six children to stand up and hold the flashcards so that the rest of the class can't see. Move Mimi along the line and have her choose one of the flashcards at random. The child turns it around and the class says *Look! It's (a pencil).*

Game: ***Where's the eraser?***

- Stick all the flashcards on the board facing the children. Divide the class into two teams. Choose a child from each team to come and stand in front of the flashcards. Say *Where's the (eraser)?* The first child to touch it and say *Here!* gets a point for the team. Repeat several times.

Watch the story video.

- Children watch the story video. Ask *Who finds Mimi's book, pencil, eraser and crayon in the story? Is Mimi happy or sad at the end of the story?*

Table time

Student's Book p 23

Listen, point and say.

- Say e.g. *Find the table!* and children point to the pictures.
- Play the audio. Children listen, point to the classroom objects and say the words.

CD1 Track 41

Mimi: I'm the teacher! Can you remember the classroom objects, Dylan?
Dylan: Yes, I can. Book.
Mimi: Book.
Dylan: Pencil.
Mimi: Pencil.
Dylan: Eraser.
Mimi: Eraser.
Dylan: Crayon.
Mimi: Crayon.
Dylan: Table.
Mimi: Table.
Dylan: Chair.
Mimi: Chair. Great job, Dylan. Very good!

Color the words you know.

- Children color the classroom objects they know.

Stick the star sticker.

- Children stick on the star sticker for achievement.
- Monitor and encourage children to think positively about their progress.

Ask and say.

- Children say sentences and ask and answer questions about the classroom objects, e.g. *Look! It's a pencil! / Where's your eraser? Here.*

Activity Book p 23

Color the faces to show the classroom objects you know. Ask and say.

- Children color the faces next to the classroom objects they know. They ask and answer about the objects.

Think and color the stars to show your progress.

- Children color the number of stars that they feel shows their progress in this unit.

Closing time

Learning review (see TB p 18)
Closing routines (see TB p 16)
Bye bye song and puppet (CD1 Track 3; see TB p 17 & 21)

Use the **Navio App** to review what children have learned in this unit, and encourage children to do the same at home.

Project

COOPERATIVE LEARNING

Classroom

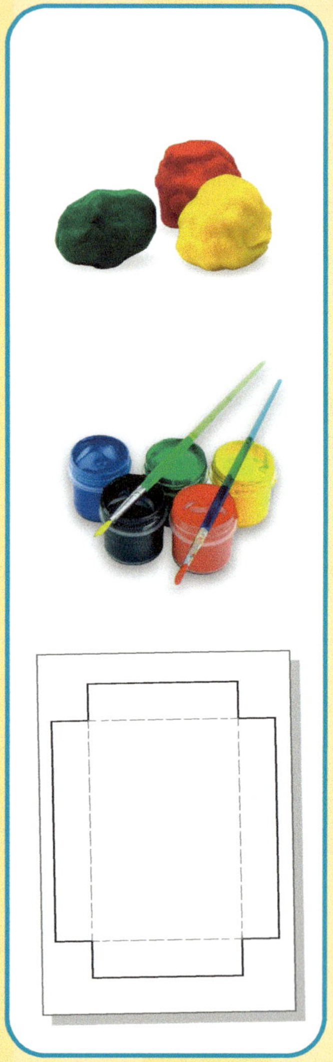

1

2

3

Make some crayons and paint a tray. Put your crayons together in the trays. Ask and say.
Language: crayon, tray; colors; It's (a crayon). It's (red). Where's the (blue) crayon? Here.
What color is your (crayon)? It's (green). I put the crayon in the tray.

24

Learning objectives

- Work together to do a collaborative project
- Make a tray of crayons
- Talk about the crayons and colors in the display
- Express enjoyment of the crayons display
- Count classroom objects and say how many

Materials

- Class CDs, Mimi puppet, project template, finger paints, modeling clay, glue/tape
- optional: crayons

Main vocabulary

- crayon, tray; colors

Key language

- It's (a crayon). It's (red). Where's the (blue) crayon? Here. What color is your (crayon)? It's (green). I put the crayon in the tray.

Teacher's tip: Developing fine motor skills

COOPERATIVE LEARNING

Rolling a ball of modeling clay into a long thin shape helps develop the muscles in the fingers and hands, which in turn leads to improved fine motor skills. Demonstrate that the children should roll the modeling clay backwards and forwards until it starts to take the shape of a crayon. Be ready to encourage and praise their efforts.

Circle time

Hello song & puppet (CD1 Track 2; see TB p 17 & 21)
Opening routines (see TB p 16)
Recycling activity (see TB p 19)
Lesson aims (see TB p 18)

Prepare for your project.

- Say *Let's do a project and make a tray of crayons!*
- Show children the copies of the tray templates that you have prepared.
- Demonstrate using finger paints to paint the tray templates.
- Demonstrate rolling the modeling clay into a crayon shape.

Table time

COOPERATIVE LEARNING

Student's Book p 24

- Say e.g. *We're going to make a tray of crayons like this. Look at what we need for our project: tray template, finger paints, modeling clay.* Children listen and point to the pictures.

Make some crayons and paint a tray.

- Divide the children into groups or tables of six children. Give out one tray template to each group and some modeling clay to each child.
- Children choose the color of modeling clay (red, yellow, green, blue, pink, orange) for their crayon or you can assign this. Make sure that each group prepares one crayon of each color.
- Make sure children have finger paints, modeling clay and glue available.
- Children paint the tray template. You will need to help them fold up and glue (or tape) the sides. They roll the modeling clay into a crayon shape.

Put your crayons together in the trays.

- When they are ready, children put their completed crayons into their trays. Each table or group makes one tray of six crayons.
- Display all the trays of crayons on a table where everyone can see.

Ask and say.

- Children talk about the crayons and name the colors.
- Ask children *Do you like our crayons?* Make the point that everyone helped make the trays of crayons and that they couldn't have made such a beautiful display of crayons and colors on their own.

Alternative version of project

- Children could use crayons instead of finger paints to color their tray.

Activity Book p 24

Draw and color objects to take to school.

- Children draw and color classroom objects (pencils, crayons, erasers) inside the pencil case.

Count the objects. Point, ask and say.

- Children count the objects and say how many. They point, ask and answer about the objects they drew.

Closing time

Learning review (see TB p 18)
Closing routines (see TB p 16)
Bye bye song and puppet (CD1 Track 3; see TB p 17 & 21)

My face

Splash!

Vocabulary and language

- **Main vocabulary:** ears, eyes, hair, mouth, nose, teeth
- **Key language:** I have (a nose). I have (two) (eyes). I have (a red) (mouth).
- **Content language:** hear, see; ears, eyes; I (see) with my (eyes).
- **Other language:** boy, girl, water, happy, special; It's a (boy) in the water. My (eyes) are special. Here is my (nose). Here are my (eyes). Where's (Maria)? Here. What color is your (nose)? It's (pink).

Unit objectives

- Identify and name parts of your face
- Sing the language song *I have two eyes*
- Say parts of the face you have
- Understand and join in the story *Splash!*
- Sing and act out the story song *Two eyes, two ears*
- Sing the values song *I'm happy I'm me*
- Develop self-esteem
- Identify and name what you use to hear and see with
- Sing and act out the traditional song *Here are my ears*
- Review your learning and progress
- Participate in a collaborative project

Story

CD2 Track 6

Picture 1

Narrator: It's hot and sunny. Mimi and Dylan are in a little boat.
Mimi: Look, Dylan. It's a girl in the water. Two eyes … two ears … a nose … and a mouth. Oh wow! I have two eyes … two ears … a nose … and a mouth!
Dylan: Amazing!
Mommy: Be careful Mimi and Dylan.
Daddy: Don't rock the boat.

Picture 2

Dylan: And look, Mimi. It's a boy in the water. Two eyes … two ears … a nose … and a mouth. Oh wow! I have two eyes … two ears … a nose … and a mouth!
Mimi: Amazing!
Mommy: Be careful, Mimi and Dylan.
Daddy: Don't rock the boat.

Picture 3

Mimi: Look, Daddy. It's a girl in the water. Two eyes … two ears … a nose … and a mouth.
Daddy: Oh, Mimi. It's you!
Mimi: Me? Oh yes.
Dylan: Look, Mommy. It's a boy in the water. Two eyes … two ears … a nose … and a mouth.
Mommy: Oh, Dylan. It's you!
Dylan: Me? Oh yes.
Mommy: Be careful, Mimi and Dylan.
Daddy: Don't rock the boat.

Picture 4

Mimi & Dylan: Oh … oh … oh …
Mimi: Ha, ha. I'm in the water now! I have two eyes … two ears … a nose … and a mouth!
Dylan: And I'm in the water now! I have two eyes … two ears … a nose … and a mouth!
Daddy: And you're wet!
Mommy: Oh … Come on. Let's go home.

Songs

Language song

I have two eyes CD2 Track 4

I have two eyes, two eyes (Point to both eyes)
Just like you (Point to a child)
I have a nose, a nose (Point to nose)
I have hair too (Point to hair)

I have two ears, two ears (Point to both ears)
Just like you (Point to a child)
I have a mouth, a mouth (Point to mouth)
I have teeth too (Open mouth and point to teeth)

I have two eyes, two eyes (Point to both eyes)
Just like you (Point to a child)
I have a nose, a nose (Point to nose)
I have hair too (Point to hair)

I have two ears, two ears (Point to both ears)
Just like you (Point to a child)
I have a mouth, a mouth (Point to mouth)
I have teeth too (Open mouth and point to teeth)

Story song

Two eyes, two ears CD2 Track 7

Two eyes, two ears, (Point to eyes and then ears)
A nose and a mouth. (Point to nose and then mouth)
It's a girl in the water. (Point to a girl)
Be careful. Be careful. (Hold up one hand)
Don't rock the boat! (Rock from side to side)
Oh, oh, oh! Splash! (Throw arms out)
I'm in the water now! (Jump in place)
Two eyes, two ears, (Point to eyes and then ears)
A nose and a mouth (Point to nose and then mouth)
It's a boy in the water. (Point to a boy)
Be careful. Be careful. (Hold up one hand)
Don't rock the boat! (Rock from side to side)
Oh, oh, oh! Splash! (Throw arms out)
I'm in the water now! (Jump in place)

Values song

I'm happy I'm me CD2 Track 10

I'm happy I'm me (Point to self and smile)
I'm happy I'm me
My hair and my eyes (Point to hair and eyes)
My ears and my nose (Point to ears and nose)
My mouth and my teeth (Point to mouth and teeth)
Are special (Open arms and move from side to side)
I'm happy, (Smile broadly)
I'm happy I'm me (Point to self and smile)
(Repeat)

Culture song

Here are my ears. CD2 Track 12

Here are my ears. (Point to ears)
Here is my nose. (Point to nose)
Here are my hands. (Hold up hands)
Here are my toes. (Point to toes)
Here are my eyes. (Point to eyes)
Both open wide. (Open eyes wide)
Here is my mouth. (Open mouth)
With teeth inside. (Smile showing teeth)
(Repeat)

My face

Splash!

Vocabulary

Lesson 1

Listen, point and repeat. Listen and play. Stick the face stickers. Say.
Language: ear, eye, mouth, nose; blue, green, pink, red

25

My face

Lesson 1 Vocabulary

Learning objectives

- Identify and name parts of the face
- Listen and point to parts of the face
- Listen and play *Round and round and round*

Materials

- Class CDs, flashcards, *Ferris Wheel* mat, Mimi puppet

Main vocabulary

- ear, eye, mouth, nose; blue, green, pink, red

Teacher's tip: Recognizing facial features in a mirror

If possible, take several small, unbreakable mirrors into class. Invite children to look at themselves in the mirrors. As you name the vocabulary, point to your own facial features and get the rest of the class to do the same. Encourage the children with the mirrors to look at their facial features in the mirror and say the words. Repeat with different children.

Circle time

Hello song & puppet (CD1 Track 2; see TB p 17 & 21)
Opening routines (see TB p 16)
Lesson aims (see TB p 18)

Introduce parts of the face.

- Introduce parts of the face by pointing to the puppet's features and your own. Say the words and encourage children to repeat them with you. Repeat for all the words.
- Put the *Ferris Wheel* mat on the floor or board with the flashcards face down (one on each color). Use the puppet to turn them over and name them. Children point to their own facial features and repeat the words.

Game: *Touch your nose!*

- Point to the flashcards in turn. Use the puppet to give instructions. Children touch the parts of their face.

Game: *Say the color!*

- Name the parts of the face on the Ferris Wheel and children name the color. Then the reverse.

Game: *Guess the word!*

- Turn the flashcards face down and mix them up so that they are on different colors of the wheel.
- Point to one flashcard. Children guess what it is. Then say *Let's find out!* Turn the flashcard over and children say the word. Repeat with all the flashcards.

Table time

Student's Book p 25

Listen, point and repeat.

- Play the audio. Children listen and point to each part of the face as they hear it.

CD2 Track 1

Mimi: Look, Dylan! Nose … ear… mouth … eye … hee, hee, hee! Repeat, Dylan!
Dylan: Yes, Mimi! Nose … ear … mouth … eye … hee, hee, hee!
Mimi: Very good, Dylan. Let's say the words together.
Both: Nose … ear … mouth … eye … hee, hee, hee!

- Play the audio again. Children listen and repeat the words.

Listen and play.

- Hold up your index finger and move it around clockwise like a wheel. Children do the same. Play the audio. Children listen, point to the color when they hear it, and say the word.

CD2 Track 2

Mimi: Round and round and round: red … nose!
Dylan: Nose!
Mimi: Round and round and round: pink … mouth!
Dylan: Mouth!
Mimi: Round and round and round: blue … ear!
Dylan: Ear!
Mimi: Round and round and round: green … eye!
Dylan: Eye!

- Play the game with you and/or individual children naming colors and others saying the words.

Stick the face stickers.

- Children put on the face stickers.

Say.

- Children point and say the parts of the face.

Activity Book p 25

Trace Dylan's eyes and mouth and Mimi's ears and nose.

- Children trace the parts of Mimi and Dylan's faces.

Point and say.

- They point and say the words.

Closing time

Learning review (see TB p 18)
Closing routines (see TB p 16)
Bye bye song and puppet (CD1 Track 3; see TB p 17 & 21)

Use the **Navio App** to play the vocabulary game, and encourage children to do the same at home.

Listen and find the new parts of the face. Listen, point and sing *I have two eyes*. Trace to match Sophie's hair and Tom's teeth. Say. Language: ears, eyes, hair, mouth, nose, teeth; I have (a nose). I have (two) (eyes).

Learning objectives

- Talk about parts of your face
- Identify and name two new parts of the face
- Sing the language song *I have two eyes*
- Say what parts of the face you have

Materials

- Class CDs, flashcards, *Ferris Wheel* mat, Mimi puppet

Main vocabulary

- ears, eyes, hair, mouth, nose, teeth

Key language

- I have (a nose). I have (two) (eyes).

Teacher's tip: Adding variety to pronunciation practice

When practicing the pronunciation of the words, add variety by asking the children to say the words in a happy way and then in a sad way. Alternate between happy and sad, encouraging them to change the tone as well as their expression when they say the words.

Circle time

Hello song & puppet (CD1 Track 2; see TB p 17 & 21)

Opening routines (see TB p 16)

Recycling activity (four face words from Lesson 1) (see TB p 19)

Lesson aims (see TB p 18)

Introduce the new parts of the face.

- Put all six face flashcards on the floor or board. Children identify the two new parts of the face.
- Use the puppet to point to and say the words in turn. Children repeat in chorus and point to their own hair and teeth.
- Turn the two new flashcards face down. Mix them up. Point to one and ask *Hair or teeth?* Children guess. Repeat several times

Introduce *I have (a nose).*

- Hold up the flashcards in turn. Point to your own facial features and say, e.g. *I have hair. / I have a nose.*
- Repeat. Children point to their own facial features and repeat the sentences with you in chorus.

Game: *Sentence chain!*

- Show a flashcard and say e.g. *I have two eyes*, and touch your eyes. Children repeat the sentence and do the same.
- Show another flashcard and say e.g. *I have two eyes. I have two ears.* Point to both flashcards and to your eyes and ears in turn. Children do the same.
- Repeat cumulatively with the other flashcards, e.g. *I have two eyes. I have two ears. I have a nose. I have a mouth,* until children are saying sentences with you about all six facial features.

***I have two eyes* song**

CD2 Track 4

- Put the flashcards face up on the floor or board in the order of the song.
- Play the audio. Children listen and point to the flashcards with you as they hear them in the song.
- Play the audio again. Children stand up, point to their own facial features and join in singing the song (see TB p 77).

Table time

Student's Book p 26

Listen and find the new parts of the face.

- Hold up your book. Point to the photo of Tom and Sophie and say the names.
- Play the audio. Children listen and find the two new parts of the face. Repeat and children say the words.

CD2 Track 3

Tom: Find … hair! Hair!
Sophie: Hair! Here!
Tom: Find … teeth! Teeth!
Sophie: Teeth! Here!

Listen, point and sing *I have two eyes.*

CD2 Track 4

- Play the song. Children listen, sing and point to the parts of Tom and Sophie's faces in the photo.
- Remember that you can use the karaoke version of the song when the children are confident.

Trace to match Sophie's hair and Tom's teeth.

- Hold up your book and demonstrate matching the pictures of the hair and the mouth to Sophie and Tom's faces in the photo.
- Children trace the lines.

Say.

- Children talk about all the parts of their face.

Activity Book p 26

Draw and color your hair. Trace the teeth and color your eyes.

- Children draw and color their hair on the face. Then they trace the teeth and color the eyes the same color as their eyes.

Point and say.

- They point and say sentences about all the parts of the face.

Closing time

Learning review (see TB p 18)

Closing routines (see TB p 16)

Bye bye song and puppet (CD1 Track 3; see TB p 17 & 21)

Use the **Navio App** to listen to the song, and encourage children to do the same at home.

Lesson 3 Story

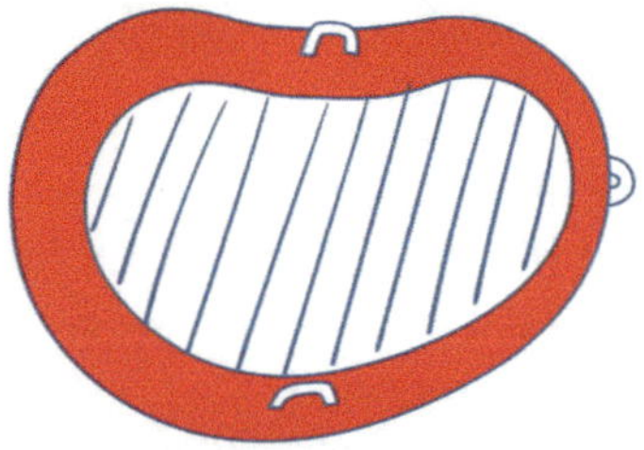

Watch. Listen to the story *Splash!* Color the boat from the story. Stick the story sticker. Say. Language: ears, eyes, mouth, nose; boy, girl; water; I have (a mouth).
I have (two) (eyes). It's (a boy) in the water.

Learning objectives

- Watch, understand and enjoy the story *Splash!*
- Make a prediction about the story
- Look and find parts of the face
- Color the boat from the story

Materials

- Class CDs, printable story cards, flashcards, *Ferris Wheel* mat, Mimi puppet

Main vocabulary

- ears, eyes, mouth, nose; boy, girl; water

Key language

- I have a (mouth). I have (two) (eyes). It's (a boy) in the water.

Teacher's tip: Being aware of safety in boats

Life skills

Use the children's shared language to ask if they have ever been in a boat. Make sure they understand that it's important to sit down and hold on so that they don't fall in like Mimi and Dylan. Have children sit on the floor in groups of 4–6 as if they are in the boat. Say in turn *Rock the boat! / Don't rock the boat!* and children respond by swaying from side to side or sitting still.

Circle time

Hello song & puppet (CD1 Track 2; see TB p 17 & 21)
Opening routines (see TB p 16)
Recycling activity (*I have* ... and parts of the face) (see TB p 19)
Lesson aims (see TB p 18)

Introduce the story *Splash!*

- Say *It's story time!* Play the *Story rhyme* (CD1 Track 4; see TB p 17).
- Say *Tom and Sophie are listening to a story about Mimi and Dylan. Mimi and Dylan are in a little boat.* Explain or draw a picture on the board. *What does Mimi see in the water? What does Dylan see in the water?* Demonstrate what you mean and encourage children to guess.

Watch or listen to the story.

CD2 Track 6

- Play the audio, watch the video or read the story using the printable story cards. Pause, repeat words, point to the pictures, ask questions.
- Ask again *What does Mimi see in the water? (a girl) What does Dylan see in the water? (a boy)* Ask *Who is it in the water? (Mimi and Dylan).*
- Repeat the story. Encourage children to join in with the words and phrases in the story.
- Ask *Do you want to go on a boat?*

Look and find.

- Say e.g. *Find Mimi's eyes!* Children look at the story, point to a picture of Mimi's eyes and repeat the word.
- Repeat with other facial features of Mimi and Dylan.

Table time

Student's Book p 27

Watch. Listen to the story *Splash!*

Story questions

Picture 1
What's in the water? *(A girl)*
Does Mimi have (two eyes/two ears/a nose/a mouth)? *(Yes)*

Picture 2
What's in the water? *(A boy)*
Does Dylan have (two eyes/two ears/a nose/a mouth)? *(Yes)*

Picture 3
Who's the girl in the water? *(Mimi)*
Who's the boy in the water? *(Dylan)*

Picture 4
Where are Mimi and Dylan now? *(The water)*
Are they wet? *(Yes)*

CD2 Track 6

- Read or play the story again. Children listen and point to the pictures in their books.

Color the boat from the story.

- Demonstrate coloring the boat from the story.

Stick the story sticker.

- Children stick on the story sticker.

Say.

- Children point and say, e.g. *I have (two) (eyes).*

Activity Book p 27

Trace the paths to connect the story pictures in order. Color a circle to show your favorite picture in the story. Say.

- Children connect the story pictures in the correct order. They color a circle to show their favorite picture.
- They point and say sentences from the story.

Closing time

Learning review (see TB p 18)
Closing routines (see TB p 16)
Bye bye song and puppet (CD1 Track 3; see TB p 17 & 21)

Use the **Navio App** to watch the video, and encourage children to do the same at home.

Lesson 4 Story Song

My face

Watch. Listen, point and sing *Two eyes, two ears*. Follow and draw paths to match the pictures of Mimi and Dylan. Color the splashes in the water. Point and say.
Language: ears, eyes, mouth, nose; boy, girl; It's (a boy) in the water.

28

My face

Lesson 4 Story Song

Learning objectives

- Watch, sing and act out the story song *Two eyes, two ears*
- Listen to the story again and identify parts of the face
- Play *Mirror, mirror!*
- Point and say who is in the water

Materials

- Class CDs, printable story cards, flashcards, *Ferris Wheel* mat, Mimi puppet

Main vocabulary

- ears, eyes, mouth, nose; boy, girl

Key language

- It's (a boy) in the water.

Teacher's tip: Calming children down

Use a calming technique to regain children's attention after the lively story song. Ask the children to be as calm as they can while you count down from three: *Three, two, one!* Use your fingers for visual reinforcement and encourage them to join in with you. At the end, make it clear that you expect them to be completely still and silent.

Circle time

Hello song & puppet (CD1 Track 2; see TB p 17 & 21)
Opening routines (see TB p 16)
Recycling activity (parts of the face vocabulary) (see TB p 19)
Lesson aims (see TB p 18)

Retell the story *Splash!*

- Play the audio, video or read the story using the printable story cards.
- Demonstrate that children should wave their arms in the air every time they hear a face word in the story.

Game: *Mirror, mirror!*

- Have ready a small face mirror. Explain in the children's shared language that when Mimi and Dylan see themselves in the water, it's similar to when you see yourself in a mirror.
- Hold up and look in the mirror and name one or two features that you see, e.g. *Two eyes, a nose.*
- Pass the mirror around the circle. Children take turns looking at their reflection and identifying one or two parts of their face.

***Two eyes, two ears* song**

CD2 Track 7

- Ask *Who's in the water?* Children watch the video and respond.
- Play the video or audio of the story song again. Children point to their facial features, mime rocking the boat, and jump in place as if into the water in the chorus (see TB p 77).
- Repeat. If you like, ask all the girls to act out the first verse and the boys to act out the second verse.

Pretend to be Mimi and Dylan.

- Children choose if they want to be Mimi or Dylan on the boat and make two groups.
- Children take turns pointing to their faces, miming and saying with you, e.g. *Two eyes, two ears, a nose and a mouth. Splash!* (Children jump in place). *I'm the girl / boy in the water.*

Table time

Student's Book p 28

Watch. Listen, point and sing *Two eyes, two ears.*

CD2 Track 7

- Play the audio of the song. Children listen, sing and point to the pictures.
- Remember that you can use the karaoke version of the song when the children are confident.

Follow and draw paths to match the pictures of Mimi and Dylan. Color the splashes in the water.

- Children follow and draw the lines to match the pictures of Mimi and Dylan. Demonstrate with your finger first.
- Then they color the splashes in the water.

Point and say.

- Children point and say, e.g. *It's a (girl) in the water.*

Activity Book p 28

Color Mimi's eyes and mouth and Dylan's ears and nose.

- Children color the parts of Mimi and Dylan's faces.

Point and say.

- They point and say, e.g. *It's a (boy) in the water.*

Closing time

Learning review (see TB p 18)
Closing routines (see TB p 16)
Bye bye song and puppet (CD1 Track 3; see TB p 17 & 21)

Use the **Navio App** to watch the video, and encourage children to do the same at home.

Lesson 5 **Speaking** Life skills

My face

Watch. Listen and point. Color the puppet's eyes and nose. Say. **Language:** ears, eyes, hair, mouth, nose; colors; I have (a red) (mouth). I have (two) (green) (ears).

29

Learning objectives

- Say what parts of the face you have
- Watch, understand and enjoy a video
- Identify parts of the puppet's face

Materials

- Class CDs, flashcards, *Ferris Wheel* mat, Mimi puppet

Main vocabulary

- ears, eyes, hair, mouth, nose; colors

Key language

- I have (a red) (mouth). I have (two) (green) (ears).

Teacher's tip: Creating a puppet's face

As additional practice, give children copies of a simple template of a puppet's face with hair, eyes, ears, nose, mouth. Children choose and color the puppet's features. They then take turns showing their puppet's face to the class and saying, e.g. *I have a blue nose.*

Circle time

Hello song & puppet (CD1 Track 2; see TB p 17 & 21)
Opening routines (see TB p 16)
Recycling activity (story song) (CD2 Track 7; see TB p 19)
Lesson aims (see TB p 18)

Game: *Name the flashcard*

- Give out the face flashcards to individual children without others seeing.
- Children take turns to pointing to the part of their own face that is on their flashcard. Other children say what it is.

Watch the video.

- Explain that Auntie Jenny is showing Tom and Sophie her puppet.
- Play the video of Auntie Jenny, Tom and Sophie.
- Ask *What color are the puppet's eyes/ears/nose/ mouth?*
- Watch again. Pause and children repeat what Auntie Jenny's puppet says.
- Ask *Do you like Auntie Jenny's puppet?*

Table time

Student's Book p 29 Life skills

Watch. Listen and point.

- Children identify Auntie Jenny, Tom and Sophie.
- Play the audio or video. Children listen and point to the parts of the puppet's face.

Color the puppet's eyes and nose.

- Children look at the puppet and color the eyes and the nose.
- Play the audio again. Pause and children repeat the parts of the face.

CD2 Track 9

Auntie Jenny: Look at my puppet!
Sophie: Oh, it's great.
Auntie Jenny: My puppet says: I have two blue eyes.
Tom & Sophie: Two blue eyes.
Auntie Jenny: I have an orange nose.
Tom & Sophie: An orange nose.
Auntie Jenny: I have two green ears.
Tom & Sophie: two green ears.
Auntie Jenny: I have a red mouth.
Tom & Sophie: A red mouth.
Auntie Jenny: I have yellow hair.
Tom & Sophie: Yellow hair.
Auntie Jenny: I love you, Sophie! I love you, Tom!
Tom & Sophie: Oh wow! Your puppet is fantastic!

Say.

- Ask *What does Auntie Jenny's puppet say?* Point to the features in turn and children say the sentences, e.g. *I have a ... .*

Activity Book p 29

Trace and color the ears, eyes, nose and mouth on the puppet.

- Children trace and color the parts of the puppet's face.

Point and say.

- They pretend to be Auntie Jenny holding the puppet, point and say, e.g. *I have two blue eyes.*

Closing time

Learning review (see TB p 18)
Closing routines (see TB p 16)
Bye bye song and puppet (CD1 Track 3; see TB p 17 & 21)

Use the **Navio App** to watch the video, and encourage children to do the same at home.

Values I'm happy I'm me

My face

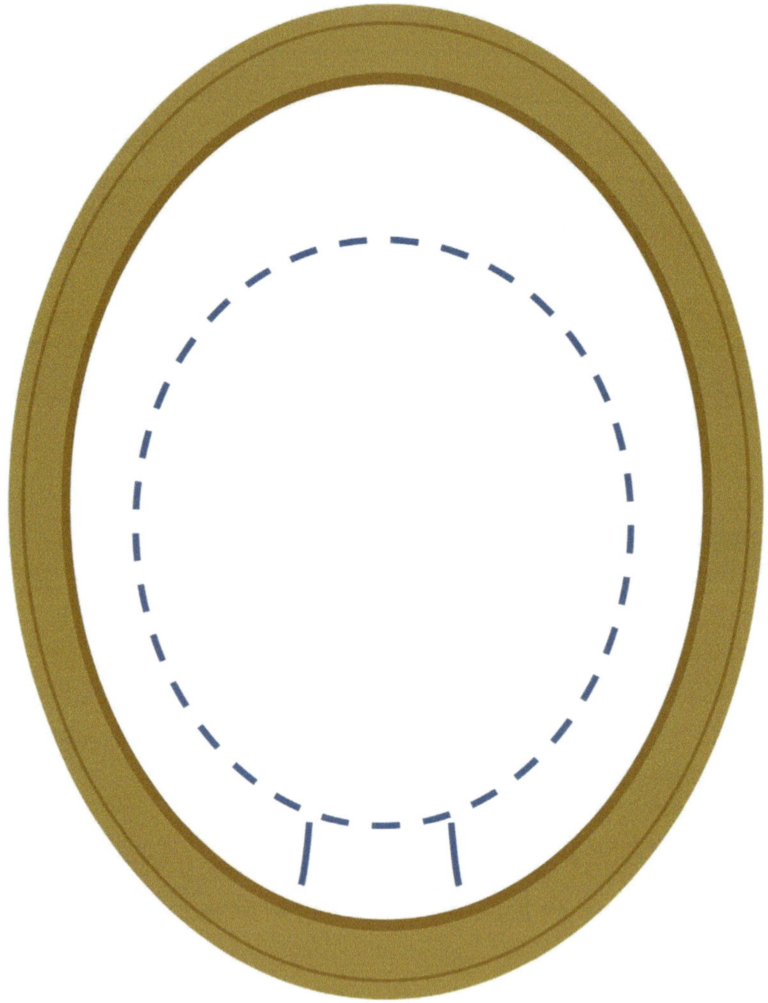

2:10

hello

Listen, point and sing *I'm happy I'm me.* Trace and draw a picture of your face. Say. **Language:** ears, eyes, hair, mouth, nose, teeth; happy, special; My (eyes) are special.

SOCIAL AND EMOTIONAL LEARNING

30

Learning objectives

- Recognize that everyone is different and develop self-esteem
- Sing the values song *I'm happy I'm me*
- Say *My (eyes) are special.*

Materials

- Class CDs, flashcards, *Ferris Wheel* mat, Mimi puppet

Main vocabulary

- ears, eyes, hair, mouth, nose, teeth; happy, special

Key language

- My (eyes) are special.

Teacher's tip: Using children's pictures to encourage a positive self-image

Once the children have completed their pictures, collect in their open books and have them sit around you as for a story. Show them a few of the self-portraits in random order saying, e.g. *Look! The eyes are special, the hair is special,* etc. and encourage the children to guess who is in each picture. Repeat on other occasions until all the children have had their pictures shown to the rest of the class, underlining how special they are.

Circle time

Hello song & puppet (CD1 Track 2; see TB p 17 & 21)
Opening routines (see TB p 16)
Recycling activity (*I have a (red) …*) (see TB p 19)
Lesson aims (see TB p 18)

Watch the *Splash!* story video.

- Play the story video.
- Children watch and repeat every time they hear a face word.
- Ask e.g. *Is Mimi special? Is Dylan special?* Use the children's shared language to explain that we all have different faces and that we are all special.

***I'm happy I'm me* song**

CD2 Track 10

- The children stand up. Pre-teach a simple dance to accompany the song.
- Play the audio. The children listen, dance and do the actions with you.
- Play the audio again. The children sing the song, dance and do the actions (see TB p 77).
- Repeat once or twice.

Table time

Student's Book p 30

Listen, point and sing *I'm happy I'm me.*

CD2 Track 10

- Play the audio of the song. Children sing and point to the pictures of Mimi and her friends.
- Use the children's shared language to make the point that Mimi's friends are all different, e.g. Eddie's "nose" and ears, Leo's teeth, and that each one is special.

Trace and draw a picture of your face.

- Children trace the head and then draw and color their own face by adding eyes, ears, hair, etc.

Say.

- Children take turns showing their pictures, naming their facial features and saying, e.g. *My (eyes) are special.*

Activity Book p 30

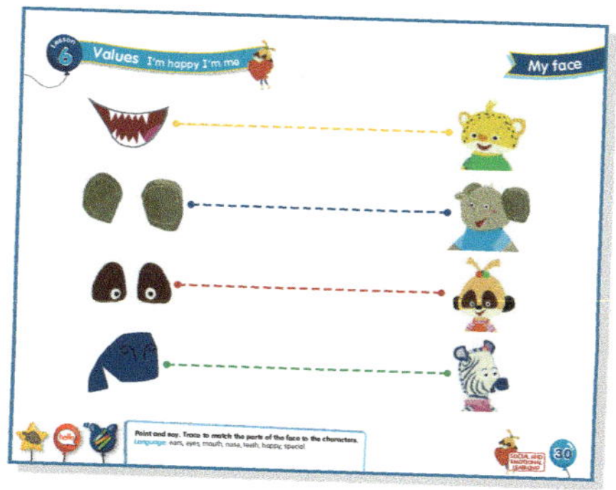

Point and say.

- Children point and name the parts of the face on the left of the page.

Trace to match the parts of the face to the characters.

- Children trace to match the parts of the face to the characters.

Closing time

Learning review (see TB p 18)
Closing routines (see TB p 16)
Bye bye song and puppet (CD1 Track 3; see TB p 17 & 21)

Use the **Navio App** to listen to the song, and encourage children to do the same at home.

Content

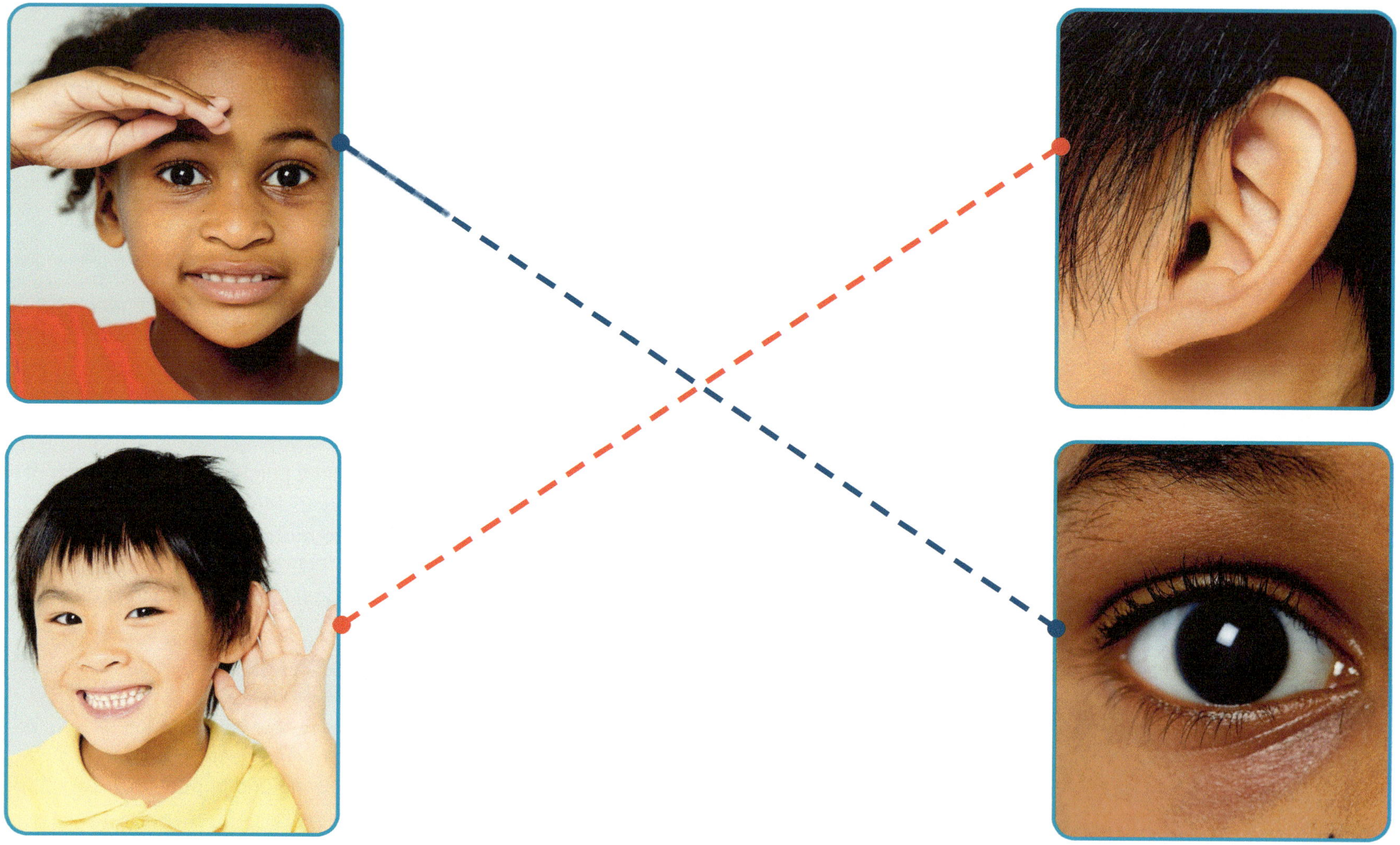

Listen and point. Trace to match the pictures. Say.
Language: hear, see; ears, eyes; I (see) with my (eyes).

Learning objectives

- Understand that we see with our eyes and hear with our ears
- Listen and understand about seeing and hearing
- Say *I (see) with my (eyes)*

Materials

- Class CDs, printable flashcards, *Ferris Wheel* mat, Mimi puppet

Main vocabulary

- hear, see; ears, eyes

Key language

- I (see) with my (eyes).

Teacher's tip: Developing children's curiosity

If space allows, set up a sensory table with objects that we use to help us see, e.g. toy binoculars, a kaleidoscope or a magnifying glass. Fill and cover some yoghurt pots with items that make different noises, e.g. dried pulses or marbles. Encourage children to look at things through the magnifying glass and shake the pots to hear the different sounds.

Circle time

Hello song & puppet (CD1 Track 2; see TB p 17 & 21)
Opening routines (see TB p 16)
Recycling activity (see TB p 19)
Lesson aims (see TB p 18)

Introduce content vocabulary.

- Use the puppet and the printable flashcards to introduce the new words (*hear, see*).
- Say the words and put your hands to your eyes and ears to mime see and hear. Children repeat the words and mime with you.
- Lay out the flashcards of eyes and ears. Say *I see with my eyes. I hear with my ears.* Children repeat the sentences with you.

Game: *See or hear!*

- Mime seeing or hearing. Children respond by saying *See!* or *Hear!*
- Alternate between showing children pictures of things that don't make a noise, e.g. a pencil, hair, and then playing a very short extract of music or making a noise, e.g. clap, knock, whistle. Children respond *See!* or *Hear!*

Table time

Student's Book p 31

Listen and point.

- Children identify Tom and Sophie in the photos. They then point and say the two parts of the face (*ear, eye*).
- Play the audio. Use the pause button after each sentence. Children listen and point to the correct part of the body in turn as Tom and Sophie speak.

CD2 Track 11

Sophie: I see with my eyes.
I see with my eyes.
I see with my eyes.
Tom: I hear with my ears.
I hear with my ears.
I hear with my ears.

- Play the audio again. Use the pause button. Children repeat the sentences.

Trace to match the pictures.

- Children trace the lines to match the pictures.
- Check children have done this correctly.

Say.

- Children point to the parts of the body in turn and say, e.g. *I see with my eyes* or *I hear with my ears* as appropriate.

Activity Book p 31

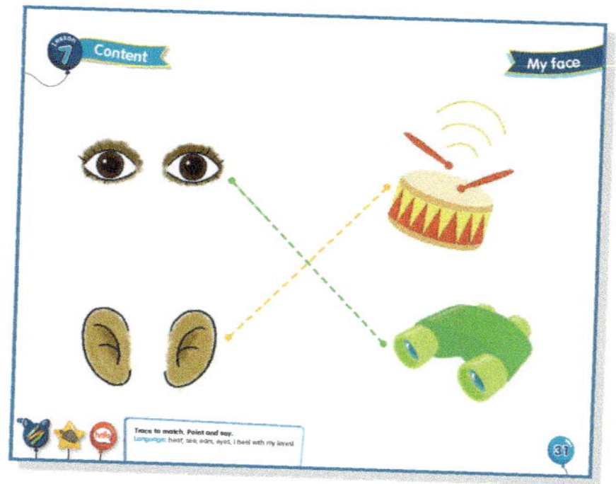

Trace to match.

- Children trace to match the eyes to the binoculars and the ears to the drum. Use mime or real objects to demonstrate that we use our eyes to see through the binoculars and our ears to hear the drum.

Point and say.

- Children point to the parts of the face and say *I (see) with my (eyes).*

Closing time

Learning review (see TB p 18)
Closing routines (see TB p 16)
Bye bye song and puppet (CD1 Track 3; see TB p 17 & 21)

Use the **Navio App** to play the vocabulary and language games, and encourage children to do the same at home.

Lesson 8 Culture

My face

Watch. Listen, point and sing *Here are my ears*. Follow and draw a path to connect the pictures in order. Say. **Language:** ears, eyes, hands, mouth, nose, teeth, toes; Here is my (nose). Here are my (eyes).

32

My face

Lesson 8 Culture

Learning objectives
- Watch, sing and act out the traditional song *Here are my ears*
- Play an action game
- Point and say *Here are my (eyes)*

Materials
- Class CDs, flashcards, *Ferris Wheel* mat, Mimi puppet

Main vocabulary
- ears, eyes, hands, mouth, nose, teeth, toes

Key language
- Here is my (nose). Here are my (eyes).

Teacher's tip: Singing in groups

Once the children are confident with joining in and acting out the song, put them into six groups. Each group should sing about one of the parts of the body in turn. Choose a confident child to "conduct" the class, pointing to the group whose turn it is next.

Circle time

Hello song & puppet (CD1 Track 2; see TB p 17 & 21)
Opening routines (see TB p 16)
Recycling activity (see TB p 19)
Lesson aims (see TB p 18)

Game: *Here are my ears.*
- Say e.g. *Here are my ears!* and point to your ears. Repeat with other parts of the face.
- Say e.g. *Here are my ears!* and point to your eyes. Demonstrate that children should correct you by saying *No! Here are my ears!*
- Repeat several times with different parts of the face.

***Here are my ears* song**

CD2 Track 12
- Play the audio. The children listen and do actions (see TB p 77).
- Play the audio again. The children sing and do the actions.

Watch the *Here are my ears* song video.
- Children watch the video and join in singing the song and doing the actions with Tom and Sophie.

Table time

Student's Book p 32

Watch. Listen, point and sing *Here are my ears.*

CD2 Track 12
- Play the audio. Children listen, sing and point to the photos of each verse.

Follow and draw a path to connect the pictures in order.
- Children first follow the path with their finger. They then draw the path to connect the pictures in order.

Say.
- Children point and say, e.g. *Here is/are my (ears).*

Activity Book p 32

Follow and draw paths to match the children showing the same body parts.
- Children draw paths to match the children who are pointing to the same body parts.

Say.
- Children point and say *Here is/are my (toes).*

Closing time

Learning review (see TB p 18)
Closing routines (see TB p 16)
Bye bye song and puppet (CD1 Track 3; see TB p 17 & 21)

Use the **Navio App** to watch the video, and encourage children to do the same at home.

Listen, point and say. Color the words you know. Stick the star sticker. Say.
Language: ears, eyes, hair, mouth, nose, teeth; I have (a mouth). I have (blue) (eyes).

My face

Review Lesson

Learning objectives
- Review your learning and progress
- Say what parts of the face you have
- Stick on a star sticker for achievement

Materials
- Class CDs, flashcards, *Ferris Wheel* mat, Mimi puppet

Main vocabulary
- ears, eyes, hair, mouth, nose, teeth

Key language
- I have (a mouth). I have (blue) (eyes).

Teacher's tip: Working with a partner

Once the children are confidently producing the sentence *I have a (mouth)* put them into pairs. Have one child say the sentence and the other point to the corresponding part of the face. Demonstrate first with one pair.

Circle time

Hello song & puppet (CD1 Track 2; see TB p 17 & 21)
Opening routines (see TB p 16)
Recycling activity (see TB p 19)
Lesson aims (see TB p 18)

Face flashcard games

- Choose one or two flashcard games with the *Ferris Wheel* mat and/or the puppet to review key vocabulary (see TB p 20 & 21).

Sing *I have two eyes.*

CD2 Track 4

- Play the audio. Children sing and point to their facial features.
- Children say sentences about their facial features e.g. *I have a nose.*

Game: *Touch your friend's (nose).*

- Have the children form pairs facing each other. Call out parts of the face, e.g. *Nose* and have them touch their friend's nose.

Game: *I have eyes.*

- Demonstrate by saying *I have eyes*. Point to your eyes and have the children say *yes* and put their arms in the air.
- Say *I have ears* and point to your mouth. Have the children fold their arms and say *no*.

Watch the story video.

- Children watch the story video. Ask *What do Mimi and Dylan see in the water?*

Table time

Student's Book p 33

Listen, point and say.

- Say e.g. *Point to the eyes!* and children point to the parts of the face in Mimi's picture.
- Play the audio. Children listen, point to the parts of the face and say the words.

CD2 Track 13

Mimi: I'm the teacher! Can you remember the parts of the face, Dylan?
Dylan: Yes, I can. Ears.
Mimi: Ears.
Dylan: Eyes.
Mimi: Eyes.
Dylan: Nose.
Mimi: Nose.
Dylan: Mouth.
Mimi: Mouth.
Dylan: Hair.
Mimi: Hair.
Dylan: Teeth.
Mimi: Teeth. Great job, Dylan. Very good!

Color the words you know.

- Children color the parts of the face they know.

Stick the star sticker.

- Children stick on the star sticker for achievement.
- Monitor and encourage children to think positively about their progress.

Say.

- Children point to their faces and say sentences e.g. *I have a mouth.*

Activity Book p 33

Color the faces to show the parts of the face you know. Point and say.

- Children color the faces next to the parts of the face they know. They point and say sentences about the parts of the face.

Think and color the stars to show your progress.

- Children color the number of stars that they feel shows their progress in this unit.

Closing time

Learning review (see TB p 18)
Closing routines (see TB p 16)
Bye bye song and puppet (CD1 Track 3; see TB p 17 & 21)

Use the **Navio App** to review what children have learned in this unit, and encourage children to do the same at home.

Project

COOPERATIVE LEARNING

My face

Paint and decorate a face. Make a faces display. Ask and say.

Language: ears, eyes, hair, mouth, nose, teeth; boy, girl; colors; It's (a girl). I have (red) (hair). I have (green) (eyes). Where's (Maria)? Here. What color is your (nose)? It's (pink).

My face

Learning objectives

- Work together to do a collaborative project
- Color and decorate a face
- Talk about the parts of the face and name the colors
- Express enjoyment of the faces display
- Look in a mirror and paint a self-portrait

Materials

- Class CDs, Mimi puppet, paper plate, finger paints, yarn, glue
- optional: project template, crayons

Main vocabulary

- ears, eyes, hair, mouth, nose, teeth; boy, girl; colors

Key language

- It's (a girl). I have (red) (hair). I have (green) (eyes). Where's (Maria)? Here. What color is your (nose)? It's (pink).

Teacher's tip: Taking responsibility for cleaning up

Life skills

Once the children have finished making their face, point out the importance of cleaning up after themselves. Provide a box for any left over yarn and encourage children to make sure there are no pieces of yarn on the floor or tables at the end of the lesson.

Circle time

Hello song & puppet (CD1 Track 2; see TB p 17 & 21)
Opening routines (see TB p 16)
Recycling activity (see TB p 19)
Lesson aims (see TB p 18)

Prepare for your project.

- Say *Let's do a project and make faces of everyone in the class!*
- Show children the paper plates.
- Demonstrate painting the parts of the face on the plate.
- Demonstrate decorating their face by gluing yarn on the paper plates for hair.

Table time

COOPERATIVE LEARNING

Student's Book p 34

- Say e.g. *We're going to make a face like this. Look at what we need for our project: a paper plate, finger paints, yarn, glue.* Children listen and point to the pictures.

Paint and decorate a face.

- Give a paper plate to each child.
- Make sure children have finger paints and pieces of colored yarn and glue available.
- Children paint the parts of their face and also glue pieces of colored yarn on the plate as hair.

Make a faces display.

- When they are ready, children show their faces to the class and say, e.g. *I have two eyes. / I have a nose.*
- Display all the faces on the class noticeboard under the heading "Our faces."

Ask and say.

- Children talk about the faces and name the parts and the colors, e.g. *I have (green) (eyes).*
- Ask children *Do you like our faces display?* Make the point that everyone helped make the display and that they couldn't have made such a beautiful display on their own.

Alternative version of project

- Children could color the photocopiable face template with crayons instead of painting a real paper plate.

Activity Book p 34

Look in a mirror. Paint a picture of you.

- Provide hand mirrors and paints. Children look in the mirror and paint a self-portrait.

Point and say.

- They point to the parts of the face on their picture and say *I have (two) (blue) (eyes).*

Closing time

Learning review (see TB p 18)
Closing routines (see TB p 16)
Bye bye song and puppet (CD1 Track 3; see TB p 17 & 21)

Clothes

Time to get dressed!

Vocabulary and language

- **Main vocabulary:** boots, coat, hat, shoes, shorts, T-shirt
- **Key language:** Put on your (hat). Where's your (coat)? Where are your (boots)? Here.
- **Content language:** rainy, sunny; It's (rainy). I put on my (coat).
- **Other language:** neat; rain, sun; spider; Take off your (hat). I'm neat. I put my (coat) away. What color is your (coat)? It's (blue). What color are your shorts? They're (red).

Unit objectives

- Identify and name clothes
- Sing the language song *The clothes song*
- Ask and say where clothes are
- Understand and join in the story *Time to get dressed!*
- Sing and act out the story song *Where's your T-shirt?*
- Sing the values song *I'm neat*
- Recognize the value of being neat
- Identify clothes for rainy and sunny weather
- Sing and act out the traditional rhyme *Itsy, bitsy spider*
- Review your learning and progress
- Participate in a collaborative project

Story

CD2 Track 19

Picture 1

Narrator: It's time to get dressed.
Mimi: Where's your T-shirt, Dylan?
Dylan: Here.
Mimi: Put on your T-shirt, Dylan.
Dylan: Yes, Mimi.
Mimi: Oh no. That's not right, Dylan. You are funny.

Picture 2

Mimi: Where are your shorts, Dylan?
Dylan: Here.
Mimi: Put on your shorts, Dylan.
Dylan: Yes, Mimi.
Mimi: Oh no. That's not right, Dylan. You are funny.

Picture 3

Mimi: Where's your hat, Dylan?
Dylan: Here.
Mimi: Put on your hat, Dylan.
Dylan: Yes, Mimi.
Mimi: Oh no. That's not right, Dylan. You are funny. Where are your shoes, Dylan?
Dylan: Here.
Mimi: Put on your shoes, Dylan.
Dylan: Yes, Mimi.
Mimi: Oh no. That's not right, Dylan. You are funny.

Picture 4

Mimi: Look, Mommy and Daddy. I'm ready! I have a T-shirt, shorts, a hat and shoes.
Dylan: Look! I'm ready too! I have a T-shirt, shorts, a hat and shoes. I'm the funny monster!
Mimi: Ha, ha! Oh yes! You're the funny monster! I like the funny monster!
Mommy: Oh, Dylan.
Daddy: Come on, Dylan. Take off your T-shirt. Take off your shorts. Take off your hat. Take off your shoes. Time to get dressed as Dylan now and not the funny monster!

Songs

Language song

The clothes song CD2 Track 17

Everybody put on your shorts, (Mime putting on shorts)
Put on your shorts.
Everybody put on your shorts,
Just like this. (Gesture to self)

Everybody put on your T-shirt, (Mime putting on a T-shirt)
Put on your T-shirt.
Everybody put on your T-shirt,
Just like this. (Gesture to self)

Everybody put on your shoes, (Mime putting on shoes)
(etc)

Everybody put on your coat, (Mime putting on a coat)
(etc)

Everybody put on your hat, (Mime putting on a hat)
(etc)

Everybody put on your boots, (Mime putting on boots)
(etc)

Story song

Where's your T-shirt? CD2 Track 20

Where's your T-shirt? (Open arms questioningly)
Here! (Point)
Put on your T-shirt! Put on your T-shirt! (Mime putting T-shirt on the wrong way)
Oh no. (Place hand on forehead)
That's not right. (Waggle index finger)
You are funny! (Pretend to giggle)

Where are your shorts? (Open arms questioningly)
(etc)

Where's your hat? (Open arms questioningly)
(etc)

Where are your shoes? (Open arms questioningly)
(etc)

Values song

I'm neat CD2 Track 23

I'm neat, I'm neat (Mime cleaning up)
I put my coat away (Point to coat flashcard)
I'm neat, I'm neat (Mime cleaning up)
I'm neat every day

I'm neat, I'm neat (Mime cleaning up)
I put my hat away (Point to hat flashcard)
I'm neat, I'm neat (Mime cleaning up)
I'm neat every day

I'm neat, I'm neat (Mime cleaning up)
I put my shoes away (Point to shoes flashcard)
I'm neat, I'm neat (Mime cleaning up)
I'm neat every day

I'm neat, I'm neat (Mime cleaning up)
I put my boots away (Point to boots flashcard)
I'm neat, I'm neat (Mime cleaning up)
I'm neat every day

Culture rhyme

Itsy, bitsy spider CD2 Track 25

Itsy, bitsy spider
Climbing up the spout (Move thumbs and index fingers in climbing action)
Down comes the rain (Hold arms high and move fingers down as rain)
And washes Itsy out (Make gesture with hands away from body)
Out comes the sun (Make big circle with arms)
And dries up all the rain
Itsy, bitsy spider (Move thumbs and index fingers in climbing action)
Climbing up again.

Clothes
Time to get dressed!
Vocabulary
Lesson 1
2:14
hello
2:15
Listen, point and repeat. Listen and play. Stick the clothes stickers. Say.
Language: hat, shoes, shorts, T-shirt; orange, pink, red, yellow
35

Clothes

Lesson 1 Vocabulary

Learning objectives

- Identify and name clothes
- Listen and point to clothes
- Listen and play *Round and round and round*

Materials

- Class CDs, flashcards, *Ferris Wheel* mat, Mimi puppet

Main vocabulary

- hat, shoes, shorts, T-shirt; orange, pink, red, yellow

Teacher's tip: Using real clothes

If possible, bring in real clothes to introduce the vocabulary. Choose volunteers to put on or hold up the items as you name them. The rest of the class then listens, points to and names the clothes in turn.

Circle time

Hello song & puppet (CD1 Track 2; see TB p 17 & 21)
Opening routines (see TB p 16)
Lesson aims (see TB p 18)

Introduce clothes.

- Use the puppet and flashcards to introduce the clothes. Children repeat the words.
- Put the *Ferris Wheel* mat on the floor or board with the clothes flashcards face down (one on each color). Use the puppet to turn them over and name them. The children repeat the words.

Game: *Say the color!*

- Name the clothes on the Ferris Wheel and children name the color. Then the reverse.

Game: *Find the clothes!*

- Stick the flashcards at the children's height on different walls around the classroom.
- Ask two to four children to stand up. Say e.g. *Find the hat!* Children respond by walking to the flashcard. Repeat with different groups of children.

Table time

Student's Book p 35

Listen, point and repeat.

- Play the audio. Children listen and point to each word as they hear it.

CD2 Track 14

Mimi: Look, Dylan! Shorts … shoes … T-shirt … hat … hee, hee, hee! Repeat, Dylan!
Dylan: Yes, Mimi! Shorts … shoes … T-shirt … hat … hee, hee, hee!
Mimi: Very good, Dylan. Let's say the words together!
Both: Shorts … shoes … T-shirt … hat … hee, hee, hee!

- Play the audio again. Children listen and repeat the words.

Listen and play.

- Hold up your index finger and move it around clockwise like a wheel. Children do the same. Play the audio. Children listen, point to the color when they hear it, and say the word.

CD2 Track 15

Mimi: Round and round and round: Red … shorts!
Dylan: Shorts!
Mimi: Round and round and round: Yellow … T-shirt!
Dylan: T-shirt!
Mimi: Round and round and round: Pink … hat!
Dylan: Hat!
Mimi: Round and round and round: Orange … shoes!
Dylan: Shoes!

- Play the game with you and/or individual children naming colors and others responding with the words.

Stick the clothes stickers.

- Children put on the clothes stickers.

Say.

- Children point to the clothes and say the words.

Activity Book p 35

Point and say.

- Children point and name the meerkats' clothes.

Color the clothes.

- They color the clothes.

Closing time

Learning review (see TB p 18)
Closing routines (see TB p 16)
Bye bye song and puppet (CD1 Track 3; see TB p 17 & 21)

Use the **Navio App** to play the vocabulary game, and encourage children to do the same at home.

Lesson 2 Language

Clothes

Listen and find the new clothes. Listen, point and sing *The clothes song*. Follow and draw paths to match the photos. Say.
Language: boots, coat, hat, shoes, shorts, T-shirt; Put on your (hat).

36

Learning objectives

- Talk about clothes
- Identify and name two new clothes
- Sing the language song *The clothes song*
- Talk about putting on clothes

Materials

- Class CDs, flashcards, *Ferris Wheel* mat, Mimi puppet

Main vocabulary

- boots, coat, hat, shoes, shorts, T-shirt

Key language

- Put on your (hat).

Teacher's tip: Varying the volume to encourage singing

Once the children are familiar with the song, play the track as normal, but turn down the volume for the last line in each verse to encourage children to sing more.

Circle time

Hello song & puppet (CD1 Track 2; see TB p 17 & 21)
Opening routines (see TB p 16)
Recycling activity (four clothes words from Lesson 1) (see TB p 19)
Lesson aims (see TB p 18)

Introduce the new clothes words.

- Put all six clothes flashcards on the floor or board. The children identify the two new clothes.
- Use the puppet to point to and say the words in turn. The children repeat in chorus.
- Turn the two new flashcards face down. Mix them up. Point to one and ask *Coat or boots?* Children guess. Repeat several times

Introduce *Put on your (hat)*.

- Have one or several hats available. Demonstrate with one child. Say *Put on your hat* and the child puts on the hat.
- Repeat several times with different children.
- If you have several hats, get children to pass them around the circle. When you say *Put on your hat,* children put on the hats.

Game: *Put on your boots!*

- Lay out the clothes flashcards and children say the words.
- Children stand up. Use the puppet to give instructions and say e.g. *Put on your boots!* Mime putting on boots and children mime with you.
- Repeat with coat and hat.

The clothes song

CD2 Track 17

- Put the flashcards of coat, hat and boots face up on the floor or board.
- Play the song. The children listen and mime putting on the clothes in each verse (see TB p 99).
- Play the song again. The children do the actions and join in singing the song.

Table time

Student's Book p 36

Listen and find the new clothes.

- Hold up your book. Point to the photos of Auntie Jenny, Tom and Sophie and say the names.
- Play the audio. Children listen and find the two new clothes. Repeat and children say the words.

CD2 Track 16

Sophie: Find the … coat! Coat!
Tom: Coat! Here!
Sophie: Find the … boots! Boots!
Tom: Boots! Here!

Listen, point and sing *The clothes song*.

CD2 Track 17

- Play the song. Children listen, sing and point to the clothes in the photos.
- Remember that you can use the karaoke version of the song when the children are confident.

Follow and draw paths to match the photos.

- Hold up your book and demonstrate matching the photos by drawing the paths with your finger. The children then draw the paths.
- Play the audio again. Pause after each verse and children name the character with the clothes in the photos, e.g. verse 1: Tom.

Say.

- Children point and say, e.g. *Put on your coat!*

Activity Book p 36

Point and say. Trace the coat and the boots and color the clothes.

- Children point and name the clothes. Then they trace the coat and the boots, and color all the clothes.

Closing time

Learning review (see TB p 18)
Closing routines (see TB p 16)
Bye bye song and puppet (CD1 Track 3; see TB p 17 & 21)

Use the **Navio App** to listen to the song, and encourage children to do the same at home.

Lesson 3 Story

2:19

hello

Watch. Listen to the story *Time to get dressed!* Color the trousers and hat on the monster. Stick the story sticker. Ask and say. Language: hat, shoes, shorts, T-shirt; Where's your (hat)? Here. Put on your (shoes). Take off your (hat).

37

Learning objectives

- Watch, understand and enjoy the story *Time to get dressed!*
- Make a prediction about the story
- Look and find clothes
- Color the monster in the story

Materials

- Class CDs, printable story cards, flashcards, *Ferris Wheel* mat, Mimi puppet

Main vocabulary

- hat, shoes, shorts, T-shirt

Key language

- Where's your (hat)? Here. Put on your (shoes). Take off your (hat).

Teacher's tip: Pausing the audio to aid listening

Pause the audio after each story frame to check that the class is following. Ask questions, e.g. *Where's Dylan's T-shirt? Is it on right?* and encourage the children to point to the different clothes as the story progresses.

Circle time

Hello song & puppet (CD1 Track 2; see TB p 17 & 21)
Opening routines (see TB p 16)
Recycling activity (*Put on your …* and clothes vocabulary) (see TB p 19)
Lesson aims (see TB p 18)

Introduce the story *Time to get dressed!*

- Say *It's story time!* Play the *Story rhyme* (CD1 Track 4; see TB p 17).
- Say *Tom and Sophie are listening to a story about Mimi and Dylan. It's time to get dressed.* Briefly explain this. Ask *What does Mimi put on? What does Dylan put on?* and encourage children to guess.

Watch or listen to the story.

CD2 Track 19

- Play the audio, watch the video or read the story using the printable story cards. Pause, repeat words, point to the pictures, ask questions.
- Ask again *What does Mimi put on? (T-shirt, shorts, shoes, hat) What does Dylan put on? (T-shirt, shorts, shoes, hat).* Ask *Are Dylan's clothes on right?*
- Repeat the story. Encourage children to join in with the words and phrases in the story.
- Ask *Do you like the story? Is Dylan funny?*

Look and find.

- Say e.g. *Find Mimi's shorts!* Children look at the story and point to the picture as fast as they can.
- Repeat with other clothes in the story.

Table time

Student's Book p 37

Watch. Listen to the story *Time to get dressed!*

CD2 Track 19

- Read or play the the story again. Children listen and point to the pictures in their books.

Color the funny monster from the book in the story.

- Demonstrate coloring the monster from the book in the story.

Story questions

Picture 1
What does Dylan put on? *(A T-shirt)*
Is that right? *(No)*

Picture 2
What does Dylan put on? *(Shorts)*
Is Dylan funny? *(Yes)*

Picture 3
What does Dylan put on? *(A hat/shoes)*
What color is Dylan's hat? *(Orange)*

Picture 4
Does Dylan have shoes? *(Yes)*
Does Mimi like the funny monster? *(Yes)*

Stick the story sticker.

- Children stick on the story sticker.

Ask and say.

- Children ask and answer questions, e.g. *Where's your (hat)? Here.*
- Ask *Is Dylan good at getting dressed?* and children respond.

Activity Book p 37

Color Dylan's clothes in the correct place.

- Children color Dylan's clothes in the correct place.

Point and say.

- They point and say *Put on/Take off your (hat).*

Closing time

Learning review (see TB p 18)
Closing routines (see TB p 16)
Bye bye song and puppet (CD1 Track 3; see TB p 17 & 21)

Use the **Navio App** to watch the video, and encourage children to do the same at home.

Lesson 4 Story Song

Watch. Listen, point and sing *Where's your T-shirt?* Color the circle to show the correct way to put on the clothes. Ask and say.
Language: hat, shoes, shorts, T-shirt; Where are your (shorts)? Here. Put on your (shoes).

38

Learning objectives

- Watch, sing and act out the story song *Where's your T-shirt?*
- Listen to the story again and identify clothes
- Play *Where's your hat?*
- Ask and answer about clothes

Materials

- Class CDs, printable story cards, flashcards, *Ferris Wheel* mat, Mimi puppet

Main vocabulary

- hat, shoes, shorts, T-shirt

Key language

- Where are your (shorts)? Here. Put on your (shoes).

Teacher's tip: Recognizing how to get dressed correctly

If you have clothes available, choose two children and have one put the clothes on correctly and the other wrongly. Encourage the class to point to the correct one and say, *Like this!*

Circle time

Hello song & puppet (CD1 Track 2; see TB p 17 & 21)
Opening routines (see TB p 16)
Recycling activity (clothes vocabulary) (see TB p 19)
Lesson aims (see TB p 18)

Retell the story *Time to get dressed!*

- Play the audio, video or read the story using the story cards.
- Demonstrate that children should wave their arms in the air every time they hear the names of clothes in the story.

Game: *Where's your hat?*

- "Hide" the flashcards of T-shirt, shorts, hat and shoes in different places in the classroom.
- Use the puppet to ask, e.g. *Where's your hat?* Invite two children to stand up and find the flashcard of the hat and respond *Here.*
- Repeat with different children and flashcards.

***Where's your T-shirt?* song**

CD2 Track 20

- Play the video or audio of the story song. The children listen and mime putting on the clothes the wrong way like Dylan.
- Watch or listen again. The children do the actions and join in singing the song (see TB p 99).
- Ask e.g. *Is Dylan funny? Can you put on your clothes correctly?* and children respond.

Game: *Put on your shorts like this!*

- Use the puppet to hold up the flashcards in turn and say, e.g. *Put on your shorts like this!* The children mime putting on the clothes correctly.
- Repeat with all the clothes.

Table time

Student's Book p 38

Watch. Listen, point and sing *Where's your T-shirt?*

CD2 Track 20

- Play the audio of the song. Children listen, sing and point to the pictures.
- Remember that you can use the karaoke version of the song when the children are confident.

Color the circle to show the correct way to put on the clothes.

- Children color the circle next to the picture to show the correct way to put on the clothes (i.e. the picture on the right).

Ask and say.

- Children ask and answer questions, e.g. *Where are your (shorts)? Here.*

Activity Book p 38

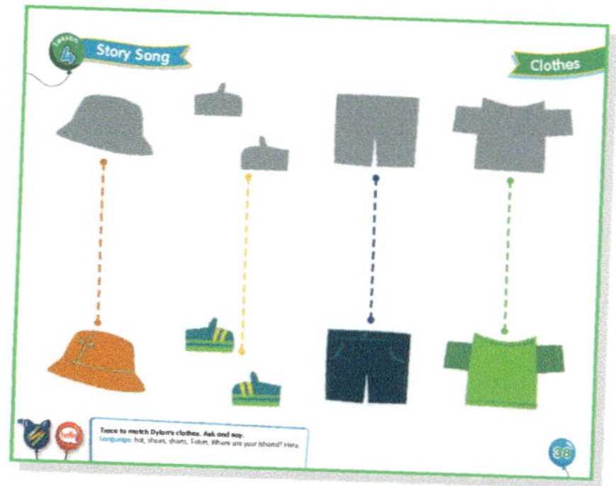

Trace to match Dylan's clothes.

- Children match the silhouettes to the pictures of Dylan's clothes.

Ask and say.

- Then they ask and answer about the clothes.

Closing time

Learning review (see TB p 18)
Closing routines (see TB p 16)
Bye bye song and puppet (CD1 Track 3; see TB p 17 & 21)

Use the **Navio App** to watch the video, and encourage children to do the same at home.

Speaking

Life skills

Watch. Listen and point. Trace to match Auntie Jenny's hat, Sophie's coat and Tom's boots. Ask and say. Language: boots, coat, hat; Where's your (coat)? Where are your (boots)? Here. Put on your (hat).

39

Learning objectives

- Talk about where clothes are and putting them on
- Watch, understand and enjoy a video
- Identify the clothes the characters put on in the video

Materials

- Class CDs, flashcards, *Ferris Wheel* mat, Mimi puppet

Main vocabulary

- boots, coat, hat

Key language

- Where's your (coat)?
  Where are your (boots)?
  Here. Put on your (hat).

Teacher's tip: Putting on a coat

Life skills

Children of this age group often need help putting their coats on. Show them how to make sure their coat is turned the right way before starting to put it on. Then, show them how to hold it and put one arm in first, then the other. If they have their own coats in the classroom, encourage them to work in pairs and help each other put their coats on and fasten them up.

Circle time

Hello song & puppet (CD1 Track 2; see TB p 17 & 21)
Opening routines (see TB p 16)
Recycling activity (story song) (CD2 Track 20; see TB p 19)
Lesson aims (see TB p 18)

Game: ***Name the flashcard***

- Give out the clothes flashcards to individual children without others seeing.
- Children take turns miming putting on the clothes on their flashcard. Other children say what it is.

Watch the video.

- Explain that Auntie Jenny, Tom and Sophie are putting on clothes to get ready to go out.
- Play the video of Auntie Jenny, Tom and Sophie.
- Ask *What does Sophie put on? (coat) What does Tom put on? (boots) What does Auntie Jenny put on? (hat)*
- Watch again. Pause and children repeat the questions and answers.
- Ask *Are they ready to go out?*

Table time

Student's Book p 39

Life skills

Watch. Listen and point.

- Children identify Auntie Jenny, Tom and Sophie.
- Play the audio or video. Children listen and point to the clothes.

CD2 Track 22

Auntie Jenny:	Come on, Tom and Sophie. It's time to go to the park. Where's your coat, Sophie?
Sophie:	Here.
Auntie Jenny:	Put on your coat, please, Sophie.
Sophie:	Yes, Auntie Jenny.
Auntie Jenny:	Where are your boots, Tom?
Tom:	Here.
Auntie Jenny:	Put on your boots, please, Tom.
Tom:	Yes, Auntie Jenny.
Sophie:	Where's your hat, Auntie Jenny?
Auntie Jenny:	Oh! Umm ... I don't know.
Sophie:	Look! Here it is! Put on your hat, please, Auntie Jenny.
Auntie Jenny:	Yes, Sophie! Come on. Let's go.

Trace to match Auntie Jenny's hat, Sophie's coat and Tom's boots.

- Children trace the lines to match the clothes to the matching items in the photo. Check they have done this correctly.
- Play the audio again. Pause and children repeat the instructions to put on the clothes.

Ask and say.

- Children pretend to be the characters in the video and ask and say, e.g. *Where's your coat? Here!*

Activity Book p 39

Follow and draw paths to match the people to their clothes.

- Children draw the paths to match each child to their clothes.

Ask and say.

- Then they ask and say about the clothes.

Closing time

Learning review (see TB p 18)
Closing routines (see TB p 16)
Bye bye song and puppet (CD1 Track 3; see TB p 17 & 21)

Use the **Navio App** to watch the video, and encourage children to do the same at home.

Values I'm neat

Listen, point and sing *I'm neat.* Color the star on the picture that shows the clothes in the correct place. Say.

Language: boots, coat, hat, shoes; neat; I'm neat. I put my (coat) away.

SOCIAL AND EMOTIONAL LEARNING

40

Learning objectives
- Recognize the value of being neat
- Sing the values song *I'm neat*
- Say *I'm neat. I put my (coat) away.*

Materials
- Class CDs, flashcards, *Ferris Wheel* mat, Mimi puppet

Main vocabulary
- boots, coat, hat, shoes; neat

Key language
- I'm neat. I put my (coat) away.

Teacher's tip:
Learning to be neat Life skills

Point out to the children the importance of being neat and putting their things away in the classroom. If they have brought a coat and/or hat to school, get them to practice putting them on their coat hook and saying *I put my coat/hat away*.

Circle time

Hello song & puppet (CD1 Track 2; see TB p 17 & 21)
Opening routines (see TB p 16)
Recycling activity (*Where's your …? / Put on your …*) (see TB p 19)
Lesson aims (see TB p 18)

Watch the *Time to get dressed* story video.
- Play the story video.
- Children watch and repeat every time they hear a clothes word.
- Hold up printable story card 1 or pause the first frame of the video. Show the meaning of *neat*. Say e.g. *Look at Dylan's shorts, hat and shoes. Is Dylan neat? Is it good to be neat? Why?* And listen to the children's response.

***I'm neat* song**

CD2 Track 23
- Lay out the flashcards of *coat, hat, shoes* and *boots* in the order of the song.
- Play the audio. The children listen and point to the flashcards.
- Play the audio again. The children mime putting away the clothes and join in singing the song (see TB p 99).
- Use children's shared language to make the point that it's important to look after your possessions and that being neat with your clothes helps you find them.

Table time

Student's Book p 40

Listen, point and sing *I'm neat.*

CD2 Track 23
- Play the song. Children sing and point to the clothes in the picture.

Color the star on the picture that shows the clothes in the correct place.
- Children color the star on the picture that shows the clothes in their correct place (i.e. the picture on the right).

Say.
- Children point to their completed pictures and say, e.g. *I'm neat. I put my (shoes) away.*

Activity Book p 40

Trace to match the clothes to the correct place.
- Children match the clothes around the picture to the clothes that have been put away.

Say.
- Then they point and say *I'm neat. I put my (shoes) away.*

Closing time

Learning review (see TB p 18)
Closing routines (see TB p 16)
Bye bye song and puppet (CD1 Track 3; see TB p 17 & 21)

Use the **Navio App** to listen to the song, and encourage children to do the same at home.

Lesson 7 Content

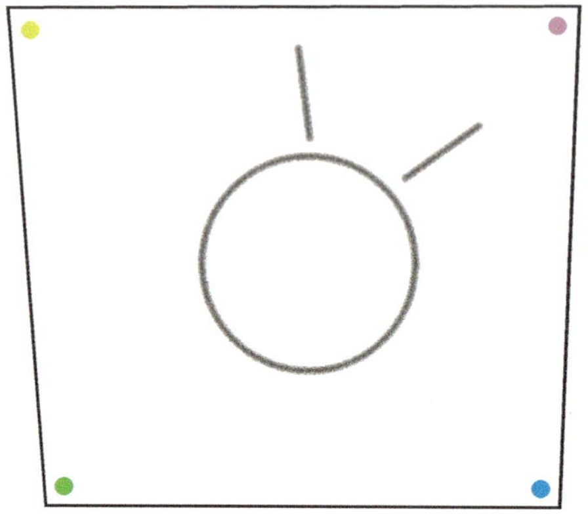

Listen and point. Draw the sunny and rainy weather in the correct place. Say.
Language: boots, coat, hat, shoes, shorts, T-shirt; rainy, sunny; It's (rainy). I put on my (coat).

41

Learning objectives

- Identify and name clothes for rainy and sunny weather
- Listen and understand about clothes for rainy and sunny weather
- Talk about the clothes you wear in different weather

Materials

- Class CDs, printable flashcards, *Ferris Wheel* mat, Mimi puppet

Main vocabulary

- boots, coat, hat, shoes, shorts, T-shirt; rainy, sunny

Key language

- It's (rainy). I put on my (coat).

Teacher's tip: Categorizing clothes

Learning to sort and categorize is an essential thinking skill that helps children establish links between groups of items. This in turn facilitates the memory process. If possible, bring in some real clothes for the children to categorize. Draw the sun on one side of the board and a rain cloud on the other. Ask volunteers to place the clothes in the correct place. Alternatively, choose two volunteers and ask one to get dressed for sunny weather and the other for rainy weather and to stand in the correct place. Encourage the rest of the class to suggest which clothes each child should wear.

Circle time

Hello song & puppet (CD1 Track 2; see TB p 17 & 21)
Opening routines (see TB p 16)
Recycling activity (see TB p 19)
Lesson aims (see TB p 18)

Introduce content vocabulary.

- Use the puppet and printable flashcards to introduce the new words (*sunny*, *rainy*). Children repeat the words.
- Say *It's sunny!* and mime this, e.g. shading your eyes with your hand.
- Say *It's rainy!* and mime this, e.g. holding up an umbrella.
- Say the sentences time about and children respond by doing mimes in the same way.
- Ask e.g. *Do you like it when it's sunny or rainy?* and listen to the children's response.

Sort the clothes.

- Lay out the flashcards of T-shirt, boots, shorts, coat and hat in jumbled order.
- Hold up the printable flashcard of "sunny" and say, e.g. *It's sunny.* Invite children to choose clothes to put on and to point to the flashcards and name the clothes.
- Repeat with *It's rainy.*

Game: *Say the weather!*

- Hold up the flashcard and say, e.g. *I put on my shorts.* Children respond by saying the weather, e.g. *It's sunny!*
- Repeat with different clothes.

Table time

Student's Book p 41

Listen and point.

- Say *Look at the photos of Tom and Sophie.* Children say the weather and name the clothes.
- Play the audio. Children listen and point to the clothes in the photos.

CD2 Track 24

Sophie: It's sunny. I put on my T-shirt and shorts. I put on my hat and shoes.
Tom: It's rainy. I put on my coat and boots.

- Play the audio again. Use the pause button. Children repeat the sentences.

Draw the sunny and rainy weather in the correct place.

- Children copy and draw the weather above the picture of the correct clothes (i.e. sunny, rainy).

Say.

- Children point to the photos and say sentences, e.g. *It's rainy. I put on my boots.*

Activity Book p 41

Circle the clothes for sunny weather in orange. Circle the clothes for rainy weather in blue.

- Children use orange to circle the clothes for sunny weather. They use blue to circle the clothes for rainy weather.

Say.

- They point and say *It's (sunny). I put on my (T-shirt).*

Closing time

Learning review (see TB p 18)
Closing routines (see TB p 16)
Bye bye song and puppet (CD1 Track 3; see TB p 17 & 21)

Use the **Navio App** to play the vocabulary and language games, and encourage children to do the same at home.

Lesson 8 Culture

Clothes

Watch. Listen, point and sing *Itsy, bitsy spider*. Trace to match the pictures to the actions. Say.
Language: spider; rain, sun

42

Learning objectives

- Watch, sing and act out the traditional rhyme *Itsy, bitsy spider*
- Play a mime game
- Point to and name the weather
- Count the legs on a spider

Materials

- Class CDs, flashcards, *Ferris Wheel* mat, Mimi puppet

Main vocabulary

- spider; rain, sun

Teacher's tip: Making a model spider to sing the rhyme

If possible, have the children make spiders out of modeling clay and pipe cleaners. Encourage them to move their model spiders up and down their arms while singing the rhyme.

Circle time

Hello song & puppet (CD1 Track 2; see TB p 17 & 21)
Opening routines (see TB p 16)
Recycling activity (see TB p 19)
Lesson aims (see TB p 18)

Mime the weather.

- Say *It's sunny!* and mime this, e.g. shading your eyes with your hand.
- Say *It's rainy!* and mime this, e.g. holding up an umbrella.
- Say the sentences and children respond by doing mimes in the same way.

***Itsy, bitsy spider* rhyme**

CD2 Track 25

- Clarify the meaning of *spider*, *spout* and *rain* by drawing simple pictures on the board. Pre-teach actions for the rhyme (see TB p 99).
- Play the audio. Children join in doing the actions with you.
- Play the audio again. Children do the actions and sing the rhyme.

Watch the *Itsy, bitsy spider* rhyme video.

- Children watch the video and join in singing the rhyme and doing the actions with Tom and Sophie.

Table time

Student's Book p 42

Watch. Listen, point and sing *Itsy, bitsy spider*.

CD2 Track 25

- Play the audio. Children listen and point to the pictures.

Trace to match the pictures to the actions.

- Play the audio again. Use the pause button after each line. Children trace the lines to match the pictures to the actions.

Say.

- Children point to the pictures and say the words *spider, rain, sun.*
- They then point to the photos below and say the rhyme.

Activity Book p 42

Trace and count the missing legs on the spider.

- Children trace the four missing legs on the spider. Then they count the missing legs.

Point and say.

- They point and say the rhyme.

Closing time

Learning review (see TB p 18)
Closing routines (see TB p 16)
Bye bye song and puppet (CD1 Track 3; see TB p 17 & 21)

Use the **Navio App** to watch the video, and encourage children to do the same at home.

Review

Clothes

Listen, point and say. Color the words you know. Stick the star sticker. Ask and say.
Language: boots, coat, hat, shoes, shorts, T-shirt; Put on your (hat). Take off your (coat). Where's your (T-shirt)? Where are your (shorts)? Here.

43

Clothes

Review Lesson

Learning objectives

- Review your learning and progress
- Ask and say where clothes are
- Stick on a star sticker for achievement

Materials

- Class CDs, flashcards, *Ferris Wheel* mat, Mimi puppet

Main vocabulary

- boots, coat, hat, shoes, shorts, T-shirt

Key language

- Put on your (hat). Take off your (coat). Where's your (T-shirt)? Where are your (shorts)? Here.

Teacher's tip: Supporting children in the review

Comprehension is likely to be ahead of production at this early stage. Be ready to encourage children to use non-verbal responses such as pointing and miming to show that they understand the vocabulary.

Circle time

Hello song & puppet (CD1 Track 2; see TB p 17 & 21)
Opening routines (see TB p 16)
Recycling activity (see TB p 19)
Lesson aims (see TB p 18)

Clothes flashcard games

- Choose one or two flashcard games with the *Ferris Wheel* mat and/or the puppet to review key vocabulary (see TB p 20 & 21).

Sing *The clothes song*.

CD2 Track 17

- Put the flashcards of coat, hat and boots face up on the floor or board.
- Play the audio. Children listen, sing and mime putting on and taking off the clothes in each verse.

Game: *Put on your hat!*

- Point to the flashcards in turn. Use the puppet to give instructions. Children mime putting on and taking off the clothes.

Game: *Where are your shoes?*

- Place two of the clothes flashcards face down on the floor or board and use the puppet to ask, *Where are your (shoes)?* Children point to one of the flashcards and say *Here*. Turn over the flashcard to check if they guessed correctly.

Watch the story video.

- Children watch the story video. Ask e.g. *Is Dylan funny?*

Table time

Student's Book p 43

Listen, point and say.

- Say e.g. *Point to the coat!* and children point to the clothes.
- Play the audio. Children listen, point to the clothes and say the words.

CD2 Track 26

Mimi: I'm the teacher! Can you remember the clothes, Dylan?
Dylan: Yes, I can. T-shirt.
Mimi: T-shirt.
Dylan: Shorts.
Mimi: Shorts.
Dylan: Shoes.
Mimi: Shoes.
Dylan: Hat.
Mimi: Hat.
Dylan: Coat
Mimi: Coat.
Dylan: Boots.
Mimi: Boots. Great job, Dylan. Very good!

Color the words you know.

- Children color the clothes they know.

Stick the star sticker.

- Children stick on the star sticker for achievement.
- Monitor and encourage children to think positively about their progress.

Ask and say.

- Children point to the clothes and ask and say, e.g. *Where's the coat? Here. Put on your coat.*

Activity Book p 43

Color the faces to show the clothes you know. Ask and say.

- Children color the faces next to the clothes they know. They ask and say about the clothes.

Think and color the stars to show your progress.

- Children color the number of stars that they feel shows their progress in this unit.

Closing time

Learning review (see TB p 18)
Closing routines (see TB p 16)
Bye bye song and puppet (CD1 Track 3; see TB p 17 & 21)

Use the **Navio App** to review what children have learned in this unit, and encourage children to do the same at home.

Project

COOPERATIVE LEARNING

1

2

3

Choose and paint a picture of clothes for sunny or rainy weather. Make a weather display.
Ask and say. **Language:** boots, coat, hat, shoes, shorts, T-shirt; rainy, sunny; colors; It's (rainy).
I put on my (coat). Where's your (hat)? Where are your (shorts)? Here. What color is your (coat)? It's (blue).

44

Learning objectives

- Work together to do a collaborative project
- Color a picture of clothes for sunny/rainy weather
- Talk about the weather and clothes on the display
- Express enjoyment of the weather display

Materials

- Class CDs, Mimi puppet, project template, finger paints, tissue paper, glue
- optional: crayons

Main vocabulary

- boots, coat, hat, shoes, shorts, T-shirt; rainy, sunny; colors

Key language

- It's (rainy). I put on my (coat). Where's your (hat)? Where are your (shorts)? Here. What color is your (coat)? It's (blue). What color are your (shorts)? They're (red).

Teacher's tip: Learning to collaborate

COOPERATIVE LEARNING

In this project, children work individually to color their child and collectively to make the tissue paper balls for the sun and rain cloud. Divide the class into two groups: one to make the sun and one to make the rain cloud. Explain and demonstrate that within their groups they should work with another child and take turns making the balls from tissue paper and gluing them on the sun or rain cloud. Give encouragement and praise and show that you value the way the children collaborate to make the finished product.

Circle time

Hello song & puppet (CD1 Track 2; see TB p 17 & 21)
Opening routines (see TB p 16)
Recycling activity (see TB p 19)
Lesson aims (see TB p 18)

Prepare for your project.

- Say *Let's do a project and make a display of clothes for sunny or rainy weather!*
- Show children the copies of the templates that you have prepared.
- Demonstrate painting the clothes for sunny or rainy weather.

Table time

COOPERATIVE LEARNING

Student's Book p 44

- Say e.g. *We're going to make a display of clothes for sunny or rainy weather like this. Look at what we need for our project: templates, tissue paper, finger paints, glue.* Children listen and point to the pictures.

Choose and paint a picture of clothes for sunny or rainy weather.

- Children choose one of the templates showing clothes for sunny or rainy weather (or you can assign these).
- Make sure children have finger paints available.
- They then paint the clothes.

Make a weather display.

- Children work together to make the sun and the rain cloud. Give out yellow and gray tissue paper for the children to roll into balls. Children help glue the yellow balls on the sun and the gray balls of tissue paper on the rain cloud.
- When they are ready, children glue their completed clothes pictures under the correct weather picture on the display you have prepared.

Ask and say.

- Children talk about the weather and clothes in the display.
- Ask children *Do you like our display of rainy and sunny weather?* Make the point that everyone helped make it and that they couldn't have made such a beautiful display on their own.

Alternative version of project

- Children could use crayons instead of finger paints to color the clothes templates.

Activity Book p 44

Glue a photo or paint a picture of you in rainy or sunny weather.

- Children glue a photo or paint a picture of themselves in rainy or sunny weather.

Point, ask and say.

- They point, ask and answer about the clothes in their picture.

Closing time

Learning review (see TB p 18)
Closing routines (see TB p 16)
Bye bye song and puppet (CD1 Track 3; see TB p 17 & 21)

Toys
The old toy box

Vocabulary and language

- **Main vocabulary:** ball, car, doll, scooter, teddy, train
- **Key language:** What's this? It's (a train). What's your favorite toy? It's (my teddy).
- **Content language:** classroom, playground; play, work; I (play) in the (playground).
- **Other language:** big, bouncy, round; numbers 1–3; Let's play with the (ball). Let's play (together). Where's the (red) (train)? Here.

Unit objectives

- Identify and name toys
- Sing the language song *What's this?*
- Ask about toys and make suggestions
- Understand and join in the story *The old toy box*
- Sing and act out the story song *Let's look in the toy box*
- Sing the values song *Let's play together*
- Recognize the value of working and playing together
- Identify and name places at school where you work and play
- Say and act out the traditional rhyme *Bouncy ball*
- Review your learning and progress
- Participate in a collaborative project

Story

CD2 Track 32

Picture 1

Narrator: Mimi and Dylan are at home. Mommy has a big, red box.
Mimi: Oh wow. What's this, Mommy?
Mommy: It's my old toy box. You can play with the toys.
Dylan: Oh, thank you. Let's look in the toy box!

Picture 2

Narrator: Mommy opens the toy box.
Dylan: What's this, Mommy?
Mommy: It's a ball.
Dylan: Let's play with the ball, Mimi.
Mimi: Yes. Bounce, bounce.
Mimi: What's this, Mommy?
Mommy: It's a train.
Mimi: Let's play with the train, Dylan!
Dylan: Yes. Choo-choo!

Picture 3

Narrator: Mommy takes one more toy out of the toy box.
Dylan: What's this, Mommy?
Mommy: It's my old teddy.
Mimi: Ahhh. Look. One ear and one eye. Poor teddy. I have an idea. Let's fix teddy.
Mommy: Oh yes, with my old T-shirt! Good idea, Mimi.

Picture 4

Narrator: Mimi and Dylan help Mommy make a new eye and a new ear for teddy.
Mommy: Look at teddy now!
Mimi: Aah. Let's hug teddy.
Dylan: And let's play with teddy, the ball and the train!
Mimi: Yes! Hurray!
Dylan: Your toy box is great, Mommy.
Mimi: And I love your old teddy.

Songs

Language song

What's this? CD2 Track 30

What's this? (Open arms questioningly)
It's a train. Choo choo (Move arms back and forth like the wheels of a train)
It's a train.

What's this? (Open arms questioningly)
It's a scooter. Zoom zoom (Mime playing on a scooter)
It's a scooter.

What's this? (Open arms questioningly)
It's a ball. Bounce, bounce (Mime bouncing a ball)
It's a ball.

What's this? (Open arms questioningly)
It's a doll. Rock, rock (Mime cradling a doll)
It's a doll.

What's this? (Open arms questioningly)
It's a car. Vroom vroom (Mime zooming a car back and forth)
It's a car.

What's this? (Open arms questioningly)
It's a teddy. Hug, hug (Mime hugging a teddy)
It's a teddy.

Story song

Let's look in the toy box CD2 Track 33

Let's look in the toy box (Point to an eye)
Let's play with the ball today (Mime bouncing a ball)
Let's look in the toy box. (Point to an eye)
Let's play with the ball. Hurray! (Throw arms up in the air)

Let's look in the toy box (Point to an eye)
Let's play with the train today (Mime pushing a toy train)
Let's look in the toy box (Point to an eye)
Let's play with the train. Hurray! (Throw arms up in the air)

Let's look in the toy box (Point to an eye)
Let's play with teddy today (Mime hugging a teddy)
Let's fix poor teddy (Mime sewing)
Let's hug teddy. Hurray! (Throw arms up in the air)

Values song

Let's play together CD2 Track 36

Let's play together (Jump and skip about)
Let's have fun (Wave arms in the air)
Let's play together (Jump and skip about)
Everyone (Arms out and spin around)

Let's work together (Mime coloring an activity sheet)
Let's have fun (Wave arms in the air)
Let's work together (Mime coloring an activity sheet)
Everyone (Arms out and spin around)

Let's play together (Jump and skip about)
Let's have fun (Wave arms in the air)
Let's play together (Jump and skip about)
Everyone (Arms out and spin around)

Let's work together (Mime coloring an activity sheet)
Let's have fun (Wave arms in the air)
Let's work together (Mime coloring an activity sheet)
Everyone (Arms out and spin around)

Culture rhyme

Bouncy ball CD2 Track 38

Here is a big, round, bouncy ball (Mime holding large ball)
I bounce it one, two, three. (Mime bouncing ball)
Here is a ball to throw. (Mime throwing ball)
I catch it, watch and see. (Mime catching ball)
Here is a ball to roll. (Mime rolling ball)
Please roll it back to me. (Point to yourself)

Here is a big, round, bouncy ball (Mime holding large ball)
I bounce it one, two, three. (Mime bouncing ball)
Here is a ball to throw. (Mime throwing ball)
I catch it, watch and see. (Mime catching ball)
Here is a ball to roll. (Mime rolling ball)
Please roll it back to me. (Point to yourself)

Listen, point and repeat. Listen and play. Stick the toy stickers. Say.
Language: ball, car, doll, teddy; blue, green, orange, yellow

Learning objectives

- Identify and name toys
- Listen and point to toys
- Listen and play *Round and round and round*

Materials

- Class CDs, flashcards, *Ferris Wheel* mat, Mimi puppet

Main vocabulary

- ball, car, doll, teddy; blue, green, orange, yellow

Teacher's tip: Associating vocabulary and real objects

If possible, introduce the key vocabulary using real toys. Use toys from the children's own classroom, allowing them to associate the new vocabulary with items they are already familiar with. Name the toy and show the flashcard and encourage different children to pick up the real toy.

Circle time

Hello song & puppet (CD1 Track 2; see TB p 17 & 21)
Opening routines (see TB p 16)
Lesson aims (see TB p 18)

Introduce toy vocabulary.

- Explain that children are going to learn about toys. Ask them to guess which toys. As they say the words in their own language, use the puppet to hold up the flashcards in turn and introduce the words. Children repeat the words.
- Put the *Ferris Wheel* mat on the floor or board with the toy flashcards face down (one on each color). Use the puppet to turn them over and name them. The children repeat the words.

Game: *Find the car!*

- Name a toy and ask one or two children to find and touch the correct flashcard as fast as they can. Repeat with the other toys.

Game: *Say the color!*

- Name the toy and children name the color. Then the reverse.

Table time

Student's Book p 45

Listen, point and repeat.

- Play the audio. Children listen and point to each toy as they hear it.

CD2 Track 27

Mimi: Look, Dylan! Doll … teddy… ball … car… hee, hee, hee! Repeat, Dylan!
Dylan: Yes, Mimi! Doll … teddy… ball … car … hee, hee, hee!
Mimi: Very good, Dylan. Let's say the words together!
Both: Doll … teddy… ball … car … hee, hee, hee!

- Play the audio again. Children listen and repeat the words.

Listen and play.

- Hold up your index finger and move it around clockwise like a wheel. Children do the same. Play the audio. Children listen, point to the color when they hear it, and say the word.

CD1 Track 28

Mimi: Round and round and round: Orange … teddy!
Dylan: Teddy!
Mimi: Round and round and round: Green … car!
Dylan: Car!
Mimi: Round and round and round: Yellow … ball!
Dylan: Ball!
Mimi: Round and round and round: Blue … doll!
Dylan: Doll!

- Play the game with you and/or individual children naming colors and others saying the words.

Stick the toy stickers.

- Children put on the toy stickers.

Say.

- Children point to the toys and say the words.

Activity Book p 45

Trace to match Mimi and Dylan to the toys.

- Children trace to match Mimi and Dylan to the toys.

Point and say.

- They point and name the toys.

Closing time

Learning review (see TB p 18)
Closing routines (see TB p 16)
Bye bye song and puppet (CD1 Track 3; see TB p 17 & 21)

Use the **Navio App** to play the vocabulary game, and encourage children to do the same at home.

Language

2:29 2:30 hello

Listen and find the new toys. Listen, point and sing *What's this?* Trace to match the scooter and the train. Ask and say.

Language: ball, car, doll, scooter, teddy, train; What's this? It's (a train).

Learning objectives

- Talk about toys
- Identify and name two new toys
- Sing the language song *What's this?*
- Ask and say what the toys are

Materials

- Class CDs, flashcards, *Ferris Wheel* mat, Mimi puppet

Main vocabulary

- ball, car, doll, scooter, teddy, train

Key language

- What's this? It's (a train).

Teacher's tip: Singing in turns

Once children are familiar with the song, line them up in pairs facing each other. Encourage one line of children to sing only the question and the other line to sing the answer. Encourage everyone to join in with the sounds of the toys and the final line of each verse.

Circle time

Hello song & puppet (CD1 Track 2; see TB p 17 & 21)
Opening routines (see TB p 16)
Recycling activity (four toy words from Lesson 1) (see TB p 19)
Lesson aims (see TB p 18)

Introduce the new toys words.

- All six toy flashcards on the floor or board.
- Children identify the two new toys.
- Use the puppet to point to and say the words in turn. Children repeat in chorus.
- Turn the two new flashcards face down. Mix them up. Point to one and ask *Train or scooter?* Children guess. Repeat several times.

Introduce *What's this? It's (a train).*

- Hold up one of the flashcards covered with the back of another flashcard. Gradually reveal the picture. Ask e.g. *What's this?* Encourage children to say, e.g. *It's a train* once it's possible to make out what's in the picture.
- Repeat with other flashcards. Children repeat the sentences.

Game: What's this?

- Lay out the toy flashcards and children say the words.
- Turn the flashcards face down. Use the puppet to ask *What's this?* Children guess e.g. *It's a doll.* Turn over the flashcard and children name the flashcard. If they guessed correctly, get everyone to clap and say *Hurray!* If not, say *Let's try again*, turn the flashcard face down and mix them up again.
- Repeat several times.

***What's this?* song**

CD2 Track 30

- Lay out the flashcards face down in the order of the song.
- Play the audio. Turn the flashcards over as the question is answered in each verse of the song. Children listen and point to the flashcards.
- Play the audio again. Children listen and join in singing and acting out the song (see TB p 121).

Table time

Student's Book p 46

Listen and find the new toys.

- Hold up your book. Point to the photos of Auntie Jenny, Tom and Sophie and children say the names.
- Play the audio. Children listen and find the two new toys. Repeat and children say the words.

CD2 Track 29

Tom: Find the … train! Train!
Sophie: Train! Here!
Tom: Find the … scooter! Scooter!
Sophie: Scooter! Here!

Listen, point and sing *What's this?*

CD2 Track 30

- Play the song. Children listen, sing and point to Tom, Sophie, Auntie Jenny and the toys in the photos.
- Remember that you can use the karaoke version of the song when the children are confident.

Trace to match the scooter and the train.

- Hold up your book and show how the pictures of the toys match the toys in the photo.
- Children trace lines to match the scooter and the train.

Ask and say.

- Children point, ask and say e.g. *What's this? It's a teddy.*

Activity Book p 46

Follow and draw paths to match the toys.

- Children draw paths to match the silhouettes to the pictures of the toys.

Point, ask and say.

- They point, ask and answer about the toys.

Closing time

Learning review (see TB p 18)
Closing routines (see TB p 16)
Bye bye song and puppet (CD1 Track 3; see TB p 17 & 21)

Use the **Navio App** to listen to the song, and encourage children to do the same at home.

Lesson 3 Story

Watch. Listen to the story *The old toy box*. Color the teddy from the story. Stick the story sticker. Ask and say. **Language:** ball, teddy, train; What's this? It's (a train). Let's play with the (ball).

Learning objectives

- Watch, understand and enjoy the story *The old toy box*
- Make a prediction about the story
- Look and find toys
- Color the teddy in the story

Materials

- Class CDs, printable story cards, flashcards, *Ferris Wheel* mat, Mimi puppet

Main vocabulary

- ball, teddy, train

Key language

- What's this? It's (a train). Let's play with the (ball).

Teacher's tip: Creating a home-school link

If possible, ask parents to send in any of their own toys from when they were young. Compare them to Mommy's toys in the story.

Circle time

Hello song & puppet (CD1 Track 2; see TB p 17 & 21)
Opening routines (see TB p 16)
Recycling activity (*What's this? It's a …* and toys) (see TB p 19)
Lesson aims (see TB p 18)

Introduce the story *The old toy box*.

- Say *It's story time!* Play the *Story rhyme* (CD1 Track 4; see TB p 17).
- Say *Tom and Sophie are listening to a story about Mommy's old toy box.* Explain or show a picture of this. Say *Guess what's in the box.* Listen to children's answers.

Watch or listen to the story.

CD2 Track 32

- Play the audio, watch the video or read the story using the printable story cards. Pause, repeat words, point to the pictures, ask questions.
- Ask again *What's in the box? (ball, train, teddy).*
- Repeat the story. Encourage children to join in with the words and phrases in the story.
- Ask *Do you like the story? Which toy does Mimi love? Which toy do you love?*

Look and find.

- Say e.g. *Find the train!* Children look at the story and point to the picture as fast as they can.
- Repeat with other toys in the story.

Table time

Student's Book p 47

Watch. Listen to the story *The old toy box*.

CD2 Track 32

- Read or play the audio of the story again. Children listen and point to the pictures in their books.

Color the teddy from the story.

- Demonstrate coloring the teddy from the story.

Story questions

Picture 1
Where are Mimi and Dylan? *(At home)*
What color is the toy box? *(Red)*

Picture 2
What does Dylan play with? *(A ball)*
What does Mimi play with? *(A train)*

Picture 3
What does Mommy have? *(A teddy)*
Does the teddy have two ears and two eyes? *(No)*

Picture 4
Does the teddy have two ears and two eyes now? *(Yes)*
Do Mimi and Dylan like Mommy's old toys? *(Yes)*

Stick the story sticker.

- Children stick on the story sticker.

Ask and say.

- Children ask and answer questions, e.g. *What's this? It's (a train).*
- Ask *Do Mimi and Dylan like Mommy's old toy box?* and children respond.

Activity Book p 47

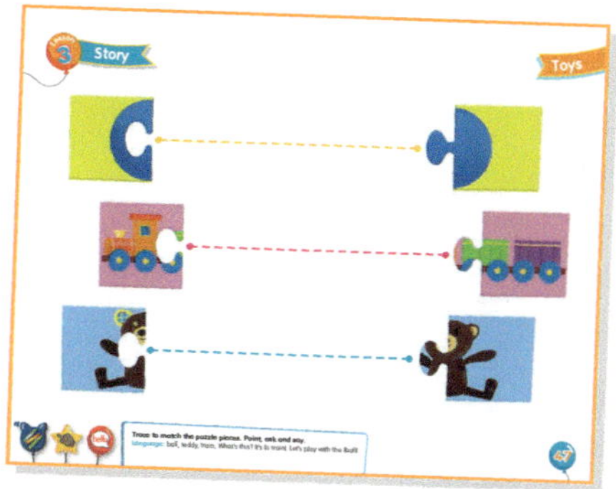

Trace to match the puzzle pieces.

- Children trace to match the puzzle pieces.

Point, ask and say.

- They point, ask and answer about the toys on the puzzle pieces.

Closing time

Learning review (see TB p 18)
Closing routines (see TB p 16)
Bye bye song and puppet (CD1 Track 3; see TB p 17 & 21)

Use the **Navio App** to watch the video, and encourage children to do the same at home.

Lesson 4 Story Song

Toys

Watch. Listen, point and sing *Let's look in the toy box.*
Find and color the toys. Say.
Language: ball, teddy, train; Let's play with the (ball).

48

Learning objectives

- Watch, sing and act out the story song *Let's look in the toy box*
- Listen to the story again and identify toys
- Play *Let's play with the car*
- Color and talk about toys

Materials

- Class CDs, printable story cards, flashcards, *Ferris Wheel* mat, Mimi puppet

Main vocabulary

- ball, teddy, train

Key language

- Let's play with the (ball).

Teacher's tip: Allowing children to burn off energy

Plan into your lesson some time for the children to burn off any excess energy. Moving about for a short while will help them regain concentration later. For example, have them stand up and sit down in quick succession, point to familiar items around them and jump in place.

Circle time

Hello song & puppet (CD1 Track 2; see TB p 17 & 21)
Opening routines (see TB p 16)
Recycling activity (toys vocabulary) (see TB p 19)
Lesson aims (see TB p 18)

Retell the story *The old toy box*.

- Play the audio, video or read the story using the printable story cards.
- Demonstrate that children should wave their arms in the air every time they hear the name of a toy in the story.

Game: ***Let's play with the car!***

- Ask children what toy they want to play with and agree on one, e.g. ball.
- Lay the flashcards face down in a pile. Use the puppet to turn them over one by one and say, e.g. *Let's play with the car!* Children respond *No!* until the puppet turns over the flashcard of the agreed toy and they respond *Yes!*
- Repeat several times with children choosing different toys each time.

***Let's look in the toy box* song**

CD2 Track 33

- Play the video or audio of the story song. The children listen and mime playing with the toys in each verse.
- Watch/listen again. The children join in singing the song and do the actions (see TB p 121).
- Ask children to make suggestions of toys to play with, e.g. *Let's play with the ball!* and others respond *Yes* or *No.*

Table time

Student's Book p 48

Watch. Listen, point and sing *Let's look in the toy box.*

CD2 Track 33

- Play the audio of the song. Children listen, sing and point to the toys.
- Remember that you can use the karaoke version of the song when the children are confident.

Find and color the toys.

- Children find the toys in the toy box and color them according to the colored dots on each one.

Say.

- Children point and say, e.g. *Let's play with the teddy Yes.*

Activity Book p 48

Choose and draw the toy you want to play with in the toy box. Color the toy.

- Children choose the toy they want to play with and draw and color it inside the toy box.

Point, ask and say.

- They point, ask and say about the toy they drew.

Closing time

Learning review (see TB p 18)
Closing routines (see TB p 16)
Bye bye song and puppet (CD1 Track 3; see TB p 17 & 21)

Use the **Navio App** to watch the video, and encourage children to do the same at home.

Speaking

Life skills

Watch. Listen and point. Trace to circle Tom's favorite toy red and Sophie's favorite toy green. Draw a picture of your favorite toy. Ask and say. **Language:** ball, car, doll, scooter, teddy, train; What's this? It's (my ball). What's your favorite toy? It's (my teddy).

49

Learning objectives

- Ask and answer questions about toys
- Watch, understand and enjoy a video
- Identify the characters' toys in the video

Materials

- Class CDs, flashcards, *Ferris Wheel* mat, Mimi puppet

Main vocabulary

- ball, car, doll, scooter, teddy, train

Key language

- What's this? It's (my ball). What's your favorite toy? It's (my teddy).

Teacher's tip: Building up children's confidence to speak

Life skills

You may find that some children are shy of participating in the speaking activities, possibly due to lack of confidence. Encourage them to whisper or use very quiet tones so that they can get used to exploring the sounds of the words before saying them out loud.

Circle time

Hello song & puppet (CD1 Track 2; see TB p 17 & 21)
Opening routines (see TB p 16)
Recycling activity (story song) (CD2 Track 33; see TB p 19)
Lesson aims (see TB p 18)

Game: *Name the toy.*

- Give out the toy flashcards to individual children without others seeing.
- Children mime playing with the toy on their flashcard. Other children say what it is.

Watch the video.

- Explain that Auntie Jenny, Tom and Sophie are looking at their toys.
- Play the video of Auntie Jenny, Tom and Sophie.
- Ask *What's Tom's favorite toy? (teddy) What's Sophie's favorite toy? (scooter) What other toys do they have? (car, doll, train, ball)*
- Watch again. Pause and children repeat the questions and answers.
- Ask *What's your favorite toy?* and listen to the children's response.

Table time

Student's Book p 49 Life skills

Watch. Listen and point.

- Children identify Auntie Jenny, Tom and Sophie.
- Play the audio or video. Children listen and point to the toys.

CD1 Track 35

Auntie Jenny:	Wow, so many toys! What's this?
Tom:	It's my teddy.
Auntie Jenny:	What's this?
Sophie:	It's my doll.
Auntie Jenny:	What's this?
Tom:	It's my train.
Auntie Jenny:	What's this?
Sophie:	It's my car. Broom, broom.
Auntie Jenny:	What's this?
Tom:	It's my ball.
Auntie Jenny:	What's your favorite toy, Tom?
Tom:	It's my teddy.
Auntie Jenny:	What's your favorite toy, Sophie?
Sophie:	It's my scooter.
Auntie Jenny:	Where's your scooter?
Sophie:	Here. Let's play in the yard.
Tom:	Yes! Great!

Trace to circle Tom's favorite toy red and Sophie's favorite toy green.

- Play the audio again. Use the pause button and children circle Tom's favorite toy (i.e. the teddy) in red and Sophie's favorite toy (i.e. the scooter) in green.
- Play the audio again. Pause and children repeat the questions and answers.

Draw a picture of your favorite toy.

- Children draw a picture of their favorite toy.

Ask and say.

- Children take turns showing each other their pictures and asking and answering questions, e.g. *What's this? It's my train.*

Activity Book p 49

Trace to circle your favorite toy in red.

- Children choose their favorite toy and circle it in red.

Ask and say. Trace to circle your friend's favorite toy in green.

- They ask a friend about their favorite toy and circle it green.

Closing time

Learning review (see TB p 18)
Closing routines (see TB p 16)
Bye bye song and puppet (CD1 Track 3; see TB p 17 & 21)

Use the **Navio App** to watch the video, and encourage children to do the same at home.

Values We play together

Listen, point and sing *Let's play together*. Trace the mouths to show working and playing together. Say.
Language: play, work; Let's (play) together.

SOCIAL AND EMOTIONAL LEARNING

50

Learning objectives

- Recognize the value of cooperating with others
- Sing the values song *Let's play together*
- Say *Let's (play) together*

Materials

- Class CDs, flashcards, *Ferris Wheel* mat, Mimi puppet

Main vocabulary

- play, work

Key language

- Let's (play) together.

Teacher's tip: Learning to play together

Children of this age group are only just beginning to understand the concept of sharing toys and materials. Encourage them to sing the song *Let's play together* when they play with toys in their classroom. Praise children who demonstrate that they can share and play nicely together, and show that you value this.

Circle time

Hello song & puppet (CD1 Track 2; see TB p 17 & 21)
Opening routines (see TB p 16)
Recycling activity (*What's this? It's a …*) (see TB p 19)
Lesson aims (see TB p 18)

Watch *The old toy box* story video.

- Play the story video.
- Children watch and repeat every time they hear the name of a toy.
- Ask e.g. *Do Mimi and Dylan look at the toy box and play together in the story? Is it good to play together? Is it good to work together? Why?* Listen to the children's responses.

***Let's play together* song**

CD2 Track 36

- Pre-teach the actions for the song. For *play* children jump and skip about. For *work*, they mime coloring an activity sheet.
- Children stand up. Play the audio. Children listen and do the actions (see TB p 121).
- Play the audio again. Children do the actions and join in singing the song.
- Use children's shared language to make the point that it's more fun when you work and play well together with others.

Table time

Student's Book p 50

Listen, point and sing *Let's play together*.

CD2 Track 36

- Play the audio of the song. Use the pause button. Children sing and point to the pictures in turn.

Trace the mouths to show working and playing together.

- Demonstrate that children should trace the mouths on the pictures showing the children not playing well (unhappy mouth) and playing well together (happy mouth).

Say.

- Children point to the picture with the happy face and say e.g. *Let's (play) together!*

Activity Book p 50

Color the circles to show how you play and work with your friends.

- Children color the circles on the pictures that show how they play and work with their friends.

Say.

- They point and say *Let's play/ work together.*

Closing time

Learning review (see TB p 18)
Closing routines (see TB p 16)
Bye bye song and puppet (CD1 Track 3; see TB p 17 & 21)

Use the **Navio App** to listen to the song, and encourage children to do the same at home.

Lesson 7 Content

Listen and point. Follow and draw paths to match the activities to the places. Say.
Language: classroom, playground; play, work; I (play) in the (playground).

Learning objectives

- Identify and name places at school where you work and play
- Listen and understand about what you do in different places
- Say *I (play) in the (playground).*

Materials

- Class CDs, printable flashcards, *Ferris Wheel* mat, Mimi puppet

Main vocabulary

- classroom, playground; play, work

Key language

- I (play) in the (playground).

Teacher's tip: Consolidating understanding of the content

Stick the printable flashcard of the playground on one wall and the printable flashcard of the classroom on another. Ask the children to stand up. Mime different activities that we do in the playground or the classroom, e.g. read, play football, draw, run, sing, etc. Encourage the children to go to and name the correct place each time.

Circle time

Hello song & puppet (CD1 Track 2; see TB p 17 & 21)
Opening routines (see TB p 16)
Recycling activity (see TB p 19)
Lesson aims (see TB p 18)

Introduce content vocabulary.

- Use the printable flashcards and the puppet to introduce the new words *(playground, classroom).* Children repeat the words.
- Say the sentences time about: *I play in the playground. / I work in the classroom.* Children listen and point to the printable flashcards.
- Repeat and children say the sentences with you.

Game: *Go to the playground!*

- Stick the printable flashcards of the classroom and playground on opposite sides of the classroom at children's height.
- Give instructions to pairs of children in turns, e.g. *Go to the playground!*
- Repeat several times with different children and alternating the places you name.

Watch and say.

- Mime typical activities that children do in the classroom, e.g. coloring, "reading" a book. Mime activities that children do in the playground, e.g. running, playing with a ball. Children respond by naming the place, i.e. *Classroom! / Playground!*
- Repeat several times.

Table time

Student's Book p 51

Listen and point.

- Point to the photos of Tom and Sophie in turn. Ask *Where are Tom and Sophie? (In the classroom/ playground.)*
- Play the audio. Children listen and point to the places in the photos on the right.

CD2 Track 37

Tom: I work in the classroom.
Sophie: I work in the classroom too.
Sophie: I play in the playground.
Tom: I play in the playground too.

Follow and draw paths to match the activities to the places.

- Play the audio again. Use the pause button and children follow and draw the lines to match the activities to the places.

Say.

- Children say sentences about each place, e.g. *I work in the classroom. / I play in the playground.*

Activity Book p 51

Trace to circle your favorite classroom activity red. Trace to circle your favorite playground activity blue.

- Children circle their favorite classroom activity in red. Then they circle their favorite playground activity in blue.

Point and say.

- They point and say *I (work) in the (classroom).*

Closing time

Learning review (see TB p 18)
Closing routines (see TB p 16)
Bye bye song and puppet (CD1 Track 3; see TB p 17 & 21)

Use the **Navio App** to play the vocabulary and language games, and encourage children to do the same at home.

Culture

2:38

hello

Watch. Listen, point and say *Bouncy ball*. Trace the line of the bouncy ball. Say.
Language: ball; big, bouncy, round; numbers 1–3

52

Learning objectives

- Watch, say and act out the traditional rhyme *Bouncy ball*
- Play with a ball
- Trace the line of the bouncy ball
- Count and say numbers 1–3

Materials

- Class CDs, flashcards, *Ferris Wheel* mat, Mimi puppet

Main vocabulary

- ball; big, bouncy, round; numbers 1–3

Teacher's tip: Improving coordination by playing with balls

Bouncing, throwing, rolling and catching balls can help improve motor skills and hand-eye coordination. Once the children are familiar with the *Bouncy ball* song, take them out into the playground and encourage them to play with a ball while singing the song.

Circle time

Hello song & puppet (CD1 Track 2; see TB p 17 & 21)
Opening routines (see TB p 16)
Recycling activity (see TB p 19)
Lesson aims (see TB p 18)

Play with a ball.

- Have ready a ball. Say *Look! I bounce the ball. I throw the ball. I catch the ball. I roll the ball.* Demonstrate each action in turn. Throw the ball in the air and catch it yourself rather than throwing it to the children.
- Repeat and children mime the actions with you.
- Say *Let's play with the ball!* Roll the ball to a child in the circle and say *Please roll it back to me.*
- Repeat several times with different children.

***Bouncy ball* rhyme**

CD2 Track 38

- Play the audio. Children join in doing the actions with you (see TB p 121).
- Play the audio again. Children mime the actions and say the rhyme.

Watch the *Bouncy ball* rhyme video.

- Children watch the video and join in saying the rhyme and doing the actions with Tom and Sophie.

Table time

Student's Book p 52

Watch. Listen, point and say *Bouncy ball.*

CD2 Track 38

- Play the audio. Children listen and point to the "bouncy ball" line with their fingers.

Trace the line of the bouncy ball.

- Children trace the line to show the movement of the bouncy ball.

Say.

- Play the audio again. Children point to the completed line and join in saying the rhyme.

Activity Book p 52

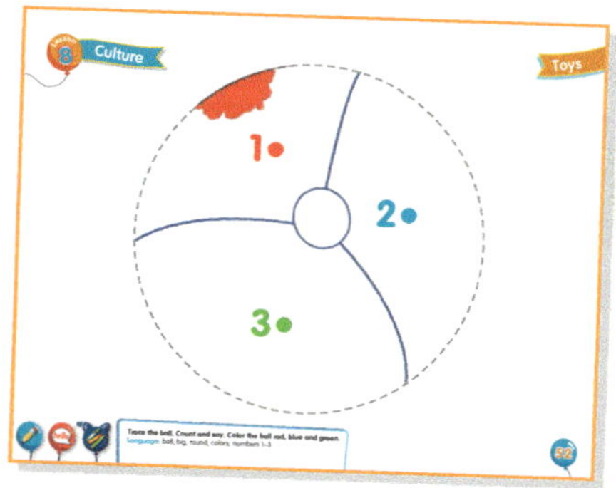

Trace the ball. Count and say.

- Children trace the outline of the ball. They count and say the numbers.

Color the ball red, blue and green.

- Children color the three sections of the ball red, blue and green.

Closing time

Learning review (see TB p 18)
Closing routines (see TB p 16)
Bye bye song and puppet (CD1 Track 3; see TB p 17 & 21)

Use the **Navio App** to watch the video, and encourage children to do the same at home.

Review

Toys

Listen, point and say. Color the words you know. Stick the star sticker. Ask and say. Language: ball, car, doll, scooter, teddy, train; What's this? It's a (train). Let's play with the (car). What's your favorite toy? It's (my doll).

53

Learning objectives

- Review your learning and progress
- Talk about toys
- Stick on a star sticker for achievement

Materials

- Class CDs, flashcards, *Ferris Wheel* mat, Mimi puppet

Main vocabulary

- ball, car, doll, scooter, teddy, train

Key language

- What's this? It's (a train). Let's play with the (car). What's your favorite toy? It's (my doll).

Teacher's tip: Encouraging children to assess their learning

Use the completed review pages to see if children themselves think they need more practice to learn the new vocabulary. If most children have colored all the items, praise them and use their shared language to ask which activities they think helped them learn the vocabulary and how.

Circle time

Hello song & puppet (CD1 Track 2; see TB p 17 & 21)
Opening routines (see TB p 16)
Recycling activity (see TB p 19)
Lesson aims (see TB p 18)

Toy flashcard games

- Choose one or two flashcard games with the *Ferris Wheel* mat and/or the puppet (see TB p 20 & 21).

Sing *What's this?*

CD2 Track 30

- Put the flashcards face down on the floor or board in the order of the song.
- Play the audio. Turn over each flashcard as the question is answered in the song. Children listen, sing and point to the flashcards in each verse.

Game: *Let's play with the (scooter).*

- Stick the flashcards at the children's height on different walls around the classroom. Have the children stand up.
- Say *Let's play with the (scooter).* Children go to the scooter flashcard and mime riding on a scooter.
- Repeat with all the toys.

Game: *What's this?*

- Have the children sit in pairs facing each other. Show one of the toy flashcards and encourage the children on the left to ask their partner, *What's this?*
- Children on the right reply, *It's (a doll).* Repeat with all the flashcards changing roles.

Watch the story video.

- Children watch the story video. Ask e.g. *Which toy does Mimi love?*

Table time

Student's Book p 53

Listen, point and say.

- Say e.g. *Point to the ball!* and children point to the toys.
- Play the audio. Children listen, point to the toys and say the words.

CD2 Track 39

Mimi: I'm the teacher! Can you remember the toys, Dylan?
Dylan: Yes, I can. Ball.
Mimi: Ball
Dylan: Car.
Mimi: Car.
Dylan: Teddy.
Mimi: Teddy.
Dylan: Doll.
Mimi: Doll.
Dylan: Train.
Mimi: Train.
Dylan: Scooter.
Mimi: Scooter. Great job, Dylan. Very good!

Color the words you know.

- Children color the toys they know.

Stick the star sticker.

- Children stick on the star sticker for achievement.
- Monitor and encourage children to think positively about their progress.

Ask and say.

- Children point to the clothes, ask and say, e.g. *What's this? It's a car. Let's play with the car! Yes!*

Activity Book p 53

Color the faces to show the toys you know. Ask and say.

- Children color the faces next to the toys they know. They ask and say about the toys.

Think and color the stars to show your progress.

- Children color the number of stars that they feel shows their progress in this unit.

Closing time

Learning review (see TB p 18)
Closing routines (see TB p 16)
Bye bye song and puppet (CD1 Track 3; see TB p 17 & 21)

Use the **Navio App** to review what children have learned in this unit, and encourage children to do the same at home.

Project

COOPERATIVE LEARNING

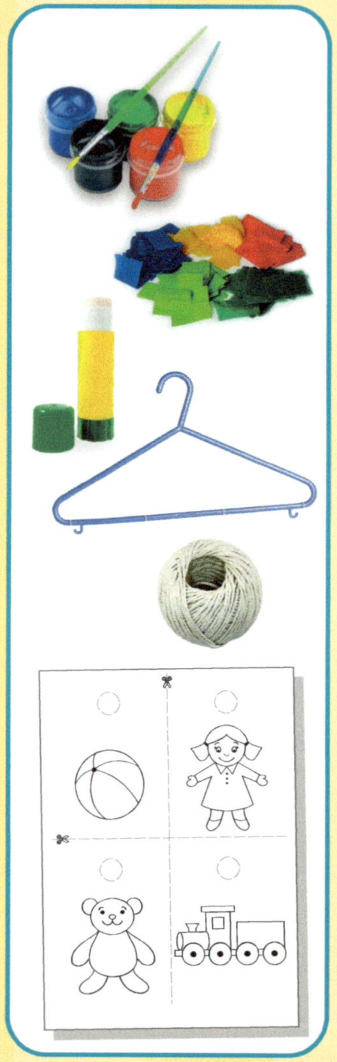

Choose, paint and decorate a toy. Make a toy mobile. Ask and say.
Language: ball, doll, teddy, train; colors; What's this? It's (a teddy). Let's play with the (ball). Where's the (red) (train)? Here. What's your favorite toy? It's (the teddy).

54

Learning objectives

- Work together to do a collaborative project
- Choose and color a toy
- Talk about the toys on the mobile
- Express enjoyment of the toy mobile
- Make a collage of toys

Materials

- Class CDs, Mimi puppet, project template, finger paints, tissue paper, glue, string, coat hangers
- optional: crayons, stickers

Main vocabulary

- ball, doll, teddy, train; colors

Key language

- What's this? It's (a teddy). Let's play with the (ball). Where's the (red) (train)? Here. What's your favorite toy? It's (the teddy).

Teacher's tip: Being positive about each other's work

Once the mobiles have been hung up, encourage the children to look at each other's work and say, e.g. *It's very good! / It's great!* Make sure all the comments are positive and discourage any negativity.

Circle time

Hello song & puppet (CD1 Track 2; see TB p 17 & 21)
Opening routines (see TB p 16)
Recycling activity (see TB p 19)
Lesson aims (see TB p 18)

Prepare for your project.

- Say *Let's do a project and make a mobile of our favorite toys!*
- Show children the copies of the toy templates that you have prepared.
- Demonstrate painting and gluing small balls of tissue paper on the toy templates.

Table time

COOPERATIVE LEARNING

Student's Book p 54

- Say e.g. *We're going to make a mobile of our favorite toys like this. Look at what we need for our project: pictures of toys, finger paints, tissue paper, glue, string, coat hangers.* The children listen and point to the pictures.

Choose, paint and decorate a toy.

- The children choose their favorite toy (from the ones on the project template). Give each child a copy of the toy they choose.
- Make sure the children have finger paints, tissue paper and glue available.
- The children paint the toys and then decorate them with balls of tissue paper.

Make a toy mobile.

- When they are ready, punch or cut a hole in the template. Then attach the finished toys to the coat hanger using string to make the mobiles.

Ask and say.

- Children talk about the toys on the mobiles, e.g. *What's this? It's (a teddy). What's your favorite toy? It's (the teddy).*
- Ask the children *Do you like the mobiles of our favorite toys?* Make the point that everyone helped make the mobiles and that they couldn't have made such a beautiful display on their own.

Alternative version of project

- Children could use crayons and stickers instead of finger paints and tissue paper to decorate their template.

Activity Book p 54

Find and glue pictures of toys.

- Children find and glue pictures of toys to make a collage.

Point, ask and say.

- Children point, ask and say about the toys in their collage.

Closing time

Learning review (see TB p 18)
Closing routines (see TB p 16)
Bye bye song and puppet (CD1 Track 3; see TB p 17 & 21)

Food
The picnic

Vocabulary and language

- **Main vocabulary:** apples, bananas, cookies, juice, sandwiches, water
- **Key language:** I like (bananas). Are you hungry? Can I have (a sandwich), please? Here you go. Thank you.
- **Content language:** drink, eat; I eat (apples). I drink (water).
- **Other language:** please, thank you; oranges; little, tree; numbers 1–10; I'm hungry. Can I have my lunch, please? (Here's a sandwich) for you. What color is the (apple)? It's (green).

Unit objectives

- Identify and name food
- Sing the language song *I like bananas*
- Ask for food and say food you like
- Understand and join in the story *The picnic*
- Sing and act out the story song *I'm hungry*
- Sing the values song *Two little words*
- Recognize the value of saying "please" and "thank you"
- Identify and name things we eat and drink
- Sing and act out the traditional song *Ten little apples*
- Review your learning and progress
- Participate in a collaborative project

Story

CD3 Track 6

Picture 1

Narrator: Mrs. Cat's class is having a picnic. The children are happy.
Mrs. Cat: Come and get your picnic lunch, children. There's a sandwich, a cookie, a banana and juice for everyone.
Mimi, Leo, Eddie, Zara: Yippee! Hurray!
Leo: Can I have my lunch, please?
Mrs. Cat: Yes. Here you go, Leo.
Leo: Thank you, Mrs. Cat. I'm hungry.
Zara: Can I have my lunch, please?
Mrs. Cat: Yes. Here you go, Zara.
Zara: Thank you, Mrs. Cat. I'm hungry.
Eddie: Can I have my lunch, please?
Mrs. Cat: Yes. Here you go, Eddie.
Eddie: Thank you, Mrs. Cat. I'm hungry.
Mimi: Can I have my lunch, please?
Mrs. Cat: Umm … oh no. Your lunch isn't here, Mimi.
Mimi: Oh no! I'm hungry too!

Picture 2

Narrator: Eddie, Zara and Leo share their lunch with Mimi.
Eddie: Oh, poor Mimi. Here's a sandwich for you, Mimi.
Mimi: Thank you, Eddie.
Zara: Here's a cookie for you, Mimi.
Mimi: Thank you, Zara.
Leo: Here's a banana for you, Mimi.
Mimi: Thank you, Leo.

Picture 3

Eddie: I'm still hungry.
Mimi: Oh no. Poor Eddie. Oh, look! It's my lunch!

Picture 4

Narrator: Mimi shares her lunch with Eddie, Zara and Leo.
Mimi: Here's a sandwich for you, Eddie.
Eddie: Thank you, Mimi. I like sandwiches.
Mimi: Here's a cookie for you, Zara.
Zara: Thank you, Mimi. I like cookies.
Mimi: Here's a banana for you, Leo.
Leo: Thank you, Mimi. I like bananas!
Mrs. Cat: Great job, children. It's good to share!
Eddie: And I'm not hungry now!

Songs

Language song

I like bananas CD3 Track 4

I like bananas (Mime peeling a banana)
I like apples too (Mime eating an apple)
I like bananas and apples (Thumbs up)
Do you? Do you? (Point to different children)

I like cookies (Mime eating a cookie)
I like sandwiches too (Mime eating a sandwich)
I like cookies and sandwiches (Thumbs up)
Do you? Do you? (Point to different children)

I like juice (Mime drinking)
I like water too (Mime drinking)
I like juice and water (Thumbs up)
Do you? Do you? (Point to different children)

Story song

I'm hungry CD3 Track 7

I'm hungry. I'm hungry. (Rub your tummy)
Here's a sandwich for you. (Gesture handing over a sandwich)
A sandwich for you. (Point to a child)
Thank you.

I'm hungry. I'm hungry. (Rub your tummy)
Here's a cookie for you. (Gesture handing over a cookie)
A cookie for you. (Point to a child)
Thank you.

I'm hungry. I'm hungry. (Rub your tummy)
Here's a banana for you. (Gesture handing over a banana)
A banana for you. (Point to a child)
Thank you.

Values song

Two little words CD3 Track 10

Two little words for every day (Hold up two fingers)
Two little words, remember to say. (Point to your brain)
Please, please, please. (Hold up the first finger)
Thank you, thank you, thank you. (Hold up the second finger)

Two little words for every day (Hold up two fingers)
Two little words, remember to say. (Point to your brain)
Please, please, please. (Hold up the first finger)
Thank you, thank you, thank you. (Hold up the second finger)

Culture song

Ten little apples CD3 Track 12

One little, two little, three little apples, (Count to three on fingers)
Four little, five little, six little apples, (Count to six on fingers)
Seven little, eight little, nine little apples, (Count to nine on fingers)
Ten little apples on the tree. (Count to ten on fingers and hold arms out like branches of a tree)
One little, two little, three little oranges, (Count to three on fingers)
Four little, five little, six little oranges, (Count to six on fingers)
Seven little, eight little, nine little oranges, (Count to nine on fingers)
Ten little oranges on the tree. (Count to ten on fingers and hold arms out like branches of a tree)

Food

The picnic

Vocabulary Lesson 1

Listen, point and repeat. Listen and play. Stick the food stickers. Say.
Language: apple, banana, cookie, sandwich; blue, green, pink, red

Learning objectives

- Identify and name food
- Listen and point to food
- Listen and play *Round and round and round*

Materials

- Class CDs, flashcards, *Ferris Wheel* mat, Mimi puppet

Main vocabulary

- apple, banana, cookie, sandwich; blue, green, pink, red

Teacher's tip: Using Mimi to help with pronunciation

If children need additional practice in pronouncing any of the new words, use Mimi to help them. Explain that Mimi is having difficulty saying the words and encourage the class to help her say the words correctly. Have Mimi say the words slowly and get the children to practice saying them with her. Repeat at more normal speed until children are pronouncing the words correctly.

Circle time

Hello song & puppet (CD1 Track 2; see TB p 17 & 21)
Opening routines (see TB p 16)
Lesson aims (see TB p 18)

Introduce food vocabulary.

- Use the puppet to say *I'm hungry*. Rub your tummy to show the meaning.
- Use the puppet to hold up the flashcards in turn, say e.g. *Mmm, banana* and introduce the words. Children repeat the words.
- Put the *Ferris Wheel* mat on the floor or board with the food flashcards face down (one on each color). Use the puppet to turn them over and name them. The children repeat the words.

Game: *Find the banana!*

- Name the food and one or two children to find and touch the correct flashcards as fast as they can.

Game: *Say the color!*

- Name the food and children name the color. Then the reverse.

Table time

Student's Book p 55

Listen, point and repeat.

- Play the audio. Children listen and point to each word as they hear it.

CD3 Track 1

Mimi: Look, Dylan! Banana … apple … cookie … sandwich … hee, hee, hee! Repeat, Dylan!
Dylan: Yes, Mimi! Banana … apple… cookie … sandwich … hee, hee, hee!
Mimi: Very good, Dylan. Let's say the words together!
Both: Banana … apple… cookie … sandwich … hee, hee, hee!

- Play the audio again. Children listen and repeat the words.

Listen and play.

- Hold up your index finger and move it around clockwise like a wheel. Children do the same. Play the audio. Children listen, point to the color when they hear it, and say the word.

CD3 Track 2

Mimi: Round and round and round:
Red … banana!
Dylan: Banana!
Mimi: Round and round and round:
Blue … apple!
Dylan: Apple!
Mimi: Round and round and round:
Pink … cookie!
Dylan: Cookie!
Mimi: Round and round and round:
Green … sandwich!
Dylan: Sandwich!

- Play the game with you and/or individual children naming colors and others saying the words.

Stick the food stickers.

- Children put on the food stickers.

Say.

- Children point to the food and say the words.

Activity Book p 55

Trace and color the food.

- Children trace and color the food.

Point and say.

- They point and say the words.

Closing time

Learning review (see TB p 18)
Closing routines (see TB p 16)
Bye bye song and puppet (CD1 Track 3; see TB p 17 & 21)

Use the **Navio App** to play the vocabulary game, and encourage children to do the same at home.

Listen and find the new food. Listen, point and sing *I like bananas*. Color the faces and trace to match them to the water and the juice. Point and say.
Language: apples, bananas, cookies, juice, sandwiches, water; I like (bananas).

56

Learning objectives

- Talk about food
- Identify and name two new foods
- Sing the language song *I like bananas*
- Say what food you like

Materials

- Class CDs, flashcards, *Ferris Wheel* mat, Mimi puppet

Main vocabulary

- apples, bananas, cookies, juice, sandwiches, water

Key language

- I like (bananas).

Teacher's tip: Developing deliberate memory

Choose three of the food items and put the flashcards on the floor or board. Say *I like bananas, apples and juice.* Choose volunteers to pick up the cards in the order you said them. Encourage the rest of the class to help.

Circle time

Hello song & puppet (CD1 Track 2; see TB p 17 & 21)

Opening routines (see TB p 16)

Recycling activity (four food words from Lesson 1) (see TB p 19)

Lesson aims (see TB p 18)

Introduce the new food words.

- Put all six food flashcards on the floor or board. Children identify the two new words.
- Use the puppet to point to and say the words in turn. Children repeat in chorus.
- Turn the two new flashcards face down. Mix them up. Point to one and ask *Juice or water?* Children guess. Repeat several times.

Introduce *I like (bananas).*

- Put the food flashcards on the floor or board. Point to one and say, e.g. *I like apples.* Smile and use mime to show what you mean.
- Repeat with one or two other flashcards.
- Repeat and this time say, e.g. *I like cookies. Do you?* Encourage children to say *Yes* or *No.*
- Get children who say "yes" to repeat the sentence.

Game: *I like sandwiches!*

- Hold up and say a sentence about one of the flashcards, e.g. *I like sandwiches.*
- Explain and demonstrate that children should wave their hands in the air and repeat the sentence if they like sandwiches too, and fold their arms and stay silent if they don't like sandwiches.
- Repeat with other flashcards.

***I like bananas* song**

CD3 Track 4

- Lay out the flashcards in the order of the song.
- Play the audio. Children listen and point to the flashcards.
- Play the audio again. Children listen and join in singing and acting out the song by pretending to eat or drink each food and pointing to a friend in the last line of each verse (see TB p 143).

Table time

Student's Book p 56

Listen and find the new food.

- Hold up your book. Point to the photos of Auntie Jenny, Tom and Sophie and children say the names.
- Play the audio. Children listen and find the two new words. Repeat and children say the words.

CD3 Track 3

Sophie: Find the … water! Water!
Tom: Water! Here!
Sophie: Find the … juice! Juice!
Tom: Juice! Here!

Listen, point and sing *I like bananas.*

CD3 Track 4

- Play the audio of the song. The children listen, sing and point to the food in the photo.
- Remember that you can use the karaoke version of the song when the children are confident.

Color the faces and trace to match them to the water and the juice.

- Hold up your book and demonstrate coloring the smiley faces to show which foods the characters like. Children color the two faces.
- Children trace the lines to match the faces to the water and juice.

Point and say.

- Children point to the colored faces for each food and say, e.g. *I like bananas.*

Activity Book p 56

Color the food and drink you like.

- Children color the food and drink they like.

Point and say.

- They point and say *I like (juice).*

Closing time

Learning review (see TB p 18)

Closing routines (see TB p 16)

Bye bye song and puppet (CD1 Track 3; see TB p 17 & 21)

Use the **Navio App** to listen to the song, and encourage children to do the same at home.

3:06

hello

Watch. Listen to the story *The picnic*. Trace to circle the picnic lunch in the story. Stick the story sticker. Ask and say. Language: banana, cookie, juice, sandwich; I'm hungry. Can I have my lunch, please? Here's (a sandwich) for you. Thank you. I like (bananas).

Learning objectives

- Watch, understand and enjoy the story *The picnic*
- Make a prediction about the story
- Look and find food
- Identify and circle the picnic lunch in the story

Materials

- Class CDs, printable story cards, flashcards, *Ferris Wheel* mat, Mimi puppet

Main vocabulary

- banana, cookie, juice, sandwich

Key language

- I'm hungry. Can I have my lunch, please? Here's (a sandwich) for you. Thank you. I like (bananas).

Teacher's tip: Managing snack time independently

Life skills

If your lesson coincides with snack time, use the opportunity to show the children how to open their juice cartons and put the straw in. Encourage them to become gradually more independent.

Circle time

Hello song & puppet (CD1 Track 2; see TB p 17 & 21)
Opening routines (see TB p 16)
Recycling activity (*I like …* and food) (see TB p 19)
Lesson aims (see TB p 18)

Introduce the story *The picnic*.

- Say *It's story time!* Play the *Story rhyme* (CD1 Track 4; see TB p 17).
- Say *Tom and Sophie are listening to a story about Mimi's class picnic*. Explain or show a picture of this. Say *Guess the food for the picnic*. Listen to children's answers.

Watch or listen to the story.

CD3 Track 6

- Play the audio, watch the video or read the story using the printable story cards. Pause, repeat words, point to the pictures, ask questions.
- Ask again *What's the food for the picnic? (sandwich, cookie, banana, juice)*.
- Repeat the story. Encourage children to join in with the words and phrases in the story.
- Ask *Is Mimi hungry at the end of the story? Does Mimi get a picnic lunch?*

Look and find.

- Say e.g. *Find a sandwich!* Children look at the story and point to the picture as fast as they can.
- Repeat with other food in the story.

Table time

Student's Book p 57

Watch. Listen to the story *The picnic*.

- Read or play the audio of the story again. Children listen and point to the pictures in their books.

Trace to circle the picnic lunch in the story.

- Demonstrate circling the picnic lunch in the story (i.e. the one on the right).

Story questions

Picture 1
What is there for lunch? *(A sandwich/a cookie/a banana/juice)*
Does Mimi have her lunch? *(No)*

Picture 2
Do Eddie, Zara and Leo share their lunch with Mimi? *(Yes)*
What does Eddie share with Mimi? *(A sandwich)*

Picture 3
Is Eddie hungry? *(Yes)*
What does Mimi see? *(Her lunch)*

Picture 4
Does Mimi share her lunch with Eddie, Zara and Leo? *(Yes)*
Is Eddie hungry now? *(No)*

Stick the story sticker.

- Children stick on the story sticker.

Ask and say.

- Children ask and say e.g. *Can I have my lunch, please? Here's (a sandwich) for you. Thank you.*
- Ask *Does Mimi share her lunch? Is Eddie hungry at the end of the story?* and children respond.

Activity Book p 57

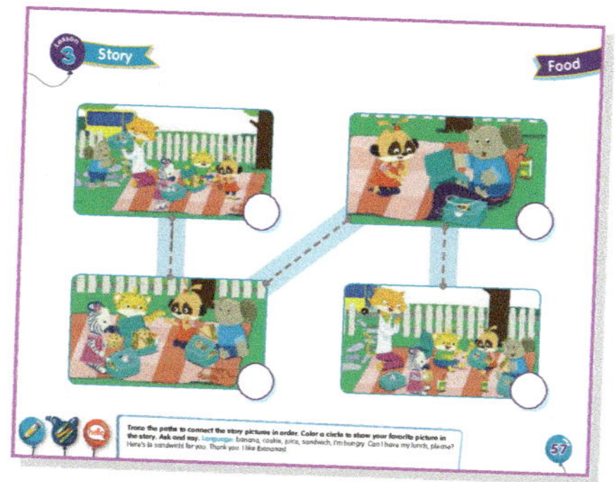

Trace the paths to connect the story pictures in order. Color a circle to show your favorite picture in the story.

- Children connect the story pictures in order. They color the circle on their favorite picture.

Ask and say.

- They ask and say phrases from the story.

Closing time

Learning review (see TB p 18)
Closing routines (see TB p 16)
Bye bye song and puppet (CD1 Track 3; see TB p 17 & 21)

Use the **Navio App** to watch the video, and encourage children to do the same at home.

Story Song

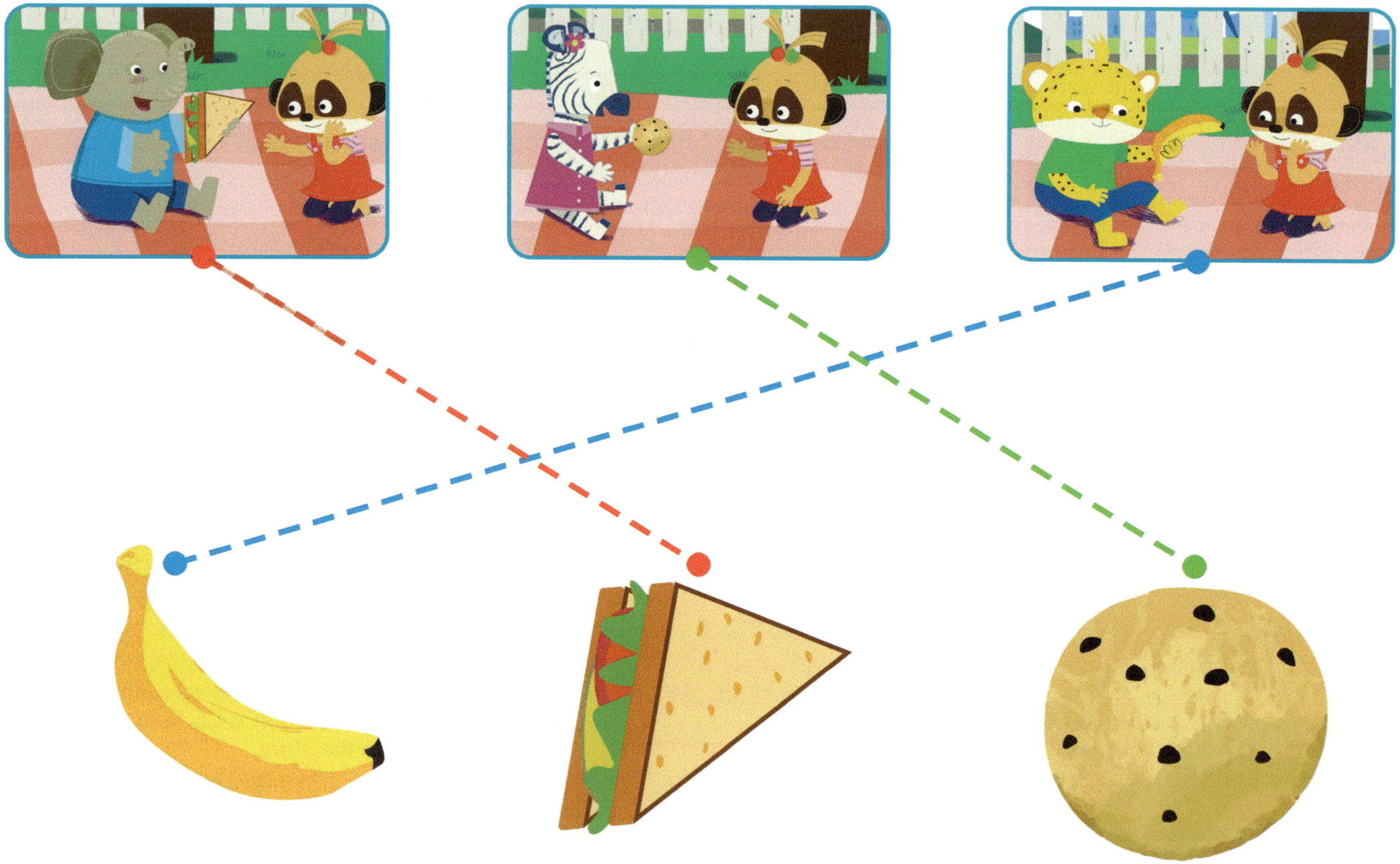

Watch. Listen, point and sing *I'm hungry*. Trace to match the characters to the food they give Mimi. Point and say. **Language:** banana, cookie, sandwich; I'm hungry. Here's (a sandwich) for you. Thank you.

3:07

58

Learning objectives
- Watch, sing and act out the story song *I'm hungry*
- Listen to the story again and identify the food
- Play *Can I have a sandwich, please?*
- Color, match and talk about food

Materials
- Class CDs, printable story cards, flashcards, *Ferris Wheel* mat, Mimi puppet

Main vocabulary
- banana, cookie, sandwich

Key language
- I'm hungry. Here's (a sandwich) for you. Thank you.

Teacher's tip: Incorporating the song into snack time routines

If your lesson coincides with snack time, encourage the children to rub their tummies and say *I'm hungry*. Either use yourself, or encourage your helper to use chunks from the song when giving out the snacks, e.g. *Here's (a sandwich) for you*. Make sure everyone says, *Thank you* on receiving their snack.

Circle time

Hello song & puppet (CD1 Track 2; see TB p 17 & 21)
Opening routines (see TB p 16)
Recycling activity (food vocabulary) (see TB p 19)
Lesson aims (see TB p 18)

Retell the story *The picnic*.
- Play the audio, video or read the story using the printable story cards.
- Demonstrate that children should wave their arms in the air every time they hear the name of a food in the story.

Game: *Can I have a sandwich, please?*
- Lay out the food flashcards face up.
- Ask the puppet, e.g. *Can I have a sandwich, please?* Use the puppet to pick up the flashcard of the sandwich, give it to you and say *Here you go*. Take the flashcard and say *Thank you*.
- Repeat several times asking individual children for different food in the same way. Children respond by giving you the flashcard and saying *Here you go* and you say *Thank you*.
- Repeat several times with different children and food.

***I'm hungry* song**

CD3 Track 7
- Play the video or audio of the story song. Children watch/listen and mime being hungry and asking for and giving each other the food in each verse (see TB p 143).
- Play the song again. Children do the actions and join in singing the song.
- Children point to the flashcards and take turns pointing and saying *Thank you*.

Table time

Student's Book p 58

Watch. Listen, point and sing *I'm hungry*.

CD3 Track 7
- Play the audio of the song. Children listen, sing and follow the lines to show the food the characters give to Mimi.
- Remember that you can use the karaoke version of the song when the children are confident.

Trace to match the characters to the food they give Mimi.
- Children trace the lines to match the characters to the food they give Mimi.

Point and say.
- Children pretend to be Mimi and the other characters and ask and say, e.g. *I'm hungry. Here's (a sandwich) for you. Thank you.*

Activity Book p 58

Find and color the food in the lunchbox.
- Children find and color the food in the lunchbox according to the colored dots.

Point and say.
- They point and say *Here's (a banana) for you.*

Closing time

Learning review (see TB p 18)
Closing routines (see TB p 16)
Bye bye song and puppet (CD1 Track 3; see TB p 17 & 21)

Use the **Navio App** to watch the video, and encourage children to do the same at home.

Lesson 5 Speaking

Life skills

Food

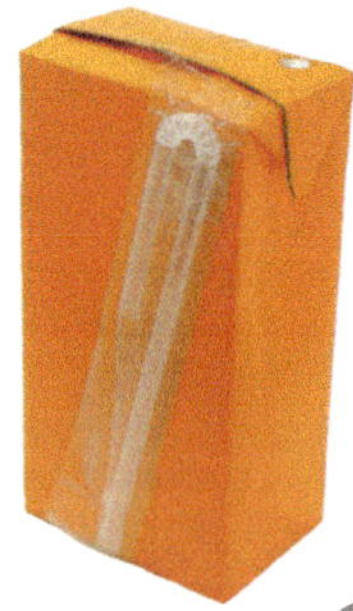

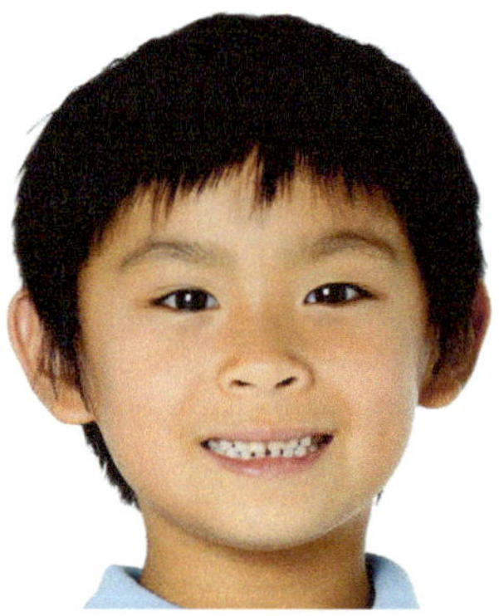

Watch. Listen and point. Trace to circle what Sophie asks for in red and what Tom asks for in blue. Ask and say. Language: banana, juice, sandwich, water; Are you hungry? Can I have (a sandwich), please? Here you go. Thank you. I like (bananas).

Learning objectives

- Ask and answer questions about food
- Watch, understand and enjoy a video
- Identify the food the characters want in the video

Materials

- Class CDs, flashcards, *Ferris Wheel* mat, Mimi puppet

Main vocabulary

- banana, juice, sandwich, water

Key language

- Are you hungry? Can I have (a sandwich), please? Here you go. Thank you. I like (bananas).

Teacher's tip: Acting out a mini role-play

Life skills

After watching the video and/or listening to the audio, add fun and realism to the speaking activity by performing a mini role-play. Put the children into threes (Tom, Sophie, Auntie Jenny) and get them to sit on the floor as if for a picnic. Demonstrate that Tom and Sophie take turns asking Auntie Jenny, e.g. *Can I have a (sandwich), please?* Auntie Jenny pretends to give it to them and says *Here you go.*

Circle time

Hello song & puppet (CD1 Track 2; see TB p 17 & 21)
Opening routines (see TB p 16)
Recycling activity (story song) (CD3 Track 7; see TB p 19)
Lesson aims (see TB p 18)

Game: *Yes or No?*

- Place the food flashcards face down in a pile.
- Demonstrate the game. Ask children e.g. *Can I have a banana, please?* Ask a child to turn over the top flashcard. If it is a banana, they give you the flashcard and say *Here you go!* If it isn't a banana, they say *No, sorry!*
- Repeat several times with different children and food.

Watch the video.

- Explain that Auntie Jenny, Tom and Sophie are having a picnic.
- Play the video. Ask *What does Tom ask for? (banana, water) What does Sophie ask for? (sandwich, juice).*
- Watch again. Pause and children repeat the questions and answers.
- Ask *What food do you like for a picnic?*

Table time

Student's Book p 59

Life skills

Watch. Listen and point.

- Children identify Auntie Jenny, Tom and Sophie in the photo and the food in the pictures.
- Play the audio. Children listen and point to the food.

CD3 Track 9

Sophie:	I like picnics!
Tom:	Me too!
Auntie Jenny:	Are you hungry?
Sophie:	Oh yes, I am. Can I have a sandwich, please, Auntie Jenny?
Auntie Jenny:	Here you go, Sophie.
Sophie:	Thank you. Mmm. I like sandwiches.
Tom:	Can I have a banana, please, Auntie Jenny?
Auntie Jenny:	Here you go, Tom.
Tom:	Thank you. Mmm. I like bananas. Can I have water, please, Auntie Jenny?
Auntie Jenny:	Here you go, Tom.
Tom:	Thank you.
Sophie:	Can I have juice, please, Auntie Jenny?
Auntie Jenny:	Here you go, Sophie.
Sophie:	Thank you. This is a great picnic!
Auntie Jenny:	Oh no! Rain!

Trace to circle what Sophie asks for in red and what Tom asks for in blue.

- Play the audio again. Use the pause button and children trace to circle what Sophie asks for in red and what Tom asks for in blue.
- Play the audio again. Pause and children repeat the questions and answers.

Ask and say.

- Children take turns pointing to the pictures and asking and saying, e.g. *Can I have a sandwich, please? Here you go. Thank you. I like sandwiches.*

Activity Book p 59

Choose and draw your picnic. Color.

- Children choose what they want for their picnic and draw and color the food on the picnic blanket.

Ask and say.

- They pretend to have a picnic and act out a mini role-play.

Closing time

Learning review (see TB p 18)
Closing routines (see TB p 16)
Bye bye song and puppet (CD1 Track 3; see TB p 17 & 21)

Use the **Navio App** to watch the video, and encourage children to do the same at home.

Lesson 6 Values I say 'please' and 'thank you'

3:10

hello

Listen, point and sing *Two little words*. Color the star yellow for 'please' and pink for 'thank you'. Say.
Language: please, thank you

SOCIAL AND EMOTIONAL LEARNING

60

Learning objectives

- Recognize the value of saying "please" and "thank you"
- Sing the values song *Two little words*
- Say *please* and *thank you*

Materials

- Class CDs, flashcards, *Ferris Wheel* mat, Mimi puppet

Main vocabulary

- please, thank you

Teacher's tip: Saying "please" and "thank you"

An important part of social and emotional learning is beginning to think of others. Incorporate the ideas and language from the song *Two little words* into your daily routines. Make sure children always say *please* and *thank you* when asking for or being given classroom items or receiving help.

Circle time

Hello song & puppet (CD1 Track 2; see TB p 17 & 21)
Opening routines (see TB p 16)
Recycling activity *(Can I have a ...? I like ...)* (see TB p 19)
Lesson aims (see TB p 18)

Watch *The picnic* story video.

- Play the story video.
- Children watch and repeat every time they hear the name of a food.
- Ask e.g. *What little word do Eddie, Zara and Leo say when they ask Mimi for food? (please) What do they say when Mimi gives them food? (Thank you) What do they say when Mimi is hungry and thirsty and doesn't have any food? (Sorry).* Explain that it's polite to use these words. Ask *Is it important to be polite?* Listen to the children's response.

***Two little words* song**

CD3 Track 10

- Children hold up two fingers. Play the audio. Children listen and do the actions (see TB p 143).
- Play the audio again. Children do the actions and join in singing the song.
- Use children's shared language to make the point that it's important to be polite and to say these words when appropriate in their own language as well as in English.

Table time

Student's Book p 60

Listen, point and sing *Two little words*.

CD3 Track 10

- Children look at the pictures and identify in which one Mimi is saying "please" and in which one she is saying "thank you."
- Play the audio of the song. Use the pause button. Children sing and point to the pictures in turn.

Color the pictures of Mimi saying 'please' and 'thank you'.

- Demonstrate that children should color Mimi saying "please" (in picture 1) and "thank you" (in picture 2).

Say.

- Children point to their completed pictures and say the words.

Activity Book p 60

Draw pictures of you saying 'please' and 'thank you'.

- Children draw themselves in the pictures saying "please" and "thank you."

Point and say.

- They point to the pictures and *say please / thank you.*

Closing time

Learning review (see TB p 18)
Closing routines (see TB p 16)
Bye bye song and puppet (CD1 Track 3; see TB p 17 & 21)

Use the **Navio App** to listen to the song, and encourage children to do the same at home.

Lesson 7 Content

Food

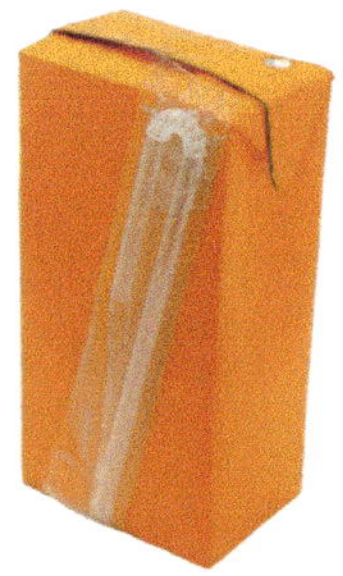

3:11

Listen and point. Color the circles green to show what we eat and blue to show what we drink. Say. Language: drink, eat; apples, bananas, cookies, juice, sandwiches, water; I eat (cookies). I drink (water).

Learning objectives

- Identify and name things we eat and drink
- Listen and understand about things we eat and drink
- Talk about what you eat or drink

Materials

- Class CDs, printable flashcards, *Ferris Wheel* mat, Mimi puppet

Main vocabulary

- drink, eat; apples, bananas, cookies, juice, sandwiches, water

Key language

- I eat (cookies). I drink (water).

Teacher's tip: Categorizing food and drink

Use any available plastic food from the children's classroom and small, unopened cartons of juice, milk or bottles of water. If possible, have two hoops available. Place the apple flashcard in one hoop and the juice flashcard in the other hoop. Have the children categorize the food and drink according to whether we eat or drink it. As they place each item in the hoop, encourage them to say *Eat* or *Drink* as appropriate.

Circle time

Hello song & puppet (CD1 Track 2; see TB p 17 & 21)
Opening routines (see TB p 16)
Recycling activity (see TB p 19)
Lesson aims (see TB p 18)

Introduce content vocabulary.

- Use the printable flashcards and the puppet to introduce the new words *(eat, drink)*. Children repeat the words.
- Alternate miming the actions and saying sentences *I eat. / I drink.* Children point to the flashcards.
- Repeat and children say the sentences with you.

Game: *Eat or drink!*

- Hold up one of the food flashcards, e.g. *bananas*. Have children respond *I eat bananas.* Then hold up the flashcard of water and children say *I drink water.*
- Repeat with different flashcards.

Sort the flashcards.

- Put the printable flashcard of *eat* on one side of the circle and the printable flashcard of *drink* on the other.
- Lay out the food flashcards and children name them.
- Ask children to help you sort the flashcards and place the items you eat next to the *eat* printable flashcard (*banana, apple, sandwich, cookie*) and the items you drink next to the *drink* printable flashcard (*juice, water*).
- Children say sentences about all the items.

Table time

Student's Book p 61

Listen and point.

- Children identify all the food in the photos.
- Play the audio. Children listen and point to the photos.

CD3 Track 11

Auntie Jenny: We need to eat and drink every day.
Sophie: I eat apples. I eat sandwiches.
Tom: I eat cookies. I eat bananas.
Tom: I drink water.
Sophie: I drink juice.
Auntie Jenny: Yes, me too. I eat apples, sandwiches, cookies and bananas. And I drink water and juice!

- Play the audio again. Use the pause button.

Color the circles green to show what we eat and blue to show what we drink.

- Children color the spots green to show what we eat and the spots blue to show the things we drink.

Say.

- Children point to the pictures of the food and drink and say, e.g. *I eat apples.*

Activity Book p 61

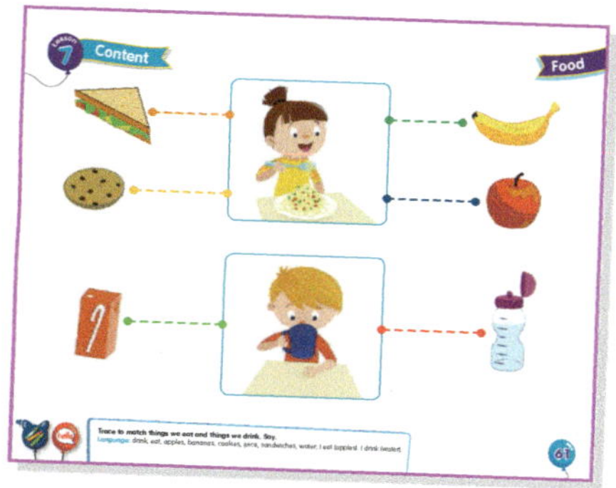

Trace to match things we eat and things we drink.

- Children trace to match the foods to the girl eating and the drinks to the boy drinking.

Say.

- They point and say *I (drink) (water).*

Closing time

Learning review (see TB p 18)
Closing routines (see TB p 16)
Bye bye song and puppet (CD1 Track 3; see TB p 17 & 21)

Use the **Navio App** to play the vocabulary and language games, and encourage children to do the same at home.

Lesson 8

Culture

Food

Watch. Listen, point and sing *Ten little apples.* Color and count the apples and oranges. Say.

Language: apple, orange; little; tree; numbers 1–10

62

Learning objectives

- Watch, sing and act out the traditional song *Ten little apples*
- Play *Pass the flashcard*
- Color and count the apples and oranges
- Identify pictures showing the same number of apples and oranges

Materials

- Class CDs, flashcards, *Ferris Wheel* mat, Mimi puppet

Main vocabulary

- apple, orange; little; tree; numbers 1–10

Teacher's tip: Singing alternative versions of the song

Once the children are familiar with the song, encourage them to suggest and sing creative, alternative versions using other vocabulary they know, e.g. Ten little bananas. Children can also invent actions to go with their version(s) of the song.

Circle time

Hello song & puppet (CD1 Track 2; see TB p 17 & 21)
Opening routines (see TB p 16)
Recycling activity (see TB p 19)
Lesson aims (see TB p 18)

Game: *Pass the flashcard*

- Have ready the food flashcards in a pile. Pick up one, say e.g. *I like apples,* and pass the flashcard to the child next to you. They say *I like apples* and pass the flashcard to the child next to them in the same way. If they don't like apples, they stay silent and just pass on the flashcard.
- Repeat by introducing different flashcards into the circle after three or four turns.

Ten little apples song

CD3 Track 12

- Say *Let's sing the song "Ten little apples."* Use mime and pictures to explain the meaning of *little* and *tree*.
- Play the audio. Children join in doing actions (see TB p 143).
- Play the audio again. Children do actions and join in singing the song.

Watch the *Ten little apples* song video.

- Children watch the video and join in singing the song and doing the actions with Tom and Sophie.

Table time

Student's Book p 62

Watch. Listen, point and sing *Ten little apples.*

CD3 Track 12

- Play the audio. Children listen and point to the apple and oranges.

Color and count the apples and oranges.

- Children color the apples red and the oranges orange. They then count the apples and oranges on each tree.

Say.

- Play the audio again. Children point to the apples and oranges and sing the song.

Activity Book p 62

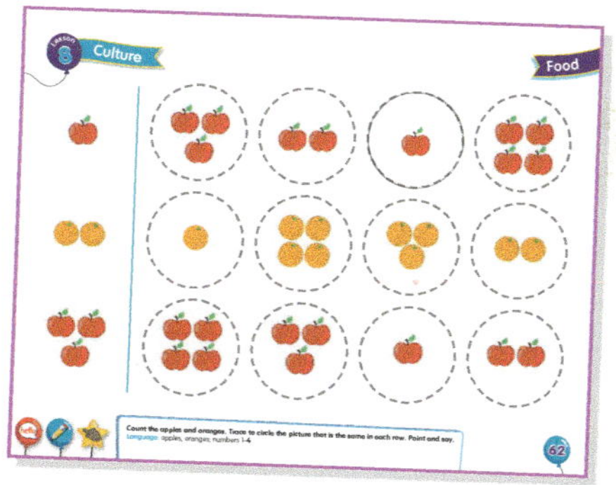

Count the apples and oranges. Trace to circle the picture that is the same in each row.

- Children look at the pictures on the left and count. They find and circle the picture in each row that is the same.

Point and say.

- They point and say, e.g. *Three apples.*

Closing time

Learning review (see TB p 18)
Closing routines (see TB p 16)
Bye bye song and puppet (CD1 Track 3; see TB p 17 & 21)

Use the **Navio App** to watch the video, and encourage children to do the same at home.

Listen, point and say. Color the words you know. Stick the star sticker. Ask and say.
Language: apple, banana, cookie, juice, sandwich, water; I'm hungry. Are you hungry? Can I have (a cookie), please? Here you go. Here's (a banana) for you. Thank you. I like (sandwiches).

Learning objectives

- Review your learning and progress
- Talk about food
- Stick on a star sticker for achievement

Materials

- Class CDs, flashcards, *Ferris Wheel* mat, Mimi puppet

Main vocabulary

- apple, banana, cookie, juice, sandwich, water

Key language

- I'm hungry. Are you hungry? Can I have (a cookie), please? Here you go. Here's (a banana) for you. Thank you. I like (sandwiches).

Teacher's tip: Reflecting on what you know

Once the children have colored the words they know, encourage them to show their completed review to a friend and compare what they know. Remind them to be positive and help each other if they colored only a few items. Ask them to think about what helped them learn the words they know and listen to their response.

Circle time

Hello song & puppet (CD1 Track 2; see TB p 17 & 21)
Opening routines (see TB p 16)
Recycling activity (see TB p 19)
Lesson aims (see TB p 18)

Food flashcard games

- Choose one or two flashcard games with the *Ferris Wheel* mat and/or the puppet (see TB p 20 & 21).

Sing *I like bananas.*

CD3 Track 4

- Lay out the flashcards in the order of the song.
- Play the audio. Children listen, sing and point to the flashcards in each verse.

Game: *Can I have a (cookie)?*

- Have the children sit in pairs facing each other. Show one of the food flashcards and encourage one child to ask *Can I have a (cookie), please?*
- The other child replies *Here you go* and mimes giving their partner a cookie. Repeat and change roles.

Game: *I like (juice).*

- Hold up one of the food flashcards covered by the back of another flashcard so that children can't see what's in the picture. Lower the back of the flashcard down slowly to gradually reveal the picture. Demonstrate that children should say, e.g. *I like (juice)!* as soon as they can tell what the picture is.
- Repeat several times with different flashcards.

Watch the story video.

- Children watch the story video. Ask e.g. *What does Mrs. Cat's class have for the picnic?*

Table time

Student's Book p 63

Listen, point and say.

- Say e.g. *Point to the apple!* and children point to the food.
- Play the audio. Children listen, point to the pictures and say the words.

CD3 Track 13

Mimi: I'm the teacher! Can you remember the food, Dylan?
Dylan: Yes, I can. Apple.
Mimi: Apple.
Dylan: Cookie.
Mimi: Cookie.
Dylan: Sandwich.
Mimi: Sandwich.
Dylan: Banana.
Mimi: Banana.
Dylan: Juice.
Mimi: Juice.
Dylan: Water.
Mimi: Water. Great job, Dylan. Very good!

Color the words you know.

- Children color the food they know.

Stick the star sticker.

- Children stick on the star sticker for achievement.
- Monitor and encourage children to think positively about their progress.

Ask and say.

- Children point to the food and ask and say, e.g. *Can I have an apple, please? Here you go. Thank you. I like apples.*

Activity Book p 63

Color the faces to show the food you know. Ask and say.

- Children color the faces next to the food they know. They ask and say about the food.

Think and color the stars to show your progress.

- Children color the number of stars that they feel shows their progress in this unit.

Closing time

Learning review (see TB p 18)
Closing routines (see TB p 16)
Bye bye song and puppet (CD1 Track 3; see TB p 17 & 21)

Use the **Navio App** to review what children have learned in this unit, and encourage children to do the same at home.

Project

COOPERATIVE LEARNING

Food

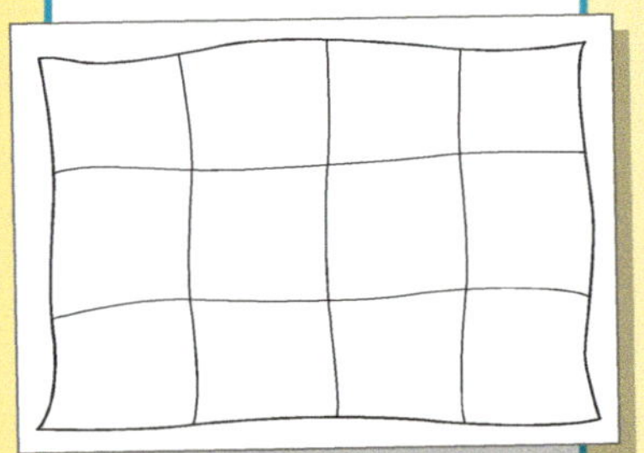

1

2

3

Make food you like for a picnic. Paint a picnic blanket. Make a picnic display. Ask and say.
Language: apple, banana, cookie, juice, sandwich, water; I'm hungry. Are you hungry? Can I have (a cookie), please? Here you go. Here's (a cookie) for you. Thank you. I like (sandwiches). What color is the (apple)? It's (green).

64

Learning objectives

- Work together to do a collaborative project
- Make food items and color a picnic blanket
- Talk about the picnic display
- Express enjoyment of the picnic display
- Count apples and bananas and circle the correct number

Materials

- Class CDs, Mimi puppet, project template, finger paints, modeling clay
- optional: crayons

Main vocabulary

- apple, banana, cookie, juice, sandwich, water

Key language

- I'm hungry. Are you hungry? Can I have (a cookie), please? Here you go. Here's (a cookie) for you. Thank you. I like (sandwiches). What color is the (apple)? It's (green).

Teacher's tip: Developing hand to eye coordination

Playing with modeling clay helps children of pre-primary age develop their hand-eye coordination as they squash and squeeze the modeling clay into food shapes. Monitor while they are working, encouraging them to show you their efforts and tell you what they are making.

Circle time

Hello song & puppet (CD1 Track 2; see TB p 17 & 21)
Opening routines (see TB p 16)
Recycling activity (see TB p 19)
Lesson aims (see TB p 18)

Prepare for your project.

- Say *Let's do a project and make food you like for a picnic!*
- Show children the copies of the picnic blanket templates that you have prepared.
- Demonstrate using modeling clay to make food for the picnic.
- Demonstrate painting the picnic blanket.

Table time

Student's Book p 64

- Say e.g. *We're going to make food we like for a picnic and a picnic blanket. Look at what we need for our project: pictures of the picnic blanket, modeling clay, finger paints.* Children listen and point to the pictures.

Make food you like for a picnic. Paint a picnic blanket.

- Give each child a copy of the picnic blanket template.
- Make sure children have different colored modeling clay available.
- Children use the modeling clay to make food of their choice for their picnic. They then paint their picnic blanket.
- When they are ready, children put their completed food on top of their completed picnic blanket.

Make a picnic display.

- Make a display of all the children's picnic blankets.

Ask and say.

- Children talk about their picnics.
- Ask children *Do you like our picnics?* Make the point that everyone helped make a picnic and that they couldn't have prepared such a beautiful class display on their own.

Alternative version of project

- Children could use crayons instead of finger paints to color their picnic blanket.

Activity Book p 64

Paint the bananas and apples. Count and circle the correct number.

- Children paint the apples and bananas. Then they count them and circle the correct number (3 apples, 5 bananas).

Point, ask and say.

- Children point and act out a mini role-play.

Closing time

Learning review (see TB p 18)
Closing routines (see TB p 16)
Bye bye song and puppet (CD1 Track 3; see TB p 17 & 21)

Pets
The little dog

Vocabulary and language

- **Main vocabulary:** bird, cat, dog, fish, mouse, rabbit
- **Key language:** I have a (mouse). Is this your (fish)? Yes, it is. / No, it isn't. This is my (fish). My fish is (orange).
- **Content language:** fly, swim; Birds fly. Fish swim.
- **Other language:** mommy; happy, sad; blue, nose; little; Is this your mommy? It's (a rabbit). I'm (happy). I'm kind to you. I help you. Little Peter Rabbit has a fly on his nose. What's this? Where's the (yellow) (rabbit)? Here. What color is your (fish)? It's (orange).

Unit objectives

- Identify and name pets
- Sing the language song *I have a cat*
- Ask and say if something is yours
- Understand and join in the story *The little dog*
- Sing and act out the story song *I'm a little dog*
- Sing the values song *I'm kind to you*
- Recognize the value of being kind to others
- Identify and name animals that swim or fly
- Sing and act out the traditional song *Little Peter Rabbit*
- Review your learning and progress
- Participate in a collaborative project

Story

CD3 Track 19

Picture 1

Narrator: Mimi and Dylan see a little dog.
Little dog: I'm sad. I want my mommy.
Mimi: Oh no. Poor little dog.
Dylan: Let's look for your mommy.
Mimi: Yes. Come on. We can help.

Picture 2

Narrator: Mimi and Dylan look everywhere for the little dog's mommy.
Dylan: Is this your mommy?
Little dog: No, it isn't.
Mimi: Oh, Dylan. It's a cat. It's a cat!
Little dog: Oh no. I'm sad. My mommy isn't here. I want my mommy.

Picture 3

Dylan: Is this your mommy?
Little dog: No, it isn't.
Mimi: Oh, Dylan. It's a rabbit. It's a rabbit!
Dog: Oh no. I'm sad. My mommy isn't here. I want my mommy.
Mimi: I have an idea. Let's ask Mommy and Daddy to help.
Dylan: Yes. Come with us, little dog. Don't be sad. Mommy and Daddy can help.

Picture 4

Narrator: Mimi and Dylan take the little dog to Mommy and Daddy.
Mimi: Hello, Mommy.
Dylan: Hello, Daddy.
Mommy: Hello, Mimi and Dylan. Come and meet our new neighbor, Mrs. Dog!
Mimi: Oh, look, little dog! Is this your mommy?
Little dog: Oh yes, it is! Hurray! Hello, Mommy.
Mrs. Dog: Hello, little dog.
Little dog: I have my mommy now. I'm happy.
Mimi: I'm happy too. You're our new neighbor and we can be friends!
Little dog: Oh yes! Thank you, Mimi!

Songs

Language song

I have a cat CD3 Track 17

I have a cat. Meow, meow. (Mime licking the back of your hand like a cat)
I have a cat.
I have a fish. Splash, splash. (Move your arm in a wavy line like a fish swimming)
I have a fish.
I have a rabbit. Hop, hop. (Mime hopping like a rabbit)
I have a rabbit.
I have a bird. Tweet, tweet. (Mime flapping your arms like a bird)
I have a bird.
I have a dog. Woof, woof. (Wave your hand behind you like a dog's tail)
I have a dog.
I have a mouse. Squeak, squeak. (Put your fingers by your nose like whiskers)
I have a mouse.

Story song

I'm a little dog CD3 Track 20

I'm a little dog (Make your hands into dog ears)
I'm sad. I want my mommy (Make a sad face)
I'm a little dog (Make your hands into dog ears)
I'm sad. I want my mommy. (Make a sad face)
Is this your mommy? (Point to the cat flashcard)
No, it isn't. (Waggle your index finger)
It's a cat. It's a cat. (Mime stroking whiskers like a cat)
Is this your mommy? (Point to the rabbit flashcard)
No, it isn't. (Waggle your index finger)
It's a rabbit. It's a rabbit. (Make your hands into bunny ears and jump in place)
Is this your mommy? (Point to the dog flashcard)
Yes, it is. (Nod enthusiastically)
It's a dog. It's a dog. (Make your hands into dog ears)
I'm a little dog (Make your hands into dog ears)
I'm happy. Hello, Mommy (Smile and wave)
I'm a little dog (Make your hands into dog ears)
I'm happy. Hello, Mommy. (Smile and wave)

Values song

I'm kind to you CD3 Track 23

I'm kind to you. (Point to your friend)
You're kind to me. (Point to yourself)
This is the way (Hold hands and dance together)
We like to be.
I help you. (Point to your friend)
You help me. (Point to yourself)
This is the way (Hold hands and dance together)
We like to be.
I'm kind to you. (Point to your friend)
You're kind to me. (Point to yourself)
This is the way (Hold hands and dance together)
We like to be
I help you. (Point to your friend)
You help me. (Point to yourself)
This is the way (Hold hands and dance together)
We like to be.

Culture song

Little Peter Rabbit CD3 Track 25

Little Peter Rabbit has a fly on his nose, (Make your hands into bunny ears then tap nose)
Little Peter Rabbit has a fly on his nose,
Little Peter Rabbit has a fly on his nose,
And he flips it, and he flops it (Mime shooing the fly away with one hand and then the other)
And it flies away. (Make flying movements with both hands)
Little Peter Rabbit has a fly on his nose, (Make your hands into bunny ears then tap nose)
Little Peter Rabbit has a fly on his nose,
Little Peter Rabbit has a fly on his nose,
And he flips it, and he flops it (Mime shooing the fly away with one hand and then the other)
And it flies away. (Make flying movements with both hands)

Pets
The little dog

Vocabulary Lesson 1

3:14 hello 3:15

Listen, point and repeat. Listen and play. Stick the pet stickers. Say.
Language: bird, fish, mouse, rabbit; orange, pink, red, yellow

Learning objectives

- Identify and name pets
- Listen and point to pets
- Listen and play *Round and round and round*

Materials

- Class CDs, flashcards, *Ferris Wheel* mat, Mimi puppet

Main vocabulary

- bird, fish, mouse, rabbit; orange, pink, red, yellow

Teacher's tip: Using actions to help children learn vocabulary

Introducing an action for each animal will help children memorize the new vocabulary. As you name the pets, do an action at the same time, e.g. two hands by the side of your head for rabbit ears, flap your arms like wings for bird, etc. Encourage the children to do the action as they say each word.

Circle time

Hello song & puppet (CD1 Track 2; see TB p 17 & 21)

Opening routines (see TB p 16)

Lesson aims (see TB p 18)

Introduce pet vocabulary.

- Say *Let's learn about pets.* Explain that pets are animals that you keep in the home.
- Use the puppet to hold up the flashcards in turn and introduce the words. Children repeat the words.
- Put the *Ferris Wheel* mat on the floor or board with the pet flashcards face down (one on each color). Use the puppet to turn them over and name them. The children repeat the words.

Game: *Find the fish!*

- Name the pet and one or two children to find and touch the correct flashcard as fast as they can.

Game: *Say the color!*

- Name the pet and children name the color. Then the reverse.

Table time

Student's Book p 65

Listen, point and repeat.

- Play the audio. Children listen and point to each word as they hear it.

CD3 Track 14

Mimi: Look, Dylan! Fish … mouse… rabbit … bird … hee, hee, hee! Repeat, Dylan!
Dylan: Yes, Mimi! Fish … mouse… rabbit … bird … hee, hee, hee!
Mimi: Very good, Dylan. Let's say the words together!
Both: Fish … mouse… rabbit … bird … hee, hee, hee!

- Play the audio again. Children listen and repeat the words.

Listen and play.

- Hold up your index finger and move it around clockwise like a wheel. Children do the same. Play the audio. Children listen, point to the color when they hear it, and say the word.

CD3 Track 15

Mimi: Round and round and round: Pink … bird!
Dylan: Bird!
Mimi: Round and round and round: Yellow … rabbit!
Dylan: Rabbit!
Mimi: Round and round and round: Orange … mouse!
Dylan: Mouse!
Mimi: Round and round and round: Red … fish!
Dylan: Fish!

- Play the game with you and/or individual children naming colors and others responding with the words.

Stick the pet stickers.

- Children put on the pet stickers.

Say.

- Children point to the pets and say the words.

Activity Book p 65

Trace to match the body parts to the pets. Color the pets' body parts.

- Children trace to match the body parts to the pets. They then color the pet's body parts.

Point and say.

- Children point and name the pets.

Closing time

Learning review (see TB p 18)

Closing routines (see TB p 16)

Bye bye song and puppet (CD1 Track 3; see TB p 17 & 21)

Use the **Navio App** to play the vocabulary game, and encourage children to do the same at home.

Lesson 2 Language

3:16 3:17 hello

Listen and find the new pets. Listen, point and sing *I have a cat.* Trace to match the cat and the dog. Say.
Language: bird, cat, dog, fish, mouse, rabbit; I have a (mouse).

66

Learning objectives

- Talk about pets
- Identify and name two new pets
- Sing the language song *I have a cat*
- Talk about pets you have

Materials

- Class CDs, flashcards, *Ferris Wheel* mat, Mimi puppet

Main vocabulary

- bird, cat, dog, fish, mouse, rabbit

Key language

- I have (a mouse).

Teacher's tip: Playing an action game

Introduce actions for the two new pets and play an action game to reinforce the vocabulary before introducing the language structure. Name each pet and encourage the children to do the action. Show the flashcard to check. Change roles, do the action yourself and the children name the animal.

Circle time

Hello song & puppet (CD1 Track 2; see TB p 17 & 21)
Opening routines (see TB p 16)
Recycling activity (four pet words from Lesson 1) (see TB p 19)
Lesson aims (see TB p 18)

Introduce the new pets.

- Put all six pet flashcards on the floor or board. The children identify the two new words.
- Use the puppet to point to and say the words in turn. Children repeat in chorus.
- Turn the two new flashcards face down. Mix them up. Point to one and ask *Cat or dog?* Children guess. Repeat several times.

Introduce *I have a (mouse).*

- Put the pet flashcards on the floor or board. Hold up e.g. the dog and say, e.g. *I have a dog.* Smile and pretend to stroke the dog to show what you mean.
- Repeat with one or two other flashcards. Children repeat the sentences with you.
- Give individual children a flashcard. Get the children to take turns holding them up to the class and saying with you, e.g. *I have a fish.*

Game: *Name the pet!*

- Put the flashcards face up on the floor or board. Children name the pets as you do this.
- Make the noise of one of the pets, e.g. *Miaow!* Children point to the flashcard and name the pet.
- Repeat with other noises and pets (see TB p 165).

***I have a cat* song**

CD3 Track 17

- Put the flashcards face up in the order of the song.
- Play the audio. Children listen and point to the flashcards.
- Play the audio again. Children listen and join in singing and acting out the song by pretending to be the animal in each verse (see TB p 165).

Table time

Student's Book p 66

Listen and find the new pets.

- Hold up your book. Point to the photos of Tom and Sophie and children say the names.
- Play the audio. Children listen and find the two new words. Repeat and children say the words.

CD3 Track 16

Sophie: Find the … cat! Cat!
Tom: Cat! Here!
Sophie: Find the … dog! Dog!
Tom: Dog! Here!

Listen, point and sing *I have a cat.*

CD3 Track 17

- Play the song. Children listen, sing and point to the pets.
- Remember that you can use the karaoke version of the song when the children are confident.

Trace to match the cat and the dog.

- Hold up your book and demonstrate matching the photos of the cat and dog to Tom and Sophie's pictures.
- Play the audio again. Pause after each verse and children match the pets.

Say.

- Children point to the pets and say, e.g. *I have a dog.*

Activity Book p 66

Follow and draw paths from the children to their pets.

- Children draw paths from the children to their pets.

Point and say.

- Children point and say *I have a (dog).*

Closing time

Learning review (see TB p 18)
Closing routines (see TB p 16)
Bye bye song and puppet (CD1 Track 3; see TB p 17 & 21)

Use the **Navio App** to listen to the song, and encourage children to do the same at home.

Lesson 3 Story

Watch. Listen to the story *The little dog*. Trace to circle the animal in the story. Stick the story sticker. Ask and say. Language: cat, dog, rabbit; mommy; happy, sad; Is this your mommy? Yes, it is. / No, it isn't. It's (a rabbit). I'm (happy).

Learning objectives

- Watch, understand and enjoy the story *The little dog*
- Make a prediction about the story
- Look and find pets
- Identify and circle the animal in the story

Materials

- Class CDs, printable story cards, flashcards, *Ferris Wheel* mat, Mimi puppet

Main vocabulary

- cat, dog, rabbit; mommy; happy, sad

Key language

- Is this your mommy? Yes, it is. / No, it isn't. It's a (rabbit). I'm (happy).

Teacher's tip: Developing empathy

Ask the children how the dog feels *(sad)*. Ask them if they sometimes have a friend who feels sad. What can they do? Demonstrate listening carefully, giving the friend a hug, or playing with them to help them feel better.

Circle time

Hello song & puppet (CD1 Track 2; see TB p 17 & 21)
Opening routines (see TB p 16)
Recycling activity (*I have a …* and pets) (see TB p 19)
Lesson aims (see TB p 18)

Introduce the story *The little dog*.

- Say *It's story time!* Play the *Story rhyme* (CD1 Track 4; see TB p 17).
- Say *Tom and Sophie are listening to a story about Mimi, Dylan and a little dog. Guess who Mimi and Dylan help the little dog look for.* Listen to children's answers.

Watch or listen to the story.

CD3 Track 19

- Play the audio, watch the video or read the story using the printable story cards. Pause, repeat words, point to the pictures, ask questions.
- Ask the question again *Who do Mimi and Dylan help the little dog look for? (the little dog's mommy).*
- Repeat the story. Encourage children to join in with the words and phrases in the story.
- Ask *Do you like the story? Does the little dog find its mommy?*

Look and find.

- Say e.g. *Find a cat!* Children look at the story and point to the picture as fast as they can.
- Repeat with other animals in the story.

Table time

Student's Book p 67

Watch. Listen to the story *The little dog*.

- Read or play the story again. Children listen and follow the story by pointing to the pictures in their books.

Trace to circle the animal in the story.

- Demonstrate tracing to circle the animal in the story (i.e. the dog).

Stick the story sticker.

- Children stick on the story sticker.

Story questions

Picture 1
Who do Mimi and Dylan see? *(A little dog)*
Is the little dog happy? *(No)*

Picture 2
Is the little dog's mommy here? *(No)*
What is it? *(A cat)*

Picture 3
Is the little dog's mommy here? *(No)*
What is it? *(A rabbit)*

Picture 4
Who is the new neighbor? *(Mrs. Dog)*
Is the little dog happy? *(Yes)*

Ask and say.

- Children ask and answer questions, e.g. *Is this your mommy? No, it isn't.*
- Ask *Is the little dog happy at the end of the story? Are Mimi and the little dog friends?* and the children respond.

Activity Book p 67

Trace to circle the little dog's mommy.

- Children trace to circle the picture of the little dog's mommy.

Point, ask and say.

- Children point, ask and answer about each mommy animal.

Closing time

Learning review (see TB p 18)
Closing routines (see TB p 16)
Bye bye song and puppet (CD1 Track 3; see TB p 17 & 21)

Use the **Navio App** to watch the video, and encourage children to do the same at home.

Story Song

Watch. Listen, point and sing *I'm a little dog*. Color the little dog's mommy. Ask and say.
Language: cat, dog, rabbit; mommy; happy, sad; Is this your mommy? Yes, it is. / No, it isn't. It's (a rabbit). I'm (happy).

Learning objectives

- Watch, sing and act out the story song *I'm a little dog*
- Listen to the story again and identify the pets
- Play *Is this your mommy?*
- Ask and answer about the story characters

Materials

- Class CDs, printable story cards, flashcards, *Ferris Wheel* mat, Mimi puppet

Main vocabulary

- cat, dog, rabbit; mommy; happy, sad

Key language

- Is this your mommy? Yes, it is. / No, it isn't. It's (a rabbit). I'm (happy).

Teacher's tip: Getting children's attention

Establish a routine signal to ensure that you have the attention of the whole class before you start to give instructions. You may like to, e.g. ring a small bell, shake a maraca or count down from three. The important thing is to be consistent so that children recognize immediately when they need to stop whatever they are doing and listen.

Circle time

Hello song & puppet (CD1 Track 2; see TB p 17 & 21)
Opening routines (see TB p 16)
Recycling activity (pet vocabulary) (see TB p 19)
Lesson aims (see TB p 18)

Retell the story *The little dog*.

- Play the audio, video or read the story using the printable story cards.
- Demonstrate that children should wave their arms in the air every time they hear the name of an animal in the story.

Game: *Is this your mommy?*

- Lay out the pet flashcards face down. Make sure you know where the flashcard of the dog is so that you turn this over last.
- Mime being the little dog in the story and get children to do the same.
- Turn over one of the flashcards and ask, e.g. *Is this your mommy?* Shake your head, say *No, it isn't* and encourage children to do the same.
- Repeat with all the flashcards until you turn over the flashcard of the dog and children say with you *Yes, it is!*
- Repeat once or twice.

***I'm a little dog* song**

CD3 Track 20

- Watch the video. Children listen and mime being the little dog and looking sad until the last verse when they jump up and down with happiness.
- Watch the video again. Children join in singing the song and do the actions (see TB p 165).

Table time

Student's Book p 68

Watch. Listen, point and sing *I'm a little dog.*

CD3 Track 20

- Play the audio of the song. Children listen, sing and point to the pictures.
- Remember that you can use the karaoke version of the song when the children are confident.

Color the little dog's mommy.

- Children color the little dog's mommy (i.e. the dog in the third picture).

Ask and say.

- Children point to the pictures and ask and answer questions, e.g. *Is this your mommy? No, it isn't. / Yes, it is.*

Activity Book p 68

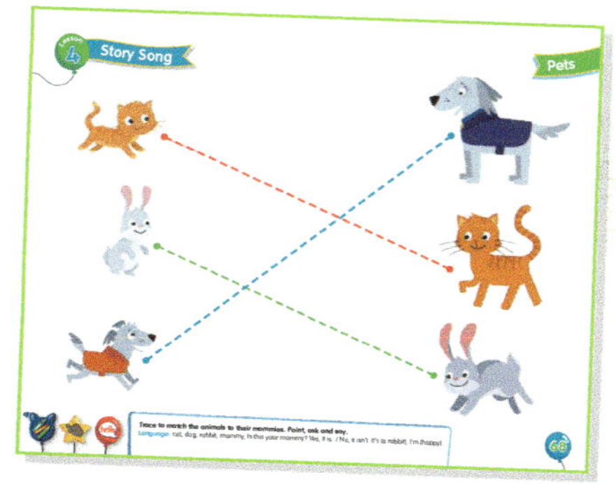

Trace to match the animals to their mommies.

- Children trace to match the animals to their mommies.

Point, ask and say.

- Children point, ask and answer about each mommy animal.

Closing time

Learning review (see TB p 18)
Closing routines (see TB p 16)
Bye bye song and puppet (CD1 Track 3; see TB p 17 & 21)

Use the **Navio App** to watch the video, and encourage children to do the same at home.

Watch. Listen and point. Color the circles to show the colors of Sophie and Tom's pets. Ask and say. Language: bird, fish; blue, orange; I have (a bird). Is this your (fish)? Yes, it is. / No, it isn't. This is my (fish). My fish is (orange).

69

Learning objectives

- Talk about your pets
- Watch, understand and enjoy a video
- Identify the characters' pets in the video

Materials

- Class CDs, flashcards, *Ferris Wheel* mat, Mimi puppet

Main vocabulary

- bird, fish; blue, orange

Key language

- I have (a bird). Is this your (fish)? Yes, it is. / No, it isn't. This is my (fish). My fish is (orange).

Teacher's tip: Caring for pets

Life skills

Ask the children if they have a pet. Use the opportunity to introduce the importance of caring for animals. Make sure the children realize that pets are our friends and that we have a responsibility to look after them. Use any toy animals in the classroom to act out different ways of caring for pets, e.g. feeding fish, brushing a dog, giving milk to a cat, etc.

Circle time

Hello song & puppet (CD1 Track 2; see TB p 17 & 21)
Opening routines (see TB p 16)
Recycling activity (story song) (CD3 Track 20; see TB p 19)
Lesson aims (see TB p 18)

Game: *I have a fish!*

- Give out the pet flashcards to different children in the circle.
- Demonstrate that children should pass the flashcards around the circle clockwise. Either play music and pause, or say *Stop!* and children who have one of the flashcards take turns holding them up and saying, e.g. *I have a cat.*
- Repeat several times.

Watch the video.

- Explain that Tom and Sophie are telling Auntie Jenny about their pets.
- Play the video of Auntie Jenny, Tom and Sophie.
- Ask *What's Sophie's pet? (fish) What color is it? (orange) What's Tom's pet? (bird) What color is it? (blue).*
- Watch again. Pause and children repeat the questions and answers starting with *Is this your …?*
- Ask *Do you like Sophie and Tom's pets?* and listen to the children's response.

Table time

Student's Book p 69

Life skills

Watch. Listen and point.

- Children identify Auntie Jenny, Tom and Sophie in the photo and the pets in the pictures.
- Play the audio. Children listen and point to the pets.

CD3 Track 22

Auntie Jenny:	Tell me about your pets.
Sophie:	I have a fish.
Auntie Jenny:	Is this your fish, Sophie?
Sophie:	Yes, it is. This is my fish. My fish is orange.
Auntie Jenny:	What a great orange fish, Sophie!
Auntie Jenny:	What about you, Tom?
Tom:	I have a bird.
Auntie Jenny:	Is this your bird?
Tom:	No, it isn't. My bird is blue.
Auntie Jenny:	Is this your bird?
Tom:	Yes, it is. This is my bird.
Auntie Jenny:	What a beautiful blue bird, Tom!
Tom:	Yes. I like my bird.
Sophie:	And I like my fish.

Color the circles to show the colors of Sophie and Tom's pets.

- Play the audio again. Use the pause button and children color the circles to show the colors of Sophie and Tom's pets (i.e. the orange fish and the blue bird). Check they have done this correctly.

Ask and say.

- Children take turns pointing to the pictures and pretending to be Sophie or Tom. They ask and say, e.g. *Is this your fish? Yes, it is. / No, it isn't.*

Activity Book p 69

Trace to match the children to their pets. Color the pets.

- Children trace to match the children to their pets. They then color the pets.

Ask and say.

- Children ask and answer about the pets.

Closing time

Learning review (see TB p 18)
Closing routines (see TB p 16)
Bye bye song and puppet (CD1 Track 3; see TB p 17 & 21)

Use the **Navio App** to watch the video, and encourage children to do the same at home.

Values I'm kind to you

Listen, point and sing *I'm kind to you*. Color the faces to show how you're kind. Say.
Language: I'm kind to you. I help you.

SOCIAL AND EMOTIONAL LEARNING

70

Learning objectives

- Recognize the value of being kind to others
- Sing the values song *I'm kind to you*
- Say how you're kind to others

Materials

- Class CDs, flashcards, *Ferris Wheel* mat, Mimi puppet

Key language

- I'm kind to you. I help you.

Teacher's tip: Being kind to others

Ask the children to tell you the different ways Mimi is kind in the four pictures (in their shared language). Then ask them to think of other ways in which they are kind to their friends and family. Ask them why it's important to be kind and help each other and listen to their ideas. From now on, whenever appropriate, say e.g. *You're kind. / Thank you for your help.* to show children how much you value these qualities.

Circle time

Hello song & puppet (CD1 Track 2; see TB p 17 & 21)
Opening routines (see TB p 16)
Recycling activity (*Is this your …? Yes, it is. / No, it isn't.*) (see TB p 19)
Lesson aims (see TB p 18)

Watch *The little dog* story video.

- Play the story video.
- Children watch and repeat every time they hear the name of an animal.
- Ask e.g. *Do Mimi and Dylan help the little dog find its mommy? (Yes) Are they kind / helpful to the little dog?* Explain the meaning of *kind* and *help*. Ask *Is it important to be kind to / to help other people?* Listen to the children's responses.

***I'm kind to you* song**

CD3 Track 23

- Children stand up with a partner. Play the audio. Children listen and do the actions (see TB p 165).
- Play the audio again. Children do the actions and join in singing the song.
- Use children's shared language to make the point that it's important to be kind and help others when we can.

Table time

Student's Book p 70

- Children look at the pictures that show different ways of being kind to others.
- Hold up your book, point to the pictures in turn and say e.g. *Mimi says: I'm kind to you* (to the little dog); *I help you* (with Dylan and the crayons); *I'm kind to you* (when Dylan is sad); *I help you* (with Dylan and the book).

Listen, point and sing *I'm kind to you.*

CD3 Track 23

- Play the audio of the song. Children sing and point to the picture for each verse.

Color the faces to show how you're kind.

- Demonstrate that children should color the smiley faces to show the ways they are kind to others. Make sure they realize there are no correct answers.

Say.

- Children point to their completed pictures and say, e.g. *I help you.*

Activity Book p 70

Choose, draw and color a picture of you being kind to others. Draw your friend.

- Children choose and draw themselves in one of the first three pictures to show how they are kind to others. They draw themselves with a friend in the final picture.

Say.

- Children say *I'm kind to you. I help you.*

Closing time

Learning review (see TB p 18)
Closing routines (see TB p 16)
Bye bye song and puppet (CD1 Track 3; see TB p 17 & 21)

Use the **Navio App** to listen to the song, and encourage children to do the same at home.

Listen and point. Color the animal that flies red. Color the animal that swims green. Say. Language: fly, swim; birds, fish; Birds fly. Fish swim.

Learning objectives

- Identify animals that swim or fly
- Listen and understand a dialogue about how birds and fish move
- Talk about how birds and fish move

Materials

- Class CDs, printable flashcards, *Ferris Wheel* mat, Mimi puppet

Main vocabulary

- fly, swim; birds, fish

Key language

- Birds fly. Fish swim.

Teacher's tip: Classifying animals

Use two large pieces of card, one blue and one green, for a classification activity. Place the fish flashcard on the blue card and the bird flashcard on the green card. Pick out animals from the toy box that fly or swim, e.g. a turtle or a parrot, and ask children to put them in the right place.

Circle time

Hello song & puppet (CD1 Track 2; see TB p 17 & 21)
Opening routines (see TB p 16)
Recycling activity (see TB p 19)
Lesson aims (see TB p 18)

Introduce content vocabulary.

- Use the printable flashcards and the puppet to introduce the new words (*swim, fly*). Children repeat the words.
- Alternate miming the actions and saying the words. Children do the same and repeat the words.
- Lay out the flashcards and children name the pets. Ask them to identify the pet that swims *(fish)* and the one that flies *(bird)*.

Game: *Mimi says … !*

- Children stand up. Demonstrate the game. Say e.g. *Mimi says "Swim!"* and children mime swimming. Then say *Mimi says "Stop!"* and children freeze in position. Repeat with *fly*.
- Alternate giving instructions several times and children respond.

Game: *Fish swim!*

- Hold up one of the pet flashcards, e.g. *fish*, and say *Fish swim!* and do the action for *swim*. Demonstrate that if the sentence is true, children should mime swimming and repeat the sentence. If it isn't true, they should fold their arms and stay silent.
- Repeat with different animals and obviously true and false sentences, e.g. *Dogs fly!* and children respond.

Table time

Student's Book p 71

Listen and point.

- Children identify the animals in the photos.
- Play the audio. Children listen and point to the photos.

CD3 Track 24

Auntie Jenny: Animals move in different ways. Some animals fly.
Sophie: Birds fly.
Auntie Jenny: Yes. Some animals swim.
Tom: Fish swim.
Auntie Jenny: Yes. Birds fly and fish swim. Very good!

Color the animal that flies red. Color the animal that swims green.

- Play the audio again. Use the pause button. Children color the animal that flies red (i.e. the bird) and the animal that swims green (i.e the fish).

Say.

- Children point to the pictures and say, e.g. *Birds fly. / Fish swim.*

Activity Book p 71

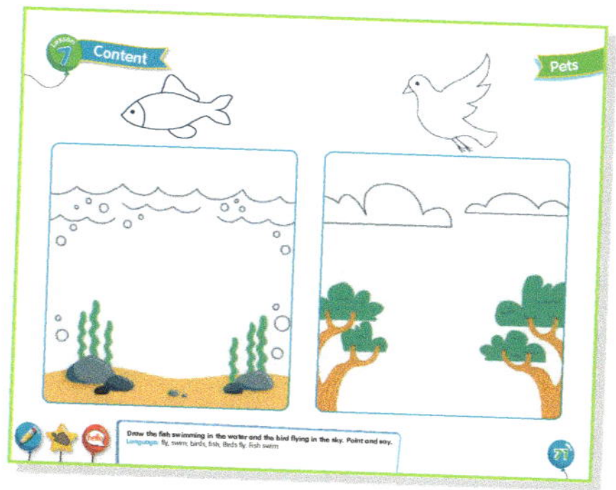

Draw the fish swimming in the water and the bird flying in the sky.

- Children draw the fish swimming in the water and the bird flying in the sky.

Point and say.

- Children point and say *Fish swim. / Birds fly.*

Closing time

Learning review (see TB p 18)
Closing routines (see TB p 16)
Bye bye song and puppet (CD1 Track 3; see TB p 17 & 21)

Use the **Navio App** to play the vocabulary and language games, and encourage children to do the same at home.

Lesson 8 Culture

Pets

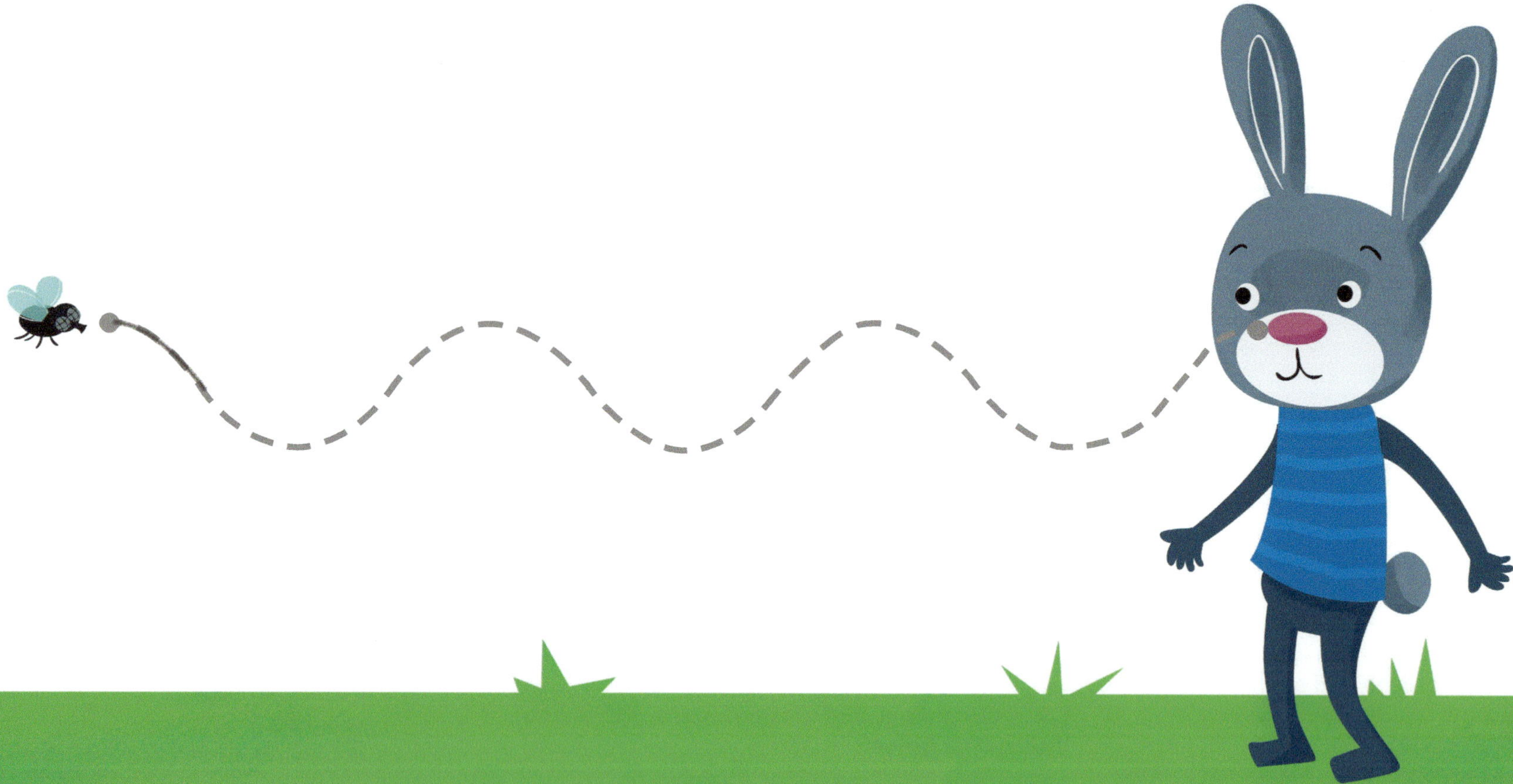

Watch. Listen, point and sing *Little Peter Rabbit*. Trace the line of the fly to Peter Rabbit's nose. Say. **Language:** fly, rabbit; nose; little; Little Peter Rabbit has a fly on his nose.

72

Learning objectives

- Watch, sing and act out the traditional song *Little Peter Rabbit*
- Play *Pass the flashcard*
- Trace the line of the fly to Peter Rabbit's nose
- Complete a dot-to-dot puzzle and count from 1–10

Materials

- Class CDs, flashcards, *Ferris Wheel* mat, Mimi puppet

Main vocabulary

- fly, rabbit; nose; little

Key language

- Little Peter Rabbit has a fly on his nose.

Teacher's tip: Performing the song

Providing children with the opportunity to give a performance helps build confidence in their ability to speak English. Prepare children to informally perform the culture song for their class teacher, parents or carers, and/or record them singing and acting out the song and allow them to enjoy watching their own performance.

Circle time

Hello song & puppet (CD1 Track 2; see TB p 17 & 21)
Opening routines (see TB p 16)
Recycling activity (see TB p 19)
Lesson aims (see TB p 18)

Game: *Pass the flashcard.*

- Have ready the pet flashcards in a pile. Pick up one, say, e.g. *I have a rabbit,* and pass the flashcard to the child next to you. They say *I have a rabbit* and pass the flashcard to the child next to them in the same way.
- Repeat by introducing different flashcards into the circle after three or four turns.

***Little Peter Rabbit* song**

CD3 Track 25

- Say *Let's sing the song "Little Peter Rabbit."*
- Children stand up. Demonstrate holding your hands to the side of your head as rabbit ears.
- Play the audio. Children join in doing actions (see TB p 165).
- Play the audio again. Children do actions and join in singing the song.

Watch the *Little Peter Rabbit* song video.

- Children watch the video and join in singing the song and doing the actions with Tom and Sophie.

Table time

Student's Book p 72

Watch. Listen, point and sing *Little Peter Rabbit*.

CD3 Track 25

- Play the audio. Children listen, sing and point to the rabbit and the fly.

Trace the line of the fly to Peter Rabbit's nose.

- Children trace the line of the fly to Peter Rabbit's nose.

Say.

- Play the audio again. Children follow the line of the fly with their finger and sing the song.

Activity Book p 72

Point and count the dots. Connect the dots in order to complete the rabbit.

- Children point to the numbers as they count the dots. Then they connect the dots in the correct order to complete the rabbit.

Color.

- Children color the rabbit.

Closing time

Learning review (see TB p 18)
Closing routines (see TB p 16)
Bye bye song and puppet (CD1 Track 3; see TB p 17 & 21)

Use the **Navio App** to watch the video, and encourage children to do the same at home.

Review

Pets

Listen, point and say. Color the words you know. Stick the star sticker. Ask and say. **Language:** bird, cat, dog, fish, mouse, rabbit; I have (a mouse). Is this your (cat)? Yes, it is. / No, it isn't. This is my (mouse).

73

Learning objectives

- Review your learning and progress
- Talk about pets
- Stick on a star sticker for achievement

Materials

- Class CDs, flashcards, *Ferris Wheel* mat, Mimi puppet

Main vocabulary

- bird, cat, dog, fish, mouse, rabbit

Key language

- I have (a mouse). Is this your (cat)? Yes, it is. / No, it isn't. This is my (mouse).

Teacher's tip: Working with different partners

COOPERATIVE LEARNING

Working with a partner helps children learn to cooperate. Ask them to complete their review with the person next to them. Once they have completed the review, encourage them to change partners and compare their results with someone different.

Circle time

Hello song & puppet (CD1 Track 2; see TB p 17 & 21)
Opening routines (see TB p 16)
Recycling activity (see TB p 19)
Lesson aims (see TB p 18)

Pet flashcard games

- Choose one or two flashcard games with the *Ferris Wheel* mat and/or the puppet to review key vocabulary (see TB p 20 & 21).

Sing *I have a cat.*

CD3 Track 17

- Lay out the flashcards in the order of the song.
- Play the audio. Children listen, sing and point to the flashcards in each verse.

Game: ***Noisy pets!***

- Hold one of the pets flashcards facing you. Name it and have the children make the corresponding noise or mime, e.g. *Miaow!* Turn the flashcard around to check.
- Then reverse roles, making the noise yourself and having the class name the pet. Repeat with all the pets.

Game: ***I have a (fish).***

- Put a flashcard on your head without looking at it. Say *I have a (fish).* If you name the flashcard correctly, children repeat the sentence and say *Hooray!* If not, they say, *No, no, no and fold their arms.*

Watch the story video.

- Children watch the story video. Ask e.g. *Who is the little dog's friend at the end of the story?*

Table time

Student's Book p 73

Listen, point and say.

- Say e.g. *Point to the cat!* and children point to the pets.
- Play the audio. Children listen, point to the pets and say the words.

CD3 Track 26

Mimi: I'm the teacher! Can you remember the pets, Dylan?
Dylan: Yes, I can. Rabbit.
Mimi: Rabbit.
Dylan: Mouse.
Mimi: Mouse.
Dylan: Fish.
Mimi: Fish.
Dylan: Bird.
Mimi: Bird.
Dylan: Dog.
Mimi: Dog.
Dylan: Cat.
Mimi: Cat. Great job, Dylan. Very good!

Color the words you know.

- Children color the pets they know.

Stick the star sticker.

- Children stick on the star sticker for achievement.
- Monitor and encourage children to think positively about their progress.

Ask and say.

- Children point to the pets and ask and say, e.g. *Is this your (cat)? Yes, it is. / No, it isn't.*

Activity Book p 73

Color the faces to show the pets you know. Ask and say.

- Children color the faces next to the pets they know. They ask and say about the pets.

Think and color the stars to show your progress.

- Children color the number of stars that they feel shows their progress in this unit.

Closing time

Learning review (see TB p 18)
Closing routines (see TB p 16)
Bye bye song and puppet (CD1 Track 3; see TB p 17 & 21)

Use the **Navio App** to review what children have learned in this unit, and encourage children to do the same at home.

Project

COOPERATIVE LEARNING

Paint and decorate your favorite pet. Make a poster of your favorite pets. Ask and say.
Language: cat, dog, fish, rabbit; colors; Is this your (cat)? Yes, it is. / No, it isn't. I have (a dog). What's this? It's (a cat). Where's the (yellow) (rabbit)? Here. This is my (fish). What color is your (fish)? It's (orange).

Pets

Project

Learning objectives

- Work together to do a collaborative project
- Choose and color your favorite pet
- Talk about the pets on the poster
- Express enjoyment of the pets poster
- Make a pets collage

Materials

- Class CDs, Mimi puppet, project template, finger paints, tissue paper, glue
- optional: crayons

Main vocabulary

- cat, dog, fish, rabbit; colors

Key language

- Is this your (cat)? Yes, it is. / No, it isn't. I have (a dog). What's this? It's (a cat). Where's the (yellow) (rabbit)? Here. This is my (fish). What color is your (fish)? It's (orange).

Teacher's tip: Coloring inside the lines

If children find it challenging to color or paint inside the lines, show them how to make smaller hand movements and to take their time when coloring and painting. Encourage their efforts and give lots of praise.

Circle time

Hello song & puppet (CD1 Track 2; see TB p 17 & 21)
Opening routines (see TB p 16)
Recycling activity (see TB p 19)
Lesson aims (see TB p 18)

Prepare for your project.

- Say *Let's do a project and make a poster of our favorite pets!*
- Show children the copies of the pet templates that you have prepared.
- Demonstrate painting and gluing small balls of tissue paper on the pet templates.

Table time

Student's Book p 74

- Say e.g. *We're going to make a poster of our favorite pets like this. Look at what we need for our project: pictures of pets, finger paints, tissue paper, glue.* Children listen and point to the pictures.

Paint and decorate your favorite pet.

- Children choose their favorite pet (from the ones on the template). Give each child a copy of the animal they choose.
- Make sure children have finger paints, tissue paper and glue available.
- Children paint and glue tissue paper on their pet.

Make a poster of your favorite pets.

- When they are ready, children glue their completed pets on the poster you have prepared.

Ask and say.

- Children talk about the pets on the poster.
- Ask children *Do you like the poster of our favorite pets?* Make the point that everyone helped make the poster and that they couldn't have made such a beautiful poster on their own.

Alternative version of project

- Children could use crayons instead of finger paints to color their pet.

Activity Book p 74

Find and glue pictures of pets.

- Children find and glue pictures of pets to make a collage.

Point, ask and say.

- Children point, ask and answer about the pets in their collage.

Closing time

Learning review (see TB p 18)
Closing routines (see TB p 16)
Bye bye song and puppet (CD1 Track 3; see TB p 17 & 21)

Beach
Five little crabs

Vocabulary and language

- **Main vocabulary:** bucket, crab, ocean, sand, shell, shovel; blue, green, orange, yellow
- **Key language:** I can see a (crab). Me too. How many (shells)? (Four). What color are the (shells)? They're (pink).
- **Content language:** land, water; cat, fish; (Fish) live in (water). (Cats) live on (land).
- **Other language:** numbers 1–10; little; trees; pink; I can see (five) little crabs. I love the (blue) (ocean). Is this your (bucket)? Yes, it is. / No, it isn't. I have (a shovel). What's this? It's (a crab). Where's the (green) (bucket)? Here.

Unit objectives

- Identify and name things at the beach
- Sing the language song *I can see the ocean*
- Say what you can see and ask how many
- Understand and act out the story *Five little crabs*
- Sing and act out the story song *One, two, three, four, five little crabs*
- Sing the values song *I love our world*
- Recognize the value of respecting nature
- Identify and name animals that live on land or in water
- Sing and act out the traditional song *One, two, three, four, five*
- Review your learning and progress
- Participate in a collaborative project

Story

CD3 Track 32

Picture 1

Narrator: It's hot and sunny. Mimi and Dylan are at the beach.
Mimi: Oh wow. Look, Dylan. I can see little crabs.
Dylan: Where?
Mimi: On the sand.
Dylan: Oh yes. How many little crabs, Mimi?
Mimi: I can see one … two … three … four … five little crabs!
Dylan: One … two … three … four … five little crabs. Oh yes! Me too!

Picture 2

Dylan: Look, Mimi. The little crabs walk like this.
Mimi: They want to go to the ocean, but the ocean is over there!
Dylan: Let's help the crabs.
Mimi: I have an idea. Where's your bucket and shovel?
Dylan: Here!

Picture 3

Narrator: The little crabs go into the bucket.
Mimi: One …
Dylan: two …
Mimi: three …
Dylan: four …
Mimi: five little crabs! Sit in the bucket, little crabs!
Dylan: Come on, let's take the crabs to the ocean.

Picture 4

Narrator: Mimi and Dylan put the little crabs in the ocean.
Mimi: One …
Dylan: two …
Mimi: three …
Dylan: four …
Mimi: five little crabs! Swim in the ocean, little crabs! Bye bye, little crabs!
Dylan: Bye bye, little crabs!
Mimi: Oh great. The little crabs are safe. I'm happy.
Dylan: Me too!

Songs

Language song

I can see the ocean CD3 Track 30

I can see the ocean, the ocean (Shade your eyes with a hand)
Me too! Me too! (Point to self)
I can see the sand, the sand (Shade your eyes with a hand)
Can you? Can you? (Open arms questioningly)
I can see a crab, a crab (Shade your eyes with a hand)
Me too! Me too! (Point to self)
I can see a shell, a shell (Shade your eyes with a hand)
Can you? Can you? (Open arms questioningly)
I can see a bucket, a bucket (Shade your eyes with a hand)
Me too! Me too! (Point to self)
I can see a shovel, a shovel (Shade your eyes with a hand)
Can you? Can you? (Open arms questioningly)

Story song

One, two, three, four, five little crabs CD3 Track 33

One, two, three, four, five little crabs (Count off five fingers)
One, two, three, four, five little crabs
One, two, three, four, five little crabs
Walk to the ocean like this (Walk sideways making pincers with fingers)
One, two, three, four, five little crabs (Count off five fingers)
One, two, three, four, five little crabs
One, two, three, four, five little crabs
Sit in the bucket like this (Pretend to sit like a crab making pincers with fingers)
One, two, three, four, five little crabs (Count off five fingers)
One, two, three, four, five little crabs
One, two, three, four, five little crabs
Swim in the ocean like this (Pretend to swim like a crab making pincers with fingers)
One, two, three, four, five little crabs (Count off five fingers)
One, two, three, four, five little crabs
One, two, three, four, five little crabs
Are safe and happy now (Wave happily as they swim)

Values song

I love our world CD3 Track 36

I love our world (Make a heart with hands)
I love the blue ocean (Move one hand up and down like waves)
Let's keep our world clean (Spread hands out sideways)
For you and me (Point to a child and then self)
I love our world (Make a heart with hands)
I love the green trees (Make upward motion with hands together)
Let's keep our world clean (Spread hands out sideways)
For you and me (Point to a child and then self)
I love our world (Make a heart with hands)
I love the blue ocean (Move one hand up and down like waves)
Let's keep our world clean (Spread hands out sideways)
For you and me (Point to a child and then self)
I love our world (Make a heart with hands)
I love the green trees (Make upward motion with hands together)
Let's keep our world clean (Spread hands out sideways)
For you and me (Point to a child and then self)

Culture song

One, two, three, four, five CD3 Track 38

One, two, three, four, five, (Hold up five fingers in turn)
Once I caught a fish alive. (Mime catching a fish in a net)
Six, seven, eight, nine, ten, (Hold up remaining fingers in turn)
Then I let it go again. (Mime letting it go)

One, two, three, four, five, (Hold up five fingers in turn)
Once I caught a crab alive. (Mime catching a crab in a net)
Six, seven, eight, nine, ten, (Hold up remaining fingers in turn)
Then I let it go again. (Mime letting it go)

(Repeat)

Beach

Five little crabs

Vocabulary Lesson 1

Listen, point and repeat. Listen and play. Stick the beach stickers. Say.

Language: crab, ocean, sand, shell; blue, green, orange, yellow

Learning objectives

- Identify and name things at the beach
- Listen and point to things at the beach
- Listen and play *Round and round and round*

Materials

- Class CDs, flashcards, *Ferris Wheel* mat, Mimi puppet

Main vocabulary

- crab, ocean, sand, shell; blue, green, orange, yellow

Teacher's tip: Recording children to build confidence

Once the children are beginning to say the new words, record them and play back the audio so that they can hear themselves speaking English. Get them to listen and give encouragement and positive feedback about their progress.

Circle time

Hello song & puppet (CD1 Track 2; see TB p 17 & 21)
Opening routines (see TB p 16)
Lesson aims (see TB p 18)

Introduce pet vocabulary.

- Say *Let's learn about the beach.*
- Use the puppet to hold up the flashcards in turn and introduce the words. Children repeat the words.
- Put the *Ferris Wheel* mat on the floor or board with the beach flashcards face down (one on each color). Use the puppet to turn them over and name them. The children repeat the words.

Game: *Find the shell.*

- Name the beach item and one or two children to find and touch the correct flashcards as fast as they can.

Game: *Say the color.*

- Name the beach item and children name the color. Then the reverse.

Table time

Student's Book p75

Listen, point and repeat.

- Play the audio. Children listen and point to each word as they hear it.

CD3 Track 27

Mimi: Look, Dylan! Shell … ocean… crab … sand … hee, hee, hee! Repeat, Dylan!
Dylan: Yes, Mimi! Shell … ocean… crab … sand … hee, hee, hee!
Mimi: Very good, Dylan. Let's say the words together!
Both: Shell … ocean… crab … sand … hee, hee, hee!

- Play the audio again. Children listen and repeat the words.

Listen and play.

- Hold up your index finger and move it around clockwise like a wheel. Children do the same. Play the audio. Children listen, point to the color when they hear it, and say the word.

CD3 Track 28

Mimi: Round and round and round: Orange … ocean!
Dylan: Ocean!
Mimi: Round and round and round: Green … sand!
Dylan: Sand!
Mimi: Round and round and round: Blue … shell!
Dylan: Shell!
Mimi: Round and round and round: Yellow … crab!
Dylan: Crab!

- Play the game with you and/or individual children naming colors and others saying the words.

Stick the beach stickers.

- Children put on the beach stickers.

Say.

- Children point to the pictures and say the words.

Activity Book p 75

Color the ocean blue, the sand yellow, the shell pink and the crab red.

- Children color the picture as instructed. If you wish, you could draw a color key on the board to help them (i.e. some blue waves, some yellow sand, a pink shell and a red crab).

Point and say.

- Children point and say the words and the colors.

Closing time

Learning review (see TB p 18)
Closing routines (see TB p 16)
Bye bye song and puppet (CD1 Track 3; see TB p 17 & 21)

Use the **Navio App** to play the vocabulary game, and encourage children to do the same at home.

Lesson 2 **Language**

Beach

3:29 3:30 hello

Listen and find the new beach words. Listen, point and sing *I can see the ocean*. Match the photos to the picture. Say.
Language: bucket, crab, ocean, sand, shell, shovel; I can see (a crab). Me too.

76

Learning objectives

- Talk about things at the beach
- Identify and name two new things at the beach
- Sing the language song *I can see the beach*
- Say what things at the beach you can see

Materials

- Class CDs, printable story cards, flashcards, *Ferris Wheel* mat, Mimi puppet

Main vocabulary

- bucket, crab, ocean, sand, shell, shovel

Key language

- I can see a (crab). Me too.

Teacher's tip: Speaking to a partner

After completing the Student's Book page and singing the song again, have the children sit with a partner and take turns pointing to the pictures and saying, e.g. *I can see a (crab).* Praise children who are taking turns and making an effort to say the sentences.

Circle time

Hello song & puppet (CD1 Track 2; see TB p 17 & 21)
Opening routines (see TB p 16)
Recycling activity (four beach words from Lesson 1) (see TB p 19)
Lesson aims (see TB p 18)

Introduce the new beach words.

- Put all six beach flashcards on the floor or board.
- Children identify the two new words.
- Use the puppet to point to and say the words in turn. Children repeat in chorus.
- Turn the two new flashcards face down. Mix them up. Point to one and ask *Bucket or shovel?* Children guess. Repeat several times.

Introduce *I can see (a crab).*

- Stick the beach flashcards around the classroom.
- Point to one of them, shade your eyes with your hand, and say, e.g. *I can see a crab.* Get children do the same and say the sentence with you.

Game: *Take a photo!*

- Leave the flashcards where they are.
- Demonstrate the game. Say e.g. *I can see the ocean! Take a photo for me, please!* Nominate two children to pretend to take a photo of the flashcard.
- Say *Show me the photo!* Demonstrate that children should pretend to show you the photo and respond, e.g. *Yes, that's very good, I can see the ocean.*
- Repeat with different children and flashcards.

***I can see the ocean* song**

CD3 Track 30

- Leave the flashcards where they are.
- Play the audio. Children stand up, listen and point to the flashcards.
- Play the audio again. Children listen and join in singing and acting out the song (see TB p 187).

Table time

Student's Book p 76

Listen and find the new beach words.

- Hold up your book. Point to the photo of Tom and Sophie at the beach and children say the names.
- Play the audio. Children listen and find the two new words. Repeat and children say the words.

CD3 Track 29

Tom: Find the … bucket! Bucket!
Sophie: Bucket! Here!
Tom: Find the … shovel! shovel!
Sophie: Shovel! Here!

Listen, point and sing *I can see the ocean.*

CD3 Track 30

- Play the audio of the song. The children listen and point to the beach items.
- Remember that you can use the karaoke version of the song when the children are confident.

Match the photos to the picture.

- Hold up your book and demonstrate matching the photos of the beach items to the equivalent items in the main picture.
- Play the audio again. Pause after each pair of lines in the song and children match the pictures.

Say.

- Children point and say, e.g. *I can see a bucket.*

Activity Book p 76

Find and color the bucket and the shovel.

- Children find and color the bucket and shovel following the colored dots.

Point and say.

- Children point and say what they can see.

Closing time

Learning review (see TB p 18)
Closing routines (see TB p 16)
Bye bye song and puppet (CD1 Track 3; see TB p 17 & 21)

Use the **Navio App** to listen to the song, and encourage children to do the same at home.

Story

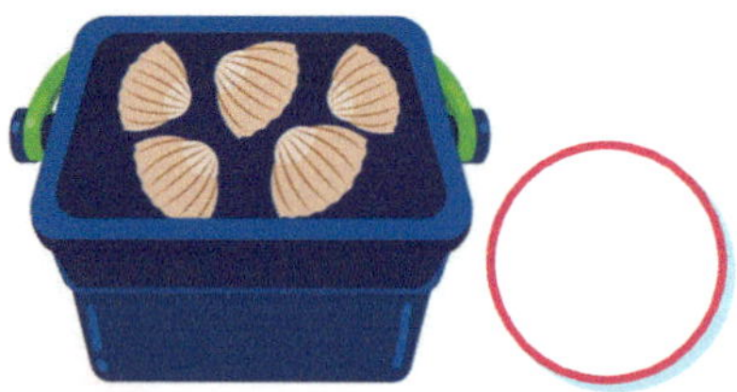

Watch. Listen to the story *Five little crabs*. Color the circle next to the bucket in the story. Stick the story sticker. Ask and say. **Language:** bucket, crab, ocean, sand, shovel; numbers 1–5; little; I can see (five) little crabs. Me too. How many little crabs? (Five).

Learning objectives

- Watch, understand and enjoy the story *Five little crabs*
- Make a prediction about the story
- Look and find things at the beach
- Identify the bucket in the story

Materials

- Class CDs, printable story cards, flashcards, *Ferris Wheel* mat, Mimi puppet

Main vocabulary

- bucket, crab, ocean, sand, shovel; numbers 1–5; little

Key language

- I can see (five) little crabs. Me too. How many little crabs? (Five).

Teacher's tip: Using the story frames to practice counting

After completing work on the story, get children to point and count the number of crabs in each story frame. Ask *Which story frame has a different number of crabs?* Repeat, getting children to count other items, e.g. hats, buckets.

Circle time

Hello song & puppet (CD1 Track 2; see TB p 17 & 21)
Opening routines (see TB p 16)
Recycling activity (*I can see …* and beach items) (see TB p 19)
Lesson aims (see TB p 18)

Introduce the story *Five little crabs*.

- Say *It's story time!* Play the *Story rhyme* (CD1 Track 4; see TB p 17).
- Say *Tom and Sophie are listening to a story about Mimi and Dylan at the beach. Guess who Mimi and Dylan help at the beach.* Listen to children's answers.

Watch or listen to the story.

CD3 Track 32

- Play the audio, watch the video or read the story using the printable story cards. Pause, repeat words, point to the pictures and ask questions.
- Ask the question again *Who do Mimi and Dylan help at the beach? (little crabs).*
- Repeat the story. Encourage children to join in with the words and phrases in the story.
- Ask *Do you like the story? How many little crabs do Mimi and Dylan help? (Five).*

Look and find.

- Say e.g. *Find a little crab!* Children look at the story and point to the picture as fast as they can.
- Repeat with other beach items in the story.

Table time

Student's Book p 77

Watch. Listen to the story *Five little crabs*.

- Read or play the story again. Children listen and point to the pictures in their books.

Color the circle next to the bucket in the story.

- Demonstrate coloring the circle next to the bucket in the story (i.e. the one on the right).

Story questions

Picture 1
Where are Mimi and Dylan? *(The beach)*
What can Mimi see? *(Little crabs)*

Picture 2
Where do the little crabs want to go? *(The ocean)*
Does Dylan want to help the little crabs? *(Yes)*

Picture 3
Where do the crabs go? *(Into the bucket)*
How many little crabs are in the bucket? *(Five)*

Picture 4
Where do Mimi and Dylan put the little crabs? *(In the ocean)*
Are Mimi and Dylan happy? *(Yes)*

Stick the story sticker.

- Children stick on the story sticker.

Ask and say.

- Children ask and answer questions, e.g. *How many crabs? Five.*
- Ask *Where are the little crabs at the end of the story? Are they safe? Are Mimi and Dylan happy?* and children respond.

Activity Book p 77

Trace the paths to connect the story pictures in order. Color a circle to show your favorite picture in the story.

- Children connect the pictures in order. They color the circle on their favorite picture.

Ask and say.

- Children ask and say about the story pictures.

Closing time

Learning review (see TB p 18)
Closing routines (see TB p 16)
Bye bye song and puppet (CD1 Track 3; see TB p 17 & 21)

Use the **Navio App** to watch the video, and encourage children to do the same at home.

Lesson 4 Story Song

Beach

Watch. Listen, point and sing *One, two, three, four, five little crabs.*
Color and count the crabs. Ask and say.
Language: bucket, crab, ocean; little; numbers 1–5; How many little crabs? (Five).

78

Lesson 4 Story Song

Learning objectives

- Watch, sing and act out the story song *One, two, three, four, five little crabs*
- Listen to the story again and identify things at the beach
- Play *How many little crabs?*
- Color and count the crabs
- Ask and say how many

Materials

- Class CDs, printable story cards, flashcards, *Ferris Wheel* mat, Mimi puppet

Main vocabulary

- bucket, crab, ocean; little; numbers 1–5

Key language

- How many little crabs? (Five).

Teacher's tip: Extending the song

Extend the song by using any of the previously learnt animals to replace the crabs in the story song. Invite the children to choose from a selection of flashcards and encourage them to join in with new verses, e.g. *One, two, three, four, five little birds … fly in the sky like this.*

Circle time

Hello song & puppet (CD1 Track 2; see TB p 17 & 21)
Opening routines (see TB p 16)
Recycling activity (beach vocabulary) (see TB p 19)
Lesson aims (see TB p 18)

Retell the story *Five little crabs.*

- Play the audio, video or read the story using the printable story cards.
- Demonstrate that children should wave their arms in the air every time they hear a beach word in the story.

Game: *How many little crabs?*

- Have ready five counters or rods to be little crabs.
- Show the counters or rods to the children and say *Let's pretend these are the little crabs in the story.*
- Lay out the five counters or rods. Point to them in turn and get children to count them with you: *One, two, three, four, five little crabs.*
- Repeat once or twice.
- Say *Close your eyes!* and remove one or two of the rods or counters. Say *Open your eyes!* Ask *How many little crabs?* Children look and count the little crabs with you.
- Repeat several times removing different numbers of counters or rods each time.

***One, two, three, four, five little crabs* song**

CD3 Track 33

- Play the video or audio of the story song. Children listen and do actions for each verse (see TB p 187).
- Watch or listen again. Children do the actions and join in singing the song.

Table time

Student's Book p 78

Watch. Listen, point and sing *One, two, three, four, five little crabs.*

CD3 Track 33

- Play the audio of the song. Children listen, sing and point to the pictures of the little crabs.
- Remember that you can use the karaoke version of the song when the children are confident.

Color and count the crabs.

- Children color the crabs and then count the crabs they have colored.

Ask and say.

- Children point to the crabs in each picture and ask and say, e.g. *How many crabs? One, two, three, four, five.*

Activity Book p 78

Count the crabs. Circle the picture that is the same in each row.

- Children count the crabs in the pictures on the left. They find and circle the picture that is the same in each row.

Point, ask and say.

- Children point, ask and say how many crabs there are.

Closing time

Learning review (see TB p 18)
Closing routines (see TB p 16)
Bye bye song and puppet (CD1 Track 3; see TB p 17 & 21)

Use the **Navio App** to watch the video, and encourage children to do the same at home.

Speaking

Life skills

Watch. Listen and point. Trace to circle the number of shells in Tom and Sophie's buckets. Ask and say. Language: bucket, ocean, sand, shell; pink; numbers 1–5; I can see (shells). How many (shells)? (Four). What color are the (shells)? They're (pink).

Learning objectives

- Talk about things you can see at the beach
- Watch, understand and enjoy a video
- Identify how many shells the characters have in the video
- Count from 1–10

Materials

- Class CDs, flashcards, *Ferris Wheel* mat, Mimi puppet

Main vocabulary

- bucket, ocean, sand, shell; pink; numbers 1–5

Key language

- I can see (shells). How many (shells)? (Four). What color are the (shells)? They're (pink).

Teacher's tip: Using real objects to create a need for communication

Life skills

If possible, bring in some real shells for the children to count. Put different quantities of shells into pots to give the children a real reason for communication. Once the first child has asked the question *How many shells?* and the second child has counted the shells, the first child should look in the pot to check the answer.

Circle time

Hello song & puppet (CD1 Track 2; see TB p 17 & 21)
Opening routines (see TB p 16)
Recycling activity (story song) (CD3 Track 33; see TB p 19)
Lesson aims (see TB p 18)

Game: *I can see a crab!*

- Hold up one of the beach flashcards covered by the back of another flashcard so that children can't see what's in the picture. Lower the back of the flashcard down slowly to gradually reveal the picture. Demonstrate that children should say, e.g. *I can see a crab!* as soon as they can tell what the picture is.
- Repeat several times with different flashcards.

Watch the video.

- Explain that Tom, Sophie and Auntie Jenny are looking at a photo of the beach. Ask *What can they see?* and children predict, e.g. ocean, sand, crab, shell.
- Play the video of Auntie Jenny, Tom and Sophie.
- Ask *What can Sophie see? (shells) How many shells? (four) What color? (pink) Where do Sophie and Tom put the shells? In Tom's (bucket).*
- Watch again. Pause and children repeat part of the dialogue from *I can see shells* to counting the shells.
- Ask *Do you like the beach? Do you like shells?* and listen to the children's responses.

Table time

Student's Book p 79 Life skills

Watch. Listen and point.

- Children identify Auntie Jenny, Tom and Sophie in the photo and name the beach items.
- Play the audio. Children listen and point to the shells in the photo.

CD3 Track 35

Sophie:	Look at our photo of the beach.
Auntie Jenny:	I love the beach.
Tom:	Me too.
Auntie Jenny:	What a beautiful photo! I can see the ocean. I can see sand. And I can see shells.
Sophie:	And look, Auntie Jenny. I have shells here in my bucket.
Auntie Jenny:	How many shells?
Sophie:	One, two, three, four shells.
Auntie Jenny:	What color are the shells?
Sophie:	They're pink.
Tom:	Oh wow. Look! I have shells too!
Auntie Jenny:	How many shells?
Tom:	One, two, three, four shells.
Auntie Jenny:	What color are the shells?
Tom:	They're pink. I have four pink shells too!

Trace to circle the number of shells in Tom and Sophie's buckets.

- Play the audio again. Use the pause button. Children circle the correct number of shells (i.e. four shells).

Ask and say.

- Children take turns pointing to the groups of shells, pretending to be Sophie, and asking and saying, e.g. *I can see shells. How many shells? One, two, three, four.*

Activity Book p 79

Color and count the shells. Circle the correct number.

- Children color the ten shells. They count and circle the correct number.

Ask and say.

- Children ask and answer about the shells.

Closing time

Learning review (see TB p 18)
Closing routines (see TB p 16)
Bye bye song and puppet (CD1 Track 3; see TB p 17 & 21)

Use the **Navio App** to watch the video, and encourage children to do the same at home.

Lesson 6 Values I love our world

Listen, point and sing *I love our world*. Color the ocean blue and the trees green. Say.

Language: ocean, trees; blue, green; I love the (blue) (ocean).

3:36

hello

SOCIAL AND EMOTIONAL LEARNING

80

Learning objectives

- Recognize the value of respecting nature
- Sing the values song *I love our world*
- Say *I love the (blue) (ocean).*

Materials

- Class CDs, flashcards, *Ferris Wheel* mat, Mimi puppet

Main vocabulary

- ocean, trees; blue, green

Key language

- I love the (blue) (ocean).

Teacher's tip: Reinforcing the value through art and craft

Encourage the children to think more about caring for the world by making a display titled: *We love our world.* Cut out a large circle to represent the world and have the children glue small squares of blue or green tissue paper on it to represent the ocean and the trees. Have each child draw a picture of themselves. Glue the pictures of the children all around the world and display it in a prominent place.

Circle time

Hello song & puppet (CD1 Track 2; see TB p 17 & 21)
Opening routines (see TB p 16)
Recycling activity *(I can see …; How many?)* (see TB p 19)
Lesson aims (see TB p 18)

Watch the *Five little crabs* story video.

- Play the story video.
- Children watch and repeat every time they hear a beach word.
- Ask e.g. *Do Mimi and Dylan love the beach? (Yes)* Use the children's shared language to explain that the beach is part of nature, as is the countryside, and that it is important for all of us to respect and look after nature and keep our world clean.
- Ask *Do you love nature?* and listen to the children's response.

***I love our world* song**

CD3 Track 36

- Show the pictures in the Student's Book. Say e.g. *Look at the blue ocean / green trees.*
- Play the audio. Children listen and do the actions (see TB p 187). Explain the meaning of *clean.*
- Play the audio again. Children sing the song and do the actions.
- Use children's shared language to make the point that it's important to respect nature and to keep our world clean.

Table time

Student's Book p 80

Listen, point and sing *I love our world.*

CD3 Track 36

- Say e.g. *I love green trees / I love the blue ocean* and children point to the correct pictures.
- Play the song. Children sing and point to the pictures.

Color the ocean blue and the trees green.

- Demonstrate that children should color the ocean blue and the trees green to show what they respect in nature.

Say.

- Children point to their completed pictures and say, e.g. *I love the blue ocean.*

Activity Book p 80

Choose, draw and color a picture of you.

- Children choose, draw and color themselves in one of the pictures.

Say.

- Children say *I love the (green) (trees).*

Closing time

Learning review (see TB p 18)
Closing routines (see TB p 16)
Bye bye song and puppet (CD1 Track 3; see TB p 17 & 21)

Use the **Navio App** to listen to the song, and encourage children to do the same at home.

Lesson 7

Content

Listen and point. Match the animals to where they live. Say.
Language: land, water; cat, crab, fish; (Fish) live in (water). (Cats) live on (land).

Learning objectives

- Identify and name animals that live on land or in water
- Listen and understand a dialogue about where animals live
- Talk about where animals live

Materials

- Class CDs, printable flashcards, *Ferris Wheel* mat, Mimi puppet

Main vocabulary

- land, water; cat, crab, fish

Key language

- (Fish) live in (water). (Cats) live on (land).

Teacher's tip: Classifying animals to reinforce the concept

If possible, lay out two large hoops on the floor with an overlap in the centre. Place the fish flashcard on one side, the cat on the other and the crab in the centre to show that it lives on land and in the water. Encourage children to classify toy animals from the children's classroom or other animal flashcards by placing them in the correct part of the hoop to reinforce the concept.

Circle time

Hello song & puppet (CD1 Track 2; see TB p 17 & 21)
Opening routines (see TB p 16)
Recycling activity (see TB p 19)
Lesson aims (see TB p 18)

Introduce content vocabulary.

- Use the printable flashcards and the puppet to introduce the new words (*water, land*). Children repeat the words.
- Say *Some animals live in water. Some animals live on land.*
- Place the flashcard of the cat (from *Pets*) by *land* and say *Cats live on land.* Then place the flashcard of the fish (from *Pets*) by *water* and say *Fish live in water.*
- Point to the flashcards in turn and children repeat the sentences.

Game: *Water or land?*

- Stick the printable flashcards of *water* and *land* on opposite sides of the classroom.
- Children stand up. Demonstrate the game. Say e.g. *Water!* and children either point to or go to the side of the room with the printable flashcard and repeat the word.
- Alternate giving instructions several times and children respond.

Game: *Cats live on land.*

- Hold up one of the animal flashcards, e.g. *cat*, and say e.g. *Cats live on land!* Demonstrate that if the sentence is true, children should repeat the sentence. If it isn't true, they should fold their arms and stay silent.
- Repeat with *fish* and *crabs.*
- Refer back to the story to help children understand that some animals, like the little crabs in the story, live on land and in water.

Table time

Student's Book p 81

Listen and point.

- Children identify the animals and water and land in the photos.
- Play the audio. Children listen and point to the photos.

CD3 Track 37

Auntie Jenny:	Some animals live in water. Some animals live on land.
Tom:	Fish live in water
Sophie:	Cats live on land
Auntie Jenny:	Crabs live in water and on land.
Sophie & Tom:	Oh wow. Amazing!

Match the animals to where they live.

- Play the audio again. Use the pause button. Children match the animals to where they live.

Say.

- Children point to the photos and say, e.g. *Cats live on land.*

Activity Book p 81

Color the animal that lives on land.

- Children color the animal that lives on land.

Point and say.

- They point and say *(Cats) live on (land).*

Closing time

Learning review (see TB p 18)
Closing routines (see TB p 16)
Bye bye song and puppet (CD1 Track 3; see TB p 17 & 21)

Use the **Navio App** to play the vocabulary and language games, and encourage children to do the same at home.

Lesson 8 Culture

Watch. Listen, point and sing *One, two, three, four, five.*
Trace to circle the animals in the song. Point and say.
Language: crab, fish, shell; numbers 1–10

Learning objectives

- Watch, sing and act out the traditional song *One, two, three, four, five*
- Count up to ten
- Identify and name the animals in the song

Materials

- Class CDs, flashcards, *Ferris Wheel* mat, Mimi puppet

Main vocabulary

- crab, fish, shell; numbers 1–10

Teacher's tip: Developing counting skills

Life skills

Help the children understand that objects can be counted in any order. Count the crab flashcards from left to right, then from top to bottom, and then spread them out randomly and count them again, to demonstrate this. Show the children that each flashcard relates to one number in the sequence by pausing when counting and making sure that the children pause with you.

Circle time

Hello song & puppet (CD1 Track 2; see TB p 17 & 21)
Opening routines (see TB p 16)
Recycling activity (see TB p 19)
Lesson aims (see TB p 18)

Count the flashcards.

- Have ready ten flashcards in a pile (don't show children the pictures).
- Use the puppet to ask children to help count the flashcards. Count them out up to five with the children. Then, optionally, continue up to ten.
- Repeat once or twice. Note: Children may already be familiar with counting 6–10. If so, they can join in but if not, don't insist and just allow them to listen to the numbers in preparation for the song.

***One, two, three, four, five* song**

CD3 Track 38

- Say *Let's sing the song "One, two, three, four, five." What beach animals are in the song?*
- Play the audio. Ask the question again and check the answer *(fish, crab)*.
- Children stand up. Pre-teach actions for the song (see TB p 187). Demonstrate pretending to catch a fish or a crab in a long net and then letting it go in the water again.
- Play the audio. Children join in doing actions.
- Play the audio again. Children do actions and join in singing the song.

Watch the *One, two, three, four, five* song video.

- Children watch the video and join in singing the song and doing the actions with Tom and Sophie.

Table time

Student's Book p 82

Watch. Listen, point and sing *One, two, three, four, five*.

- Play the audio. Children listen, sing and point to the fish and the crab.

Trace to circle the animals in the song.

- Name the animals in the picture. Children circle the animals in the song (i.e. the fish and the crab).

Point and say.

- Children point to the animals that are in the song and say the words, e.g. *crab, fish*.

Activity Book p 82

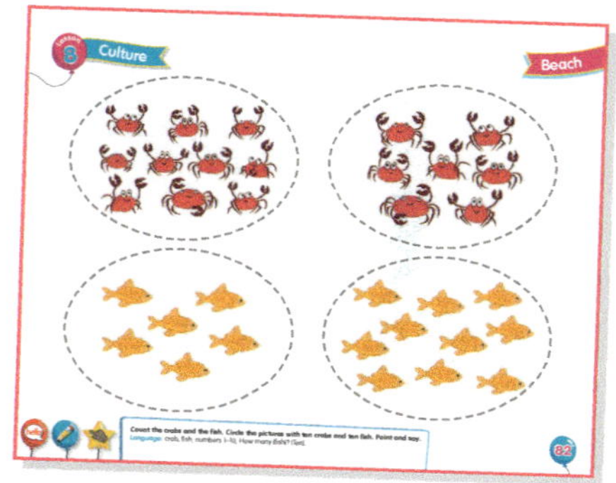

Count the crabs and the fish. Circle the pictures with ten crabs and ten fish.

- Children count the groups of crabs and fish. They circle the pictures with ten crabs and ten fish.

Point and say.

- They point and say how many crabs and fish there are in each picture.

Closing time

Learning review (see TB p 18)
Closing routines (see TB p 16)
Bye bye song and puppet (CD1 Track 3; see TB p 17 & 21)

Use the **Navio App** to watch the video, and encourage children to do the same at home.

Review

Beach

Listen, point and say. Color the words you know. Stick the star sticker. Ask and say.
Language: bucket, crab, ocean, sand, shell, shovel; numbers 1–3; colors; I can see (a bucket). Me too. How many (shells)? (Three). What color are the (shells)? They're (pink).

Learning objectives

- Review your learning and progress
- Name and talk about things at the beach
- Stick on a star sticker for achievement

Materials

- Class CDs, flashcards, *Ferris Wheel* mat, Mimi puppet

Main vocabulary

- bucket, crab, ocean, sand, shell, shovel; numbers 1–3; colors

Key language

- I can see (a bucket). Me too. How many (shells)? (Three). What color are the (shells)? They're (pink).

Teacher's tip: Developing deliberate memory

After completing the review activities, ask children to look at the picture carefully. Give them 20–30 seconds to do this. Then cover the picture and invite children to say what they can see from memory, e.g. *I can see a (bucket).* Be ready to accept words that they don't yet know in English in their shared language e.g. racket, castle, umbrella. Keep count of how many things children remember and praise their efforts. At the end, get children to look at the picture again and say what they missed.

Circle time

Hello song & puppet (CD1 Track 2; see TB p 17 & 21)
Opening routines (see TB p 16)
Recycling activity (see TB p 19)
Lesson aims (see TB p 18)

Beach flashcard games

- Choose one or two flashcard games with the *Ferris Wheel* mat and/or the puppet to review key vocabulary (see TB p 20 & 21).

Sing *I can see the ocean.*

CD3 Track 30

- Lay out the flashcards in the order of the song.
- Play the audio. Children listen, sing and point to the flashcards in each verse.

Game: *I can see a shovel.*

- Hold the pack of flashcards facing you. Quickly turn it around and back again, giving the children a glimpse of the item. Demonstrate that children should say, e.g. *I can see a (shovel)!* as soon as they see the picture.
- Repeat several times with different flashcards.

Game: *How many shells?*

- Choose a number between 1 and 5 and hold up that many fingers behind your back.
- Say *How many shells?* Children guess the number. Reveal your fingers to check, e.g. *Three!* Repeat, changing the number.

Watch the story video.

- Children watch the story video. Ask e.g. *Are the little crabs safe at the end of the story?*

Table time

Student's Book p 83

Listen, point and say.

- Say e.g. *Point to the bucket.* and children point to the beach items.
- Play the audio. Children listen, point to the beach items and say the words.

CD3 Track 39

Mimi: I'm the teacher! Can you remember the beach words, Dylan?
Dylan: Yes, I can. Ocean.
Mimi: Ocean.
Dylan: Sand.
Mimi: Sand.
Dylan: Crab.
Mimi: Crab.
Dylan: Shell.
Mimi: Shell.
Dylan: Bucket.
Mimi: Bucket.
Dylan: Shovel.
Mimi: Shovel. Great job, Dylan. Very good!

Color the words you know.

- Children color the beach words they know.

Stick the star sticker.

- Children stick on the star sticker for achievement.
- Monitor and encourage children to think positively about their progress.

Ask and say.

- Children point and say, e.g. *I can see a shell.*

Activity Book p 83

Color the faces to show the beach words you know. Ask and say.

- Children color the faces next to the beach words they know. They say what they can see.

Think and color the stars to show your progress.

- Children color the number of stars that they feel shows their progress in this unit.

Closing time

Learning review (see TB p 18)
Closing routines (see TB p 16)
Bye bye song and puppet (CD1 Track 3; see TB p 17 & 21)

Use the **Navio App** to review what children have learned in this unit, and encourage children to do the same at home.

Project

COOPERATIVE LEARNING

Beach

1

2

3

Paint and decorate an object from the beach. Make a beach display. Ask and say. **Language:** bucket, crab, ocean, sand, shell, shovel; colors; numbers; I can see (a shell). Me too. How many (crabs)? (Five). Is this your (bucket)? Yes, it is. / No, it isn't. I have (a shovel). What's this? It's (a crab). Where's the (green) (bucket)? Here.

Learning objectives

- Work together to do a collaborative project
- Choose and color a beach object
- Talk about the objects on the display
- Express enjoyment of the beach display
- Paint a picture of a beach and talk about it

Materials

- Class CDs, Mimi puppet, project template, finger paints, tissue paper, glue
- optional: crayons

Main vocabulary

- bucket, crab, ocean, sand, shell, shovel; colors; numbers

Key language

- I can see (a shell). Me too! How many (crabs)? (Five). Is this your (bucket)? Yes, it is / No, it isn't. I have (a shovel). What's this? It's (a crab). Where's the (green) (bucket)? Here.

Teacher's tip: Collaborating with a partner

When children come out to glue their finished pictures on the display, encourage them to do so in pairs. Have them work together to decide where is the best place to glue their pictures by taking turns to point and say, e.g *Where? Here!* Encourage them to thank each other for the help given.

Circle time

Hello song & puppet (CD1 Track 2; see TB p 17 & 21)
Opening routines (see TB p 16)
Recycling activity (see TB p 19)
Lesson aims (see TB p 18)

Prepare for your project.

- Say *Let's do a project and make a beach display!*
- Show children the copies of the beach templates that you have prepared.
- Demonstrate painting or gluing small balls of tissue paper on the beach templates.

Table time

Student's Book p 84

- Say e.g. *We're going to make a beach display like this. Look at what we need for our project: pictures of things at the beach, finger paints, tissue paper, glue.* Children listen and point to the pictures.

Paint and decorate an object from the beach.

- Children choose an object from the beach (from the ones on the template). Give each child a copy of the item they choose.
- Make sure children have finger paints, colored tissue paper and glue available.
- Children paint the picture of the object they have chosen or glue on small balls of colored tissue paper.

Make a beach display.

- When they are ready, children glue their completed pictures on the display you have prepared with a background of blue ocean and yellow sand.

Ask and say.

- Children talk about the objects on the display.
- Ask children *Do you like our beach display?* Make the point that everyone helped make it and that they couldn't have made such a beautiful display on their own.

Alternative version of project

- Children could use crayons instead of finger paints to color their picture.

Activity Book p 84

Paint a picture of the beach.

- Children paint the beach scene.

Ask and say.

- Children ask and say about their picture.

Closing time

Learning review (see TB p 18)
Closing routines (see TB p 16)
Bye bye song and puppet (CD1 Track 3; see TB p 17 & 21)

Colors

Listen, point and say. Color the balls so they are the same.
Language: blue, green, red, yellow

Learning objective

- Introduce, reinforce, consolidate or review colors

Materials

- Class CDs, flashcards, *Ferris Wheel* mat, Mimi puppet, feely bag

Main vocabulary

- blue, green, red, yellow

Teacher's tip: Reinforcing the concept with real objects

In addition to the flashcards, use familiar items of different colors to reinforce the concept, e.g. a lemon and a banana for yellow; a tomato and an apple for red, etc. Pass the items around and encourage the children to name the color each time.

Circle time

Hello song & puppet (CD1 Track 2; see TB p 17 & 21)
Opening routines (see TB p 16)
Lesson aims (see TB p 18)

Introduce the colors.

- Use the flashcards, puppet and feely bag to introduce or remind children of the colors.

Play flashcard games.

- Play one or two flashcard games with the *Ferris Wheel* mat and/or the puppet (see TB p 20 & 21).
- Ask children to point to, touch or bring you items of different colors in the classroom.

Table time

Student's Book p 85

Listen, point and say.

- Hold up your book. Play the audio. Point to the colors in turn.
- Play the audio again. Children join in pointing to the balls in their books and naming the colors.

CD3 Track 40

Blue … green … red … yellow
Blue … green … red … yellow
Blue … green … red … yellow

Color the balls so they are the same.

- Children color the balls so they are the same color as in the main picture.
- Children point to the balls and say the colors.

Activity Book p 85

Trace to match the children with the same color balls.

- Children trace to match the children holding the same color balls.

Point and say.

- Children point and say the colors.

Closing time

Learning review (see TB p 18)
Closing routines (see TB p 16)
Bye bye song & puppet (CD1 Track 3; see TB p 17 & 21)

Cross-curricular activities

- See also the activities in the other Colors lesson (see TB p 211).

Art and craft

Cut out six large ball shapes (one for each group or table of children). Allow them to choose from the colors introduced.

Children work at their tables or in groups and either color, paint or glue colored tissue paper on each ball. Alternatively, have them cut out pictures from magazines and glue those of the same color on the balls.

Display the balls. Children name the colors.

Colors

Listen, point and say. Color the butterfly so the wings are the same.
Language: brown, orange, pink, purple

Colors

Brown, orange, pink, purple

Learning objective

- Introduce, reinforce, consolidate or review colors

Materials

- Class CDs, flashcards, *Ferris Wheel* mat, Mimi puppet, feely bag

Main vocabulary

- brown, orange, pink, purple

Teacher's tip: Reinforcing the concept with real objects

In addition to the flashcards, use familiar items of different colors to reinforce the concept, e.g. an orange for orange, a leaf for green, etc. Pass the items around and encourage the children to name the color each time.

Circle time

Hello song & puppet (CD1 Track 2; see TB p 17 & 21)
Opening routines (see TB p 16)
Lesson aims (see TB p 18)

Introduce the colors.

- Use the flashcards, puppet and feely bag to introduce or remind children of the colors.

Play flashcard games.

- Play one or two flashcard games with the *Ferris Wheel* mat and/or the puppet (see TB p 20 & 21).
- Ask children to point to, touch or bring you items of different colors in the classroom. Highlight any colors that are new.

Table time

Student's Book p 86

Listen, point and say.

- Hold up your book. Play the audio. Point to the colors in turn.
- Play the audio again. Children join in pointing to the picture in their books and naming the colors.

CD3 Track 41

Brown … orange … pink … purple
Brown … orange … pink … purple
Brown … orange … pink … purple

Color the butterfly so the wings are the same.

- Children color the picture to make the butterfly symmetrical.
- Children point to the picture and say the colors.

Activity Book p 86

Trace to circle the butterflies in the correct colors.

- Children circle each butterfly using the same color as the butterfly's wings.

Point and say.

- Children point and say the colors.

Closing time

Learning review (see TB p 18)
Closing routines (see TB p 16)
Bye bye song & puppet (CD1 Track 3; see TB p 17 & 21)

Cross-curricular activities

- See also the activities in the other Colors lesson (see TB p 209).

Music

Play a track of lively instrumental music. Children pass around the pink flashcard. When you pause the CD, say *Touch something pink!* Whoever is holding the flashcard has to touch a pink object. Repeat with the other colors.

Maths

Continue to work on symmetry by cutting out butterfly shapes from paper and folding them in half. Children apply paint to one half of the butterfly. Fold while the paint is still wet and open again. Point out the symmetry and talk about the colors the children used.

Numbers 1 2 3 4 5

1 2 3 4 5

Listen, point and say. Color and count the crayons. Circle the correct number.
Language: one, two, three, four, five

87

Numbers 1, 2, 3, 4, 5

Learning objective

- Introduce, reinforce, consolidate or review numbers

Materials

- Class CDs, flashcards, *Ferris Wheel* mat, Mimi puppet, feely bag

Main vocabulary

- one, two, three, four, five

Teacher's tip: Helping learners identify numbers by the shape

In addition to the flashcards, use plastic, wooden or foam numbers from the children's classroom to accustom them to the correct number formation. Place the numbers 1–5 in a feely bag and encourage the children to guess which number they are touching before they remove it from the bag.

Circle time

Hello song & puppet (CD1 Track 2; see TB p 17 & 21)
Opening routines (see TB p 16)
Lesson aims (see TB p 18)

Introduce the numbers.

- Use the flashcards, puppet and feely bag to introduce or remind children of the numbers.

Play flashcard games.

- Play one or two flashcard games with the *Ferris Wheel* mat and/or the puppet (see TB p 20 & 21).
- Ask children to count different classroom objects with you.

Table time

Student's Book p 87

Listen, point and say.

- Hold up your book. Play the audio. Point to the numbers in turn.
- Play the audio again. Children join in pointing to the numbers in their books and saying the words.

CD3 Track 42

One … two … three … four … five
One … two … three … four … five
One … two … three … four … five

Color and count the crayons. Circle the correct number.

- Children color the crayons according to the colored dot on each one, and then count them.
- Children point to the crayons and say *One, two, three, four crayons.*
- They circle the number 4 at the top of the page.

Activity Book p 87

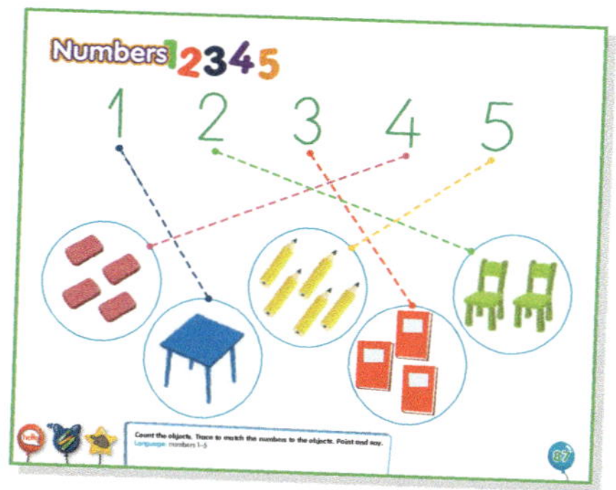

Count the objects. Trace to match the numbers to the objects.

- Children count each group of objects. They match the numbers to the objects.

Point and say.

- Children point and say the numbers.

Closing time

Learning review (see TB p 18)
Closing routines (see TB p 16)
Bye bye song & puppet (CD1 Track 3; see TB p 17 & 21)

Cross-curricular activities

- See also the activities in the other Numbers lesson (see TB p 215).

Music

Play lively dance music and encourage children to dance and move to the rhythm of the music.

Pause the music and call out a number. Children hold up that number of fingers.

Repeat with different numbers.

Physical movement

Call out different instructions to the children, e.g. *clap* or *jump*. Then ask them to do each action the number of times you say, e.g. *Two jumps. / Five claps.*

Numbers 1 2 3 4 5 6 7 8 9 10

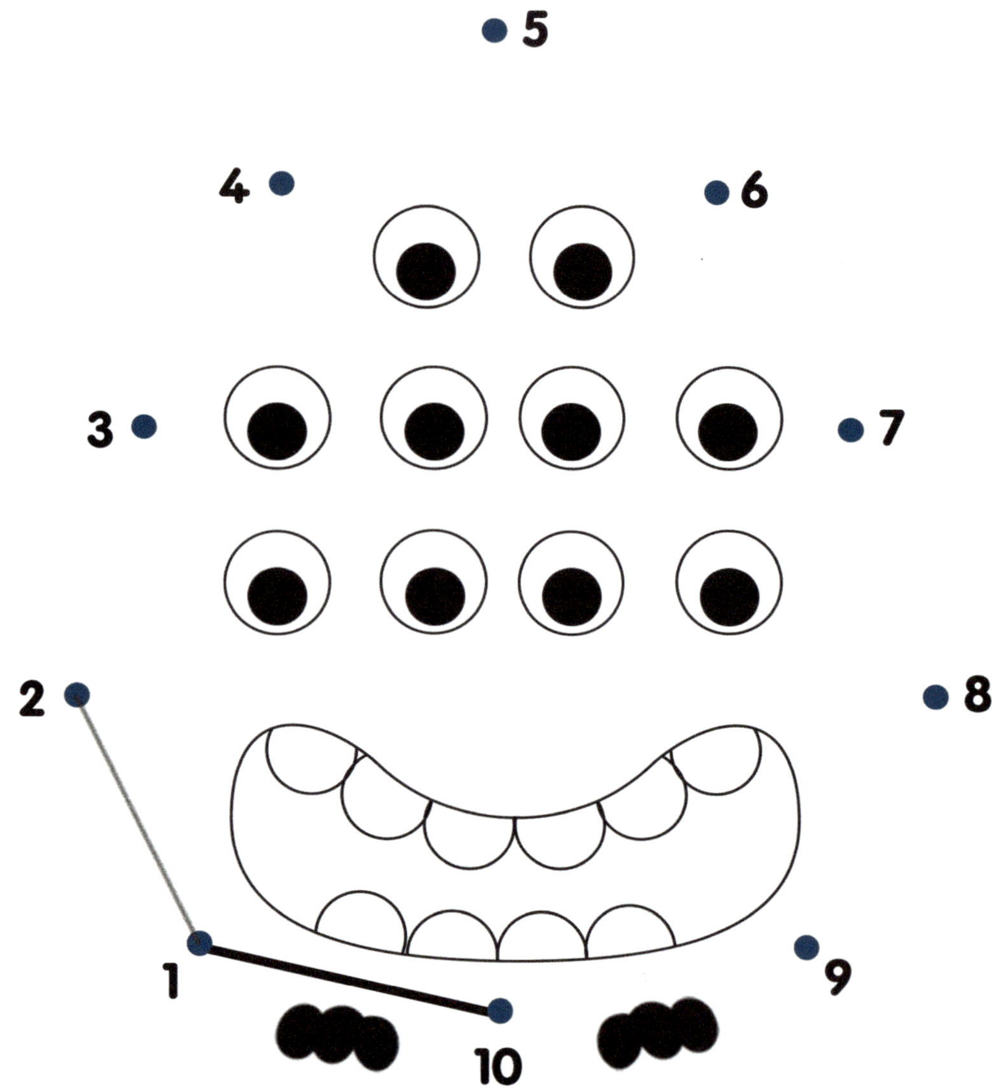

Listen, point and say. Connect the dots. Color the monster. Count the eyes and teeth.

Language: numbers 1–10

88

Learning objective

- Introduce, reinforce, consolidate or review numbers

Materials

- Class CDs, flashcards, *Ferris Wheel* mat, Mimi puppet, feely bag

Main vocabulary

- numbers 1–10

Teacher's tip: Helping learners identify numbers by the shape

In addition to the flashcards, use plastic, wooden or foam numbers from the children's classroom to accustom them to the correct number formation. Place the numbers 1–10 in a feely bag and encourage the children to guess which number they are touching before they remove it from the bag.

Circle time

Hello song & puppet (CD1 Track 2; see TB p 17 & 21)
Opening routines (see TB p 16)
Lesson aims (see TB p 18)

Introduce the numbers.

- Use the flashcards, puppet and feely bag to introduce or remind children of the numbers.

Play flashcard games.

- Play one or two flashcard games with the *Ferris Wheel* mat and/or the puppet (see TB p 20 & 21).
- Ask children to count different classroom objects with you. Highlight any numbers that are new.

Table time

Student's Book p 88

Listen, point and say.

- Hold up your book. Play the audio. Point to the numbers in turn.
- Play the audio again. Children join in pointing to the numbers in their books and saying the words.

CD3 Track 43

One … two … three … four … five … six … seven … eight … nine … ten
One … two … three … four … five ... six … seven … eight … nine … ten
One … two … three … four … five … six ... seven … eight … nine … ten

Connect the dots. Color the monster.

- Children connect the numbers to complete the monster. Then they color the monster.

Count the eyes and teeth.

- Children count and say the number of eyes and teeth on the monster (i.e. ten eyes and ten teeth).

Activity Book p 88

Trace the monster's eyes. Count the eyes and circle the correct number.

- Children trace the eyes. They count the eyes and circle the correct number (10).

Point and say.

- Children point and say the numbers.

Closing time

Learning review (see TB p 18)
Closing routines (see TB p 16)
Bye bye song & puppet (CD1 Track 3; see TB p 17 & 21)

Cross-curricular activities

- See also the activities in the other Numbers lesson (see TB p 213).

Maths

Give each table or group of children ten small plastic cups with a number from 1 to 10 on each one and sets of small objects, e.g. dried chick peas, buttons or bottle tops.

Children work together and count out the correct number of objects to put in each cup.

Children check they have put the correct number of objects in each cup by taking them out again and counting out loud.

Art and craft

Cut simple monster face shapes out of card.

Give a number flashcard and modeling clay to each group of children.

Tell them to add that number of eyes to their monster.

Shapes

Listen, point and say. Trace the circles and triangles.
Language: circle, triangle

Learning objective

- Introduce, reinforce, consolidate or review shapes

Materials

- Class CDs, flashcards, *Ferris Wheel* mat, Mimi puppet, feely bag

Main vocabulary

- circle, triangle

Teacher's tip: Touching different textures

Cut circles and triangles out of different materials: sandpaper, card, fabric, etc. Have children touch them, running their fingers over them while they say the name. Touching shapes of different textures will reinforce the concepts and help children remember the words.

Circle time

Hello song & puppet (CD1 Track 2; see TB p 17 & 21)
Opening routines (see TB p 16)
Lesson aims (see TB p 18)

Introduce the shapes.

- Use the flashcards, puppet and feely bag to introduce or remind children of circles and triangles.

Play flashcard games.

- Play one or two flashcard games with the *Ferris Wheel* mat and/or the puppet (see TB p 20 & 21).
- Get children to identify circles and triangles in classroom objects or posters.

Table time

Student's Book p 89

Listen, point and say.

- Hold up your book. Play the audio. Point to the circles and triangles in the picture.
- Play the audio again. Children join in pointing to the circles and triangles in their books and saying the words.

CD3 Track 44

Circle … triangle
Circle … triangle
Circle … triangle

Trace the circles and triangles.

- Children trace the circles and triangles in the picture.
- They then point to the circles and triangles and say the words.

Activity Book p 89

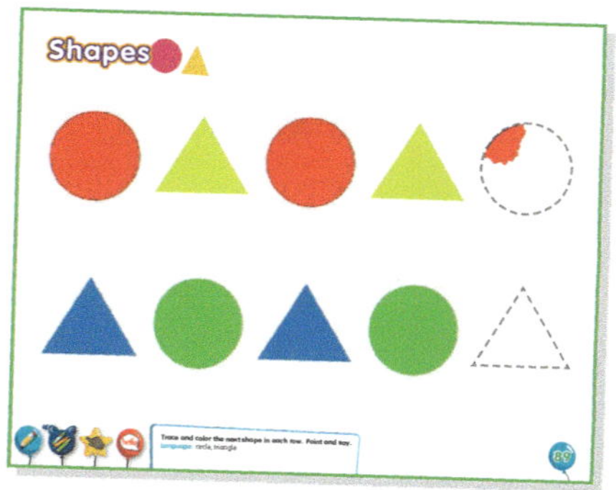

Trace and color the next shape in each row.

- Children trace the next shape in each sequence and color it.

Point and say.

- Children point and say the names of the shapes in each sequence.

Closing time

Learning review (see TB p 18)
Closing routines (see TB p 16)
Bye bye song & puppet (CD1 Track 3; see TB p 17 & 21)

Cross-curricular activities

- See also the activities in the other Shapes lesson (see TB p 219).

Maths

Give each table or group of children some modeling clay. Encourage them to flatten it. If you have circle or triangle shaped cutters, have them press down to cut out shapes from the clay.

Shapes

Listen, point and say. Trace and color the squares red and the rectangles blue.
Language: square, rectangle

90

Square, rectangle

Learning objective
- Introduce, reinforce, consolidate or review shapes

Materials
- Class CDs, flashcards, *Ferris Wheel* mat, Mimi puppet, feely bag

Main vocabulary
- rectangle, square

Teacher's tip: Touching different textures

Cut squares and rectangles out of different materials: sandpaper, card, fabric, etc. Have children touch them, running their fingers over them while they say the names. Touching shapes of different textures will reinforce the concepts and help children remember the words.

Circle time

Hello song & puppet (CD1 Track 2; see TB p 17 & 21)
Opening routines (see TB p 16)
Lesson aims (see TB p 18)

Introduce the shapes.
- Use the flashcards, puppet and feely bag to introduce or remind children of squares and rectangles.

Play flashcard games.
- Play one or two flashcard games with the *Ferris Wheel* mat and/or the puppet (see TB p 20 & 21).
- Get children to identify squares and rectangles in classroom objects or posters.

Table time

Student's Book p 90

Listen, point and say.
- Hold up your book. Play the audio. Point to the squares and rectangles in the picture.
- Play the audio again. Children join in pointing to the squares and rectangles in their books and saying the words.

CD3 Track 45

Square … rectangle
Square … rectangle
Square … rectangle

Trace and color the squares red and the rectangles blue.
- Children trace and color the squares in the picture in red. They trace and color the rectangles in blue.
- They then point to the shapes and say the words.

Activity Book p 90

Color the squares and rectangles to complete the path to the house.
- Children color the squares yellow and the rectangles green to complete the path.

Point and say.
- Children point and say the names of the shapes.

Closing time

Learning review (see TB p 18)
Closing routines (see TB p 16)
Bye bye song & puppet (CD1 Track 3; see TB p 17 & 21)

Cross-curricular activities

- See also the activities in the other Shapes lesson (see TB p 217).

Physical movement

Stand with your back to the children and draw a shape in the air, e.g. circle. Children guess and name the shape.

Repeat with the other shapes.

Ask a child to come to the front and stand with their back to you and the class. Use your finger to draw a shape on the child's back and encourage the child to guess the shape. Get the rest of the class to say if the guess is correct or not.

Repeat several times with different children.

Social science

Place some different shaped everyday objects from around the house into a feely bag.

Cut out large shapes from card and put them on the floor.

Children identify the shapes by touch, take out the item and place it on the corresponding shape on the floor.

Concepts

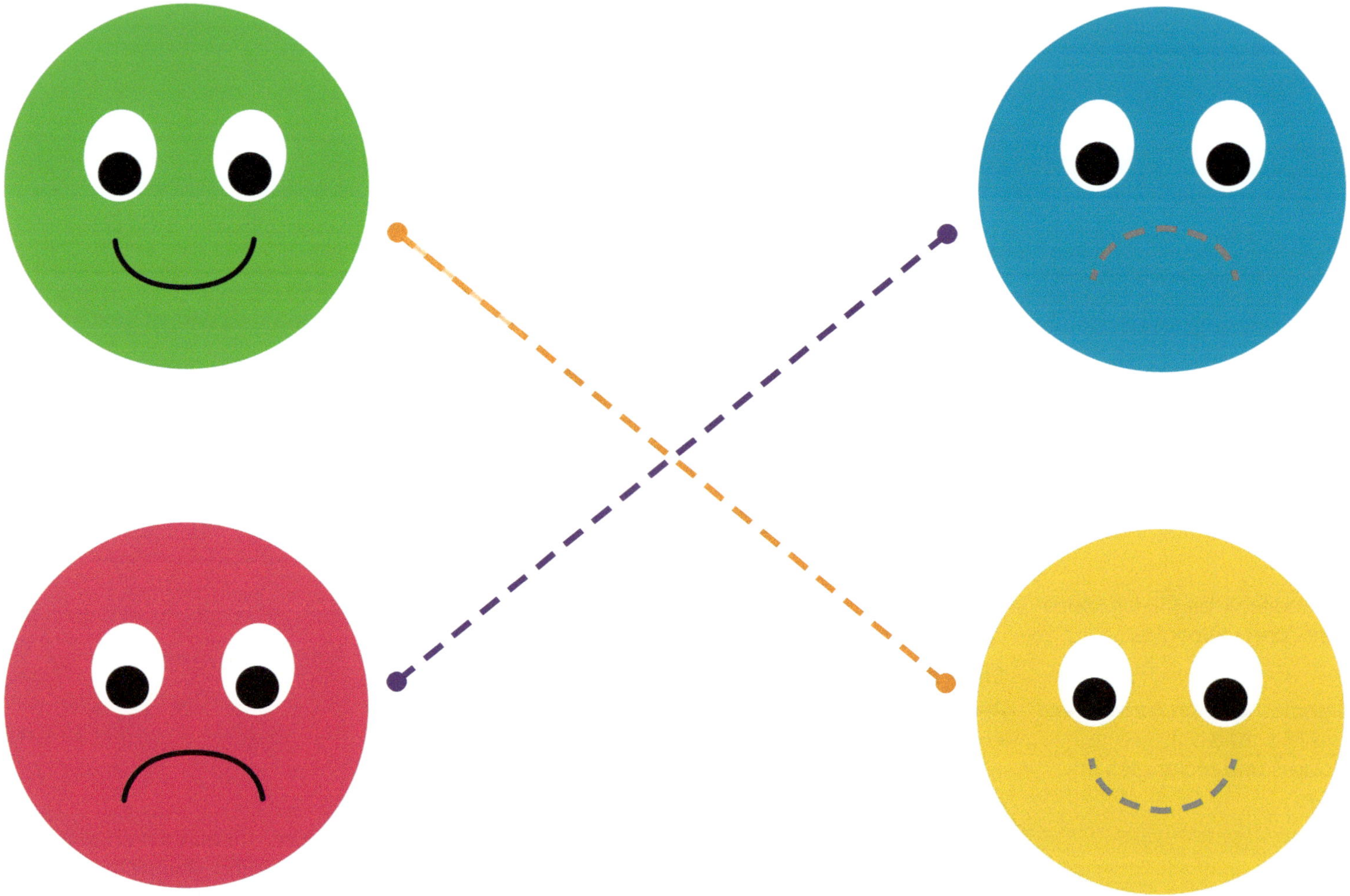

Listen, point and say. Trace to match the happy faces and the sad faces. Trace the mouths.
Language: happy, sad

91

Learning objective

- Introduce, reinforce, consolidate or review concepts

Materials

- Class CDs, flashcards, *Ferris Wheel* mat, Mimi puppet, feely bag

Main vocabulary

- happy, sad

Teacher's tip: Creating a concepts corner

If you have a vocabulary corner in the classroom, you could add a concepts corner. Use contrasting colored card for each pair of concepts and add pictures to illustrate happy and sad.

Circle time

Hello song & puppet (CD1 Track 2; see TB p 17 & 21)
Opening routines (see TB p 16)
Lesson aims (see TB p 18)

Introduce the concepts.

- Use the flashcards, puppet and feely bag to introduce or remind children of the pair of concepts.

Play flashcard games.

- Play one or two flashcard games with the *Ferris Wheel* mat and/or the puppet (see TB p 20 & 21).
- Check that children clearly recognize each concept.

Table time

Student's Book p 91

Listen, point and say.

- Hold up your book. Play the audio. Point to the pictures that show happy and sad in turn.
- Play the audio again. Children join in pointing to the pictures in their books and saying the words.

CD3 Track 46

Happy … sad
Happy … sad
Happy … sad

Trace to match the happy faces and the sad faces. Trace the mouths.

- Children trace to match the happy and sad faces. They then trace the mouths.
- Children point to the faces and say if they are happy or sad.

Activity Book p 91

Draw the mouths to show if the children are happy or sad.

- Children look at each child and complete the face next to them to show if they are happy or sad.

Point and say.

- Children point and say *happy* or *sad.*

Closing time

Learning review (see TB p 18)
Closing routines (see TB p 16)
Bye bye song & puppet (CD1 Track 3; see TB p 17 & 21)

Cross-curricular activities

- See also the activities in the other Concepts lessons (see TB p 223 & 225).

Drama

Children stand up. Explain and demonstrate that you're going to say one or other of the concepts, e.g. *Happy!* or *Sad!*, and children do a mime to show they understand, e.g. smiling to show they're happy or turning their mouth down to show they're sad.

Alternate giving instructions for the two concepts.

Concepts

Listen, point and say. Circle the small things.
Language: big, small

Concepts

Learning objective

- Introduce, reinforce, consolidate or review concepts

Materials

- Class CDs, flashcards, *Ferris Wheel* mat, Mimi puppet, feely bag

Main vocabulary

- big, small

Teacher's tip: Creating a concepts corner

If you have a vocabulary corner in the classroom, you could add a concepts corner. Use contrasting colored card for each pair of concepts and add pictures to illustrate big and small.

Circle time

Hello song & puppet (CD1 Track 2; see TB p 17 & 21)
Opening routines (see TB p 16)
Lesson aims (see TB p 18)

Introduce the concepts.

- Use the flashcards, puppet and feely bag to introduce or remind children of the pair of concepts.

Play flashcard games.

- Play one or two flashcard games with the *Ferris Wheel* mat and/or the puppet (see TB p 20 & 21).
- Check that children clearly recognize each concept.

Table time

Student's Book p 92

Listen, point and say.

- Hold up your book. Play the audio. Point to the pictures that show big and small in turn.
- Play the audio again. Children join in pointing to the pictures in their books and saying the words.

CD3 Track 47

Big … small
Big … small
Big … small

Circle the small things.

- Children circle the small thing in each set.
- They then point to the things and say if they are big or small.

Activity Book p 92

Color the things that are big. Circle the things that are small.

- Children color the big things in the picture and circle the small things.

Point and say.

- Children point and say *big* or *small*.

Closing time

Learning review (see TB p 18)
Closing routines (see TB p 16)
Bye bye song & puppet (CD1 Track 3; see TB p 17 & 21)

Cross-curricular activities

- See also the activities in the other Concepts lessons (see TB p 221 & 225).

Social science

Ask children to look around the classroom and point to something big or small, something that is up or down, etc.

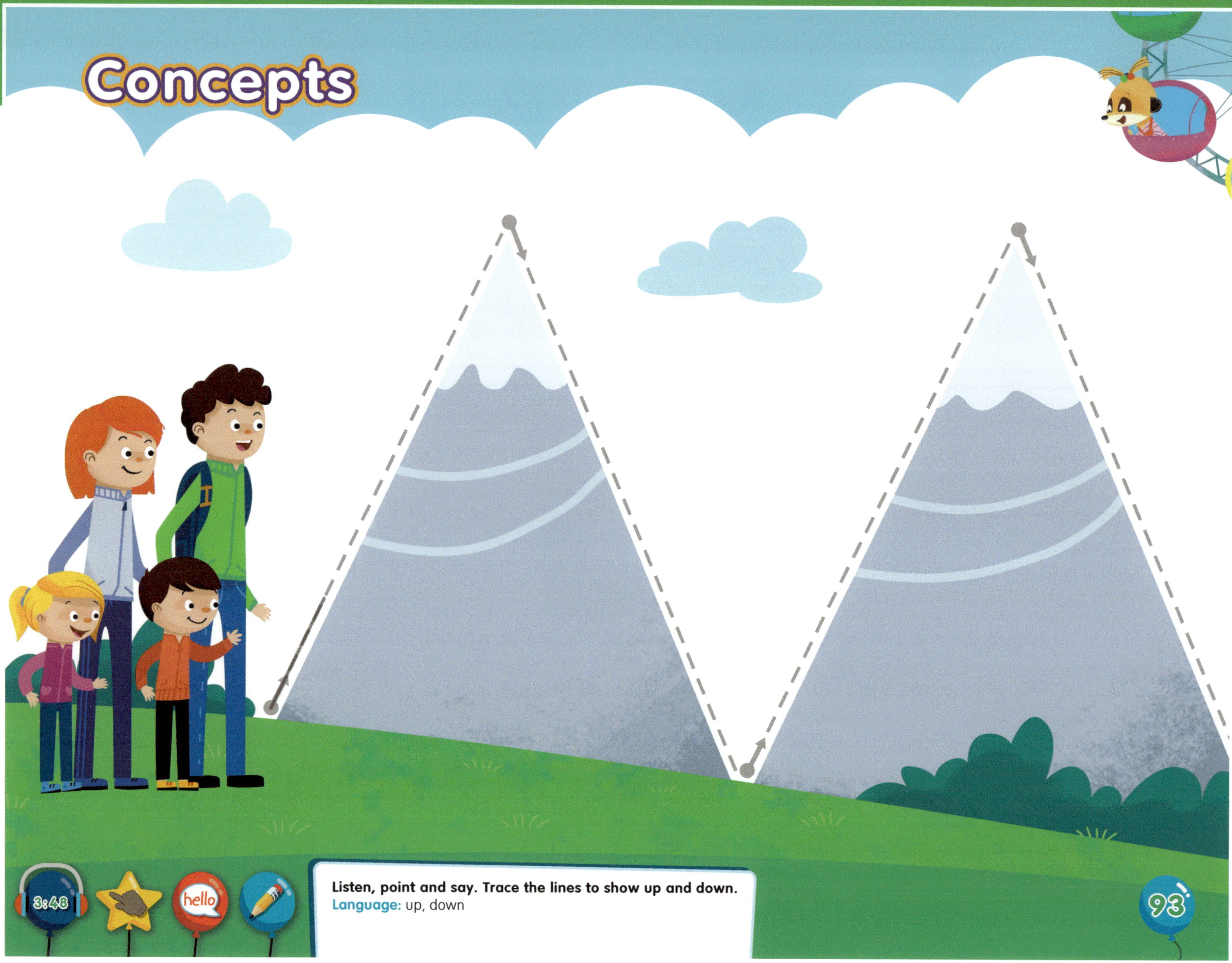

Listen, point and say. Trace the lines to show up and down.
Language: up, down

Concepts

Up, down

Learning objective

- Introduce, reinforce, consolidate or review concepts

Materials

- Class CDs, flashcards, *Ferris Wheel* mat, Mimi puppet, feely bag

Main vocabulary

- up, down

Teacher's tip: Create a concepts corner

If you have a vocabulary corner in the classroom, you could add a concepts corner. Use contrasting colored card for each pair of concepts and add pictures to illustrate up and down.

Circle time

Hello song & puppet (CD1 Track 2; see TB p 17 & 21)
Opening routines (see TB p 16)
Lesson aims (see TB p 18)

Introduce the concepts.

- Use the flashcards, puppet and feely bag to introduce or remind children of the pair of concepts.

Play flashcard games.

- Play one or two flashcard games with the *Ferris Wheel* mat and/or the puppet (see TB p 20 & 21).
- Check that children clearly recognize each concept.

Table time

Student's Book p 93

Listen, point and say.

- Hold up your book. Play the audio. Trace the lines in the picture with your finger to show up and down.
- Play the audio again. Children join in tracing the lines in their books with their finger and saying the words.

CD3 Track 48

Up … down
Up … down
Up … down

Trace the lines to show up and down.

- Children trace the lines to show up and down with a pencil or crayon.
- They then "draw" lines in the air to show up and down and say the words.

Activity Book p 93

Trace the lines to show up and down. Color the monkeys up in the trees.

- Children trace the lines to show up and down. Then they color the monkeys who are up in the trees.

Point and say.

- Children point to the monkeys and say *up* or *down*

Closing time

Learning review (see TB p 18)
Closing routines (see TB p 16)
Bye bye song & puppet (CD1 Track 3; see TB p 17 & 21)

Cross-curricular activities

- See also the activities in the other Concepts lessons (see TB p 221 & 223).

Art and craft

Take two pieces of card in contrasting colors – one for each of the concepts (happy/sad, big/small or up/down).

Give out pictures cut from magazines. Children classify them by gluing them in the right place.

Festivals

Carnival

Listen, point and say. Listen and sing *Carnival parade*. Color and count the Carnival masks.
Language: Carnival, mask, parade; dance, sing; numbers 1–5

94

Learning objectives

- Identify and name Carnival vocabulary
- Sing and act out the song *Carnival parade*
- Color and count masks
- Participate in celebrating a special day
- Paint and decorate a Carnival mask

Materials

- Class CDs, flashcards, *Ferris Wheel* mat, Mimi puppet

Main vocabulary

- Carnival, mask, parade; dance, sing; numbers 1–5

Teacher's tip: Making carnival masks

Cut out simple mask shapes from card and have the children decorate them for Carnival. Thread elastic through holes so that children can wear the masks. Alternatively, glue the masks on straws. If you wish, you could have a parade and invite parents to attend.

Circle time

Hello song & puppet (CD1 Track 2; see TB p 17 & 21)
Opening routines (see TB p 16)
Lesson aims (see TB p 18)

Introduce Carnival.

- Ask children if they want to celebrate Carnival.
- Ask them to name things they associate with Carnival in their shared language.
- Use the puppet to introduce the new words (*parade, mask, carnival, sing, dance*). Children repeat.
- Put the *Ferris Wheel* mat on the floor or board with flashcards face down on the pods. Use the puppet to turn over and name. Children repeat the words.

Game: *Say the color.*

- Name the words and children say the color of the pod. Then the reverse.

Game: *Guess and say.*

- Turn the flashcards face down and mix them up.
- Use the puppet to point to one of the flashcards and children guess what it is. Turn the flashcard over and see if they're correct.

***Carnival parade* song**

- Put the flashcards face up on the floor or board.
- Play the song. Children listen and point to the flashcards as they hear the words.
- Children stand up. Play the audio again. Children listen, do actions (see below) and join in singing the song.

CD3 Track 50

Carnival, Carnival, it's Carnival today!
Let's sing and dance (Mime dancing around holding a microphone)
In the Carnival parade (Mime marching)
Let's sing and dance (Mime dancing around holding a microphone)
It's Carnival today! (Throw your arms up excitedly)

Carnival, Carnival, it's Carnival today! (Mime marching)
Let's wear a mask (Cover your face withyour hands)
In the Carnival parade (Mime marching)
Let's wear a mask (Cover your face with you hands)
It's Carnival today! (Throw your arms up excitedly)
Carnival, Carnival, it's Carnival today! (Mime marching)

Table time

Student's Book p 94

Listen, point and say.

- Play the audio. Hold up your book. Point to the pictures in turn.
- Play the audio again. Children join in pointing to the pictures in their books and saying the words.

CD3 Track 49

It's Carnival.
Look! A mask … a parade … dance … sing!

Listen and sing *Carnival parade*.

CD3 Track 50

- Play the song. Children point to the pictures and join in singing the song.

Color and count the Carnival masks.

- Children color and count the Carnival masks.
- Say *Happy Carnival!* and encourage children to say this to each other and to you.

Activity Book p 94

Paint and decorate your Carnival mask.

- Children paint and decorate the Carnival mask using finger paints, glue and colored shapes.

Point and say.

- Children point and say about their mask.

Closing time

Learning review (see TB p 18)
Closing routines (see TB p 16)
Bye bye song and puppet (CD1 Track 3; see TB p 17 & 21)

Festivals

International Family Day

Listen, point and say. Listen and sing *Happy Family Day*. Draw a picture of your family. Language: happy, family; mommy, daddy, grandma, grandpa, brother, sister

Learning objectives

- Identify and name International Family Day vocabulary
- Sing and act out the song *Happy Family Day*
- Draw a picture of your family
- Participate in celebrating a special day
- Identify differences between two family pictures

Materials

- Class CDs, flashcards, *Ferris Wheel* mat, Mimi puppet

Main vocabulary

- happy, family; mommy, daddy, grandma, grandpa, brother, sister

Teacher's tip: Celebrating the festival after the Family unit

If timing allows, you may like to celebrate International Family Day after completing the Family unit in the main body of the Student's Book.

Circle time

Hello song & puppet (CD1 Track 2; see TB p 17 & 21)
Opening routines (see TB p 16)
Lesson aims (see TB p 18)

Introduce International Family Day.

- Explain that there is a special day each year to celebrate our family. Ask children if they want to celebrate International Family Day.
- Ask children to name family members that they know.
- Use the puppet and flashcards to review the vocabulary.
- Put the *Ferris Wheel* mat on the floor or board with the flashcards face down (on different colored pods). Use the puppet to turn them over and name them. The children repeat the words.

Game: *Guess and say.*

- Turn the flashcards face down and mix them up.
- Use the puppet to point to one of the flashcards and children guess what it is. Turn the flashcard over and see if they're correct.
- Repeat several times.

Game: *Say the color.*

- Name the family members on the *Ferris Wheel* mat and children name the color. Then the reverse.

***Happy Family Day* song**

- Say *Let's listen to the song "Happy Family Day."*
- Lay out the flashcards. Children say the words.
- Play the song. Children listen, point to the flashcards as they hear the words in each verse.
- Children stand up. Play the audio again. Children listen, sing and do the actions.
- Repeat once or twice.

CD3 Track 52

Happy Family Day to you! (Point to a child)
Happy Family Day to you! (Point to a different child)
Mommy, daddy, brother, sister (Point to the family flashcards in turn)
Happy Family Day to you! (Point to a child)

Happy Family Day to you! (Point to a child)
Happy Family Day to you! (Point to a different child)
Mommy, daddy, grandma, grandpa (Point to the family flashcards in turn)
Happy Family Day to you! (Point to a child)

Happy Family Day to you! (Point to a child)
Happy Family Day to you! (Point to a different child)
Whoever's in your family (Gesture all around)
Happy Family Day to you! (Point to a child)

Table time

Student's Book p 95

Listen, point and say.

- Play the audio. Hold up your book. Point to the pictures in turn.
- Play the audio again. Children join in pointing to the pictures in their books and saying the words.

CD3 Track 51

It's International Family Day.
Look! A happy family! Mommy … daddy … brother … sister … grandma … grandpa!

Listen and sing *Happy Family Day.*

CD3 Track 52

- Play the song. Children point to the pictures and join in singing the song.

Draw a picture of your family.

- Children draw a picture of their family inside the empty frame.
- Ask e.g. *Do you like International Family Day?* and children respond.
- Say *Happy International Family Day!* and encourage children to say this to each other and to you.

Activity Book p 95

Find and circle five differences in the pictures.

- Children find and circle five differences in the pictures.

Point and say.

- Children point and say the family members.

Closing time

Learning review (see TB p 18)
Closing routines (see TB p 16)
Bye bye song and puppet (CD1 Track 3; see TB p 17 & 21)

Festivals

Teddy Bear Day

Listen, point and say. Listen and sing *I love my teddy bear*. Trace and color the teddy bears. Color the circle of the teddy bear you like.
Language: brown; eyes, feet, fur; teddy bear

Learning objectives

- Identify and name Teddy Bear Day vocabulary
- Sing and act out the song *I love my teddy bear*
- Trace and color teddy bears
- Participate in celebrating a special day
- Identify teddy bears that are the same

Materials

- Class CDs, flashcards, *Ferris Wheel* mat, Mimi puppet

Main vocabulary

- brown; eyes, feet, fur; teddy bear

Teacher's tip: Bringing in teddy bears

Before the lesson, send home a note asking parents or carers to send a teddy bear to school with their child. Children can then celebrate Teddy Bear Day with their own teddy bears. If not all children have a teddy bear, be ready to provide an alternative, e.g. a picture of a teddy bear.

Circle time

Hello song & puppet (CD1 Track 2; see TB p 17 & 21)
Opening routines (see TB p 16)
Lesson aims (see TB p 18)

Introduce Teddy Bear Day.

- Ask children if they want to celebrate Teddy Bear Day.
- Use the puppet and flashcards to introduce the new vocabulary.
- Put the *Ferris Wheel* mat on the floor or board with the flashcards face down (on different colored pods). Use the puppet to turn them over and name them. The children repeat the words.

Game: *Guess and say!*

- Turn the flashcards face down and mix them up.
- Use the puppet to point to one of the flashcards and children guess what it is. Turn the flashcard over and see if they're correct.
- Repeat several times.

***I love my teddy bear* song**

- Say *Let's listen to the song "I love my teddy bear."*
- Lay out the flashcards. Children say the words.
- Play the song. Children listen, point to the flashcards as they hear the words in each verse.
- Children stand up. Play the audio again. Children listen, sing and do the actions in the song.
- Repeat once or twice.

CD3 Track 54

I love my teddy bear (Hug yourself)
He's so sweet
Soft, brown fur (Make a stroking motion)
Big eyes and feet (Point to your eyes and feet)
Oh, teddy bear, teddy bear
I love my teddy bear! (Hug yourself)

I love my teddy bear (Hug yourself)
She's so sweet
Soft, brown fur (Make a stroking motion)
Big eyes and feet (Point to your eyes and feet)
Oh, teddy bear, teddy bear
I love my teddy bear! (Hug yourself)

Table time

Student's Book p 96

Listen, point and say.

- Play the audio. Hold up your book. Point to the pictures in turn.
- Play the audio again. Children join in pointing to the pictures in their books and saying the words.

CD3 Track 53

It's Teddy Bear Day.
Look! Brown eyes … brown feet … brown fur!

Listen and sing *I love my teddy bear.*

CD3 Track 54

- Play the audio of the song. Children point to the pictures and join in singing the song.

Trace and color the teddy bears.

- Children trace and color the teddy bears.

Color the circle of the teddy bear you like.

- Children color the circle under the teddy bear they like.
- Use the children's shared language to ask, *e.g. Do you like Teddy Bear Day?* and children respond.
- Say *Happy Teddy Bear Day!* and encourage children to say this to each other and to you.

Activity Book p 96

Trace to circle the teddy bear that is the same in each row.

- Children look at the teddy bears on the left. They find and circle the teddy bear that is the same in each row.

Point and say.

- Children point and describe the teddy bears, e.g. *big eyes, brown fur*, etc.

Closing time

Learning review (see TB p 18)
Closing routines (see TB p 16)
Bye bye song and puppet (CD1 Track 3; see TB p 17 & 21)

Project template

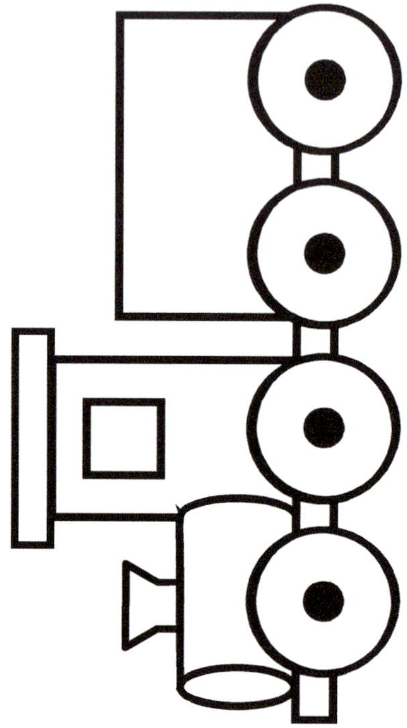

Project template

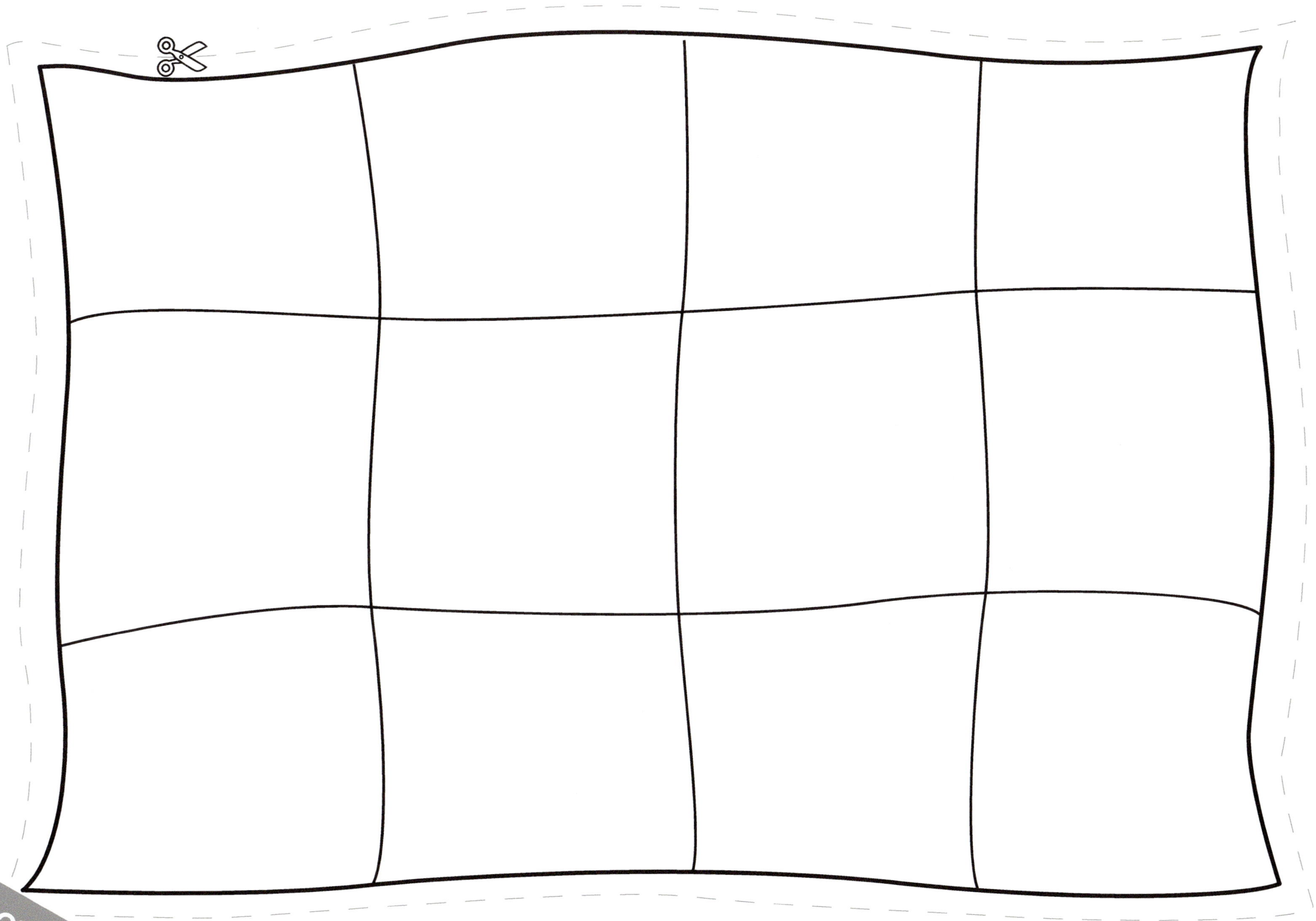

Project template